WENDY LOWER

# Hitler's Furies

German Women in the Nazi Killing Fields

**VINTAGE BOOKS**
London

Published by Vintage 2014

4 6 8 10 9 7 5 3

First published in Great Britain in 2013 by
Chatto & Windus

Vintage
Random House, 20 Vauxhall Bridge Road,
London SW1V 2SA

www.vintage-books.co.uk

Addresses for companies within The Random House Group Limited
can be found at: www.randomhouse.co.uk/offices.htm

The Random House Group Limited Reg. No. 954009

A CIP catalogue record for this book
is available from the British Library

ISBN 9780099572282

Map © Peter Palm, Berlin, Germany

The Ran                                                              ⌐ship
Council® (|                                                          ⌐isation.
Our book                                                             ⌐aper.
FSC is                                                               ⌐ding

*For my grandmothers, Nancy Morgan and Virginia Williamson*
*my mother, Mary Suzanne Liljequist*
*and my sisters, Virginia Lower and Lori Lower*

# CONTENTS

# ILLUSTRATIONS

## MAIN CHARACTERS

## Witnesses, Accomplices, Killers

INGELENE IVENS, schoolteacher from Kiel, sent to Poznań, Poland

ERIKA OHR, nurse from the village of Stachenhausen in Swabia, daughter of a sheep herder, sent to a hospital in Zhytomyr, Ukraine

ANNETTE SCHÜCKING, law student from Münster, great-granddaughter of the esteemed writer Leon Schücking, daughter of a Social Democratic Party politician and journalist, sent as a nurse to a soldiers' home in Novgorod Volynsk, Ukraine, and Krasnodar, Russia

PAULINE KNEISSLER, nurse from Duisburg in the Rhineland, born in Odessa, Ukraine, emigrated to Germany at the end of the First World War, sent to Poland and Belarus

ILSE STRUWE, secretary from the suburbs of Berlin, went with the German Armed Forces to France, Serbia and Ukraine

LISELOTTE MEIER, secretary from the town of Reichenbach, Saxony, near German-Czech border, sent to Minsk and Lida, Belarus

JOHANNA ALTVATER, secretary from Minden, Westphalia, daughter of a foundry foreman, went to Volodymyr-Volynsky, Ukraine

SABINE HERBST DICK, secretary from Gestapo headquarters in Berlin, middle-class graduate of a *Gymnasium*, went to Latvia and Belarus

GERTRUDE SEGEL LANDAU, SS commander's daughter, secretary from Gestapo headquarters in Vienna, volunteered to serve in Radom, Poland, and Drohobych, Ukraine, wife of *Einsatzkommando* squad leader and Gestapo chief Felix Landau

JOSEFINE KREPP BLOCK, typist who worked in Gestapo headquarters in Vienna and frequently visited her husband, SS Major Hans Block, the Gestapo station chief in Drohobych, Ukraine

VERA STÄHLI WOHLAUF, socialite from Hamburg, wife of Captain Julius Wohlauf, SS and Order Police company commander, Battalion 101, joined her husband in Poland

LIESEL RIEDEL WILLHAUS, typist, daughter of a senior foreman in the ironworks of the industrial Saar region, Catholic-educated, wife of Gustav Willhaus, SS commander of the Janowska concentration camp, joined her husband in Ukraine

ERNA KÜRBS PETRI, farmer's daughter and farmer's wife, grammar-school education, managed an SS agricultural estate in Ukraine with her husband, SS Second Lieutenant Horst Petri

The Nazi East

furthest German advance, 1943

Leningrad

Novgorod

Kalinin

Volga

USSR

Volga

Moscow

Vyazma

Oka

Smolensk

Vitebsk

Don

Mogilev

Voronezh

Minsk

Bobruisk

Desna

elarus

Gomel

Stalingrad

Pripyat'

Chernihiv

Kharkiv

Kiev

Novgorod Volynsk

Poltava

Voroshilovgrad

Rivne

Zhytomyr

Don

Donez

Dnepr

Berdychiv

Cherkasy

Stalino

Dnepropetrovsk

Rostov on Don

Vinnytsia

REICH COMMISSARIAT
UKRAINE

opol

Mariupol

czacz

Transnistria

Melitopol

Azov Sea

Bug

rnowitz

Krasnodar

Bessarabia

Nikolajev

Prut

Dnestr

Kerch

Iasi

Odessa

Krim

Sochi

Simferopol

ROMANIA

Sevastopol

Yalta

Donau

ucharest

Black Sea

BULGARIA

TURKEY

# INTRODUCTION

I N THE SUMMER of 1992 I bought a plane ticket to Paris, purchased an old Renault and drove with a friend to Kiev over hundreds of miles of bad Soviet roads. We had to stop often. The tyres blew on the jagged surface, there was no petrol available and curious peasants and lorry drivers wanted to look under the bonnet to see a Western car engine. On the single highway stretching from Lviv to Kiev, we visited the town of Zhytomyr, a centre of Jewish life in the former Pale of Settlement, which during the Second World War had become the headquarters of Heinrich Himmler, the architect of the Holocaust. Down the road to the south, in Vinnytsia, was Adolf Hitler's Werwolf compound. The entire region was once a Nazi playground in all its horror.

Seeking to build an empire to last a thousand years, Hitler arrived in this fertile area of Ukraine – the coveted bread basket of Europe – with legions of developers, administrators, security officials, 'racial scientists' and engineers who were tasked with colonising and exploiting the region. The Germans blitzkrieged eastwards in 1941, ravaged the conquered territory and evacuated westwards in defeat in 1943 and

1944. As the Red Army reoccupied the area, Soviet officials seized countless pages of official German reports, files of photographs and newspapers and boxes of film reels. They deposited this war booty and classified the 'trophy' documents in state and regional archives that would remain behind the Iron Curtain for decades. It was this material that I had come to Ukraine to read.

In the archives in Zhytomyr I came across pages with boot footprints and charred edges. The documents had survived two assaults: a Nazi scorched-earth evacuation that included the burning of incriminating evidence, and the destruction of the city during the fighting of November and December 1943. The files contained broken chains of correspondence, tattered scraps of paper with fading ink, decrees with pompous, illegible signatures left by petty Nazi officials, and police interrogation reports with the shaky scrawls of terrified Ukrainian peasants. I had seen many Nazi documents before, while comfortably ensconced in the microfilm reading room of the US National Archives in Washington, DC. But now, seated in the buildings that had been occupied by the Germans, I discovered something besides the rawness of the material I was sifting through. To my surprise, I also found the names of young German women who were active in the region as Hitler's empire-builders. They appeared on innocuous, bureaucratic lists of kindergarten teachers. With these leads in hand, I returned to the archives in the United States and Germany and started to look more systematically for documentation about German women who were sent east, and specifically about those who witnessed and perpetrated the Holocaust. The files began to grow, and stories started to take shape.

Researching post-war investigative records, I realised that hundreds of women had been called to testify as witnesses and that many were very forthcoming, since prosecutors were more interested in the heinous crimes of their male colleagues and husbands than in those of women. Many of the women remained callous and cavalier in their recounting of what they had seen and experienced. One former kindergarten teacher in Ukraine mentioned 'that Jewish thing during the war'. She and her female colleagues had been briefed as they crossed the border from Germany into the eastern occupied zones in 1942. She remembered that a Nazi official in a 'gold-brownish uniform' had reassured them that they should not be afraid when they heard gunfire – it was 'just that a few Jews were being shot'.

If the shooting of Jews was considered no cause for alarm during the war, then how did women respond when they actually arrived at their posts? Did they turn away, or did they want to see or do more? I read studies by pioneering historians such as Gudrun Schwarz and Elizabeth Harvey that confirmed my suspicions about the participation of German women in the Nazi system, but left open questions of wider and deeper culpability. Schwarz had uncovered violent SS wives. She mentioned one in Hrubieszow, Poland, who took the pistol from her husband's hand and shot Jews during a massacre in the local cemetery. But Schwarz provided no name for this killer. Harvey had established that women teachers were active in Poland and that, on occasion, they visited ghettos and stole Jewish property. The scope of women's participation in the massacres in the eastern territories remained unclear, however. It seemed that no one had scoured the wartime and post-war records and memoirs with these questions in mind: Did ordinary German women participate in the Nazi mass shooting of Jews? Did German women in places such as Ukraine, Belarus and Poland participate in the Holocaust in ways that they did not admit to after the war?

In the post-war investigations in Germany, Israel and Austria, Jewish survivors identified German women as persecutors, not only as gleeful onlookers, but also as violent tormentors. But by and large these women could not be named by the survivors, or after the war the women married and took on different names and could not be found. Though there were source limits to my enquiries, over time it became clear that the list of teachers and other female Nazi Party activists that I had found in 1992 in Ukraine was the tip of the iceberg. Hundreds of thousands of German women went to the Nazi East – that is, to Poland and the western territories of what was for many years the USSR, including today's Ukraine, Belarus, Lithuania, Latvia and Estonia – and were indeed integral parts of Hitler's machinery of destruction.

One of these women was Erna Petri. I discovered her name in the summer of 2005 in the archives of the United States Holocaust Memorial Museum. The museum had successfully negotiated the acquisition of microfilmed copies from the files of the former East German secret police (Stasi). Among the records were the interrogations and courtroom proceedings in a case against Erna and her husband, Horst Petri, who were both convicted of shooting Jews on their private estate in Nazi-occupied Poland. In credible detail Erna Petri described the half-naked Jewish boys who whimpered as she drew her pistol. When pressed by the interrogator as to how she, a mother, could murder these children, Petri referred to the anti-Semitism of the regime and her own desire to prove herself to the men. Her misdeeds were not those of a social renegade. To me, she looked like the embodiment of the Nazi regime.

Recorded cases of female killers were to a degree representative of a much bigger phenomenon that had been suppressed, overlooked and under-researched. Given the ideological indoctrination of the young cohort of men and women who came of age in the Third Reich, their mass mobilisation in the eastern campaign, and the culture of genocidal violence embedded in Nazi conquest and colonisation, I deduced – as a historian, not a prosecutor – that there were plenty of women who killed Jews and other 'enemies' of the Reich, more than had been documented during the war or prosecuted afterwards. Though the documented cases of direct killing are not numerous, they must be taken very seriously and not dismissed as anomalies. Hitler's Furies were not marginal sociopaths. They believed that their violent deeds were justified acts of revenge meted out to enemies of the Reich; such deeds were, in their minds, expressions of loyalty. To Erna Petri, even helpless Jewish boys fleeing from a freight wagon bound for the gas chamber were not innocent; they were the ones who almost got away.

• • •

It was not by chance that eastern Europe was where Nazis and their collaborators carried out mass murder. Historically, the terrain was home to the largest populations of Jews, many of whom had become, in Nazi thinking, dangerously 'bolshevised'. Western European Jews were deported to remote areas of Poland, Belarus, Lithuania and Latvia to be shot and gassed in broad daylight.

The history of the Holocaust is wrapped up in the Nazi imperial conquest of eastern Europe, which mobilised all Germans. In Nazi-speak, being part of the *Volksgemeinschaft,* or People's Community, meant participating in all the campaigns of the Reich, including the Holocaust. The most powerful agencies, starting with the SS and police, were the main executors; these agencies were controlled by men, but also staffed by women. In the government hierarchies, female professionals and spouses attached themselves to men of power and in turn wielded considerable power themselves, including over the lives of the regime's most vulnerable subjects. Women who were assigned to military support positions to free up men for the front had the authority to issue orders to subordinates. These women filled positions in the Nazi hierarchy from the very bottom to the very top.

Among Hitler's retinue stationed in the East were his secretaries – women like Christa Schroeder, who took dictation for the Führer in his bunker near Vinnytsia. After touring the Ukrainian countryside, where she caroused with the regional German chiefs and visited the ethnic German (*Volksdeutsche*) colonies, she pondered the future of the new German *Lebensraum* ('living space') in a wartime letter:

> Our people immigrating here do not have an easy task, but there are many possibilities to achieve great things. The longer one spends in this immense region and recognises the enormous opportunity for development, the more the question presents itself as to who will be carrying through these great projects in the future. One comes to the conclusion that the foreign people [*Fremdvolk*] are not suitable for various reasons, and ultimately because in the course of the generations an admixture of blood between the controlling strata, the German element and the foreign people

would occur. That would be a cardinal breach of our understanding of the need to preserve our Nordic racial inheritance and our future would then take a similar course to that of, for example, the Roman Empire.

Schroeder was in an extremely unusual place among a select few, of course; yet her words attest to the fact that secretaries in the field recognised their imperial role and that their understanding of the Nazi mission was articulated in the sort of racialist, colonialist terminology that is usually attributed to the male conquerors and governors.

As self-proclaimed superior rulers, German women in the Nazi East wielded unprecedented power over those designated 'subhuman'; they were given a licence to abuse and even kill those who were perceived, as one secretary near Minsk said after the war, as the scum of society. These women had proximity to power in the massive state-run machinery of destruction. They also had proximity to the crime scenes; there was no great distance between the settings of small towns, where women went about their daily routines, and the horrors of ghettos, camps and mass executions. There was no divide between the home front and the battlefront. Women could decide on the spot to join the orgy of violence.

Hitler's Furies were zealous administrators, robbers, tormentors and murderers in the bloodlands. They melded into hundreds of thousands – at least half a million – women who went east. The sheer numbers alone establish the significance of German women in the Nazi system of genocidal warfare and imperial rule. The German Red Cross trained six hundred and forty thousand women during the Nazi era, and some four hundred thousand were placed in wartime service; the majority of these were sent to the rear areas or near the battle zones in the eastern territories. They worked in field hospitals of the army and Waffen-SS, on train platforms serving refreshments to soldiers and refugees, in hundreds of soldiers' homes socialising with German troops in Ukraine, Belarus, Poland and the Baltics. The German army trained over five hundred thousand young women in support positions – as radio operators, file-card keepers, flight recorders and wire-tappers – and two hundred thousand of these served in the East. Secretaries organised, tracked and distributed the massive supplies necessary to keep the war machine running. Myriad organisations sponsored by the Nazi Party (such as the National Socialist Welfare Association) and Himmler's Race and Resettlement Office deployed German women and girls as social workers, racial examiners, resettlement advisers, educators and teaching aides. In one region of annexed Poland that was a laboratory for 'Germanisation', Nazi leaders deployed thousands of teachers. Hundreds more – including the young teachers mentioned in the files I found in Zhytomyr – were sent to other colonial enclaves of the Reich. As agents of Nazi empire-building, these women were assigned the constructive work of the German 'civilising' process. Yet the destructive and constructive practices of Nazi conquest and occupation were inseparable.

Appalled by the violence of the war and the Holocaust, most female witnesses found ways to distance themselves from it and to minimise their roles as agents of a criminal regime. But for the thirty thousand women certified by Himmler's SS and police as auxiliaries in gendarme offices, Gestapo headquarters and prisons, psychological distancing was hardly an option, and the likelihood of direct participation in mass murder was high. In the civil administration of Nazi colonial governors and commissioners, another ten thousand secretaries were spread out across the Nazis' eastern capitals and district offices in Rovno (now Rivne), Kiev, Lida, Reval (now Tallinn), Grodno, Warsaw and Radom. These offices were responsible for the dispensation of indigenous populations, including Jews, many of whom had been placed in ghettos and forced-labour assignments managed by these German male and female bureaucrats. Hitler's Furies were not always agents of the Nazi regime. Often they were mothers, girlfriends and wives who joined their sons and mates in Poland, Ukraine, Belarus, the Baltics and Russia. Some of the worst killers were in this group.

Within this mobilised mass, certain women stand out. Multitasking secretaries were both desk murderers and sadists: some not only typed up liquidation orders, but also participated in ghetto massacres and attended mass shootings. Wives and lovers of SS men not only consoled their mates when they returned from their dirty work but, in some cases, also bloodied their own hands. In Nazi thinking, rounding up and shooting Jews for several hours was hard labour, so female consolation extended beyond creating a moral sanctuary at home: women set up refreshment tables with food and drink for their men near mass-execution and -deportation sites. In a small town in Latvia, a young female stenographer distinguished herself as the life of the party as well as a mass shooter. The entanglement of sexual intimacy and violence was evident as I read the files, but in ways that were more mundane than scenes depicted in vulgar post-war pornography. Romantic outings such as a walk in the woods might bring lovers into visceral contact with the Holocaust. I read about a German commissioner and his lover-secretary in Belarus who organised a wintertime hunt. They failed to find animals, so they shot at Jewish targets who moved slowly in the snow.

Women with official roles in Hitler's Reich – such as Gertrud Scholtz-Klink, the top woman in the Nazi Party – may have been highly visible, but they were largely figureheads, wielding little political power in the formal sense. The contribution of other women in numerous other roles has, in contrast, gone largely unacknowledged and unexplored. This historical blind spot is especially glaring in regard to women in the occupied eastern territories.

All German women were required to work and contribute to the war effort, in paid and unpaid positions. They managed fatherless households, family farms and businesses. They clocked in at factories and modern office buildings. They dominated in the field of agriculture and in the white-collar 'female' professions of nursing and secretarial work. Some 25–30 per cent of the teachers in Weimar and Nazi Germany were women. As the Reich's terror apparatus expanded, new career tracks opened for women, including employment in concentration camps. While the careers and acts of female camp guards have been scrutinised by journalists and scholars, much less is known about women occupying traditional female roles – women not trained to be cruel – who by chance or design ended up serving the criminal policies of the regime.

Teachers, nurses, secretaries, welfare workers and wives – these were the women in the eastern territories, where most of the worst crimes of the Reich occurred. For ambitious young women, the possibilities for advancement lay in the emerging Nazi empire abroad. They left behind repressive laws, bourgeois mores and social traditions that made life in Germany regimented and oppressive. Women in the eastern territories witnessed and committed atrocities in a more open system, and as part of what they saw as a professional opportunity and a liberating experience.

*Hitler's Furies* focuses on the transformations of individual women in the inner workings and outer landscapes of the Holocaust – in the offices, among the occupational elite, in the killing fields. Often those who seemed the least likely to perpetrate the Holocaust's horrors became the most entangled and involved. The women featured in this book came from diverse backgrounds and regions – rural Westphalia, cosmopolitan Vienna, industrial Rhineland – but collectively they form a generational cohort (seventeen to thirty years old). They all came of age with the rise and fall of Hitler.

Sometimes a source allowed me to explore deeper questions. Why were these women violent? What were their post-war perceptions of their time in the East? Without detailed interrogation records, memoirs and private writings such as diaries or letters, as well as a number of extraordinary interviews, it would have been nearly impossible to determine what the women were thinking, what their attitudes were before, during and after the war.

After the war most German women did not speak openly about their experiences. They were too ashamed or frightened to tell their stories of what had happened or what they did. Their shame was not necessarily about culpability. Some had good memories of what was supposed to be a bad time. There were ample rations, first-time romances, servants at one's disposal, nice villas, late-night parties and plenty of land. Germany's future seemed limitless, and the country reigned over Europe. For many men and women, in fact, this time preceding Germany's military defeat marked a high point of their lives.

Their silence about Jews and other victims of the Holocaust also illustrates the selfishness of youth and ambition, the ideological atmosphere in which these German girls grew up and the post-war staying power of these formative years. As teenagers, eager professionals and newly weds, these women were immersed in their own plans, whether dreamed up on a small Swabian farm or in a bustling port city like Hamburg. They wanted respectable occupations and pay cheques. They wanted to have friends, nice clothes; they wanted to travel, to experience more freedom of action. When they admired themselves in their new Red Cross uniforms, or proudly displayed their certificates for completing a childcare course sponsored by the Nazi Party or celebrated their new typing job in a Gestapo office, they became part of the Nazi regime, intentionally or not. It is perhaps not surprising that these young women did not admit to themselves or to us, either then or many years later, in courtrooms or their own memoirs, what their participation in the Nazi regime had actually entailed.

In the immediate aftermath of the war, the stark exposure of the worst female camp guards, such as Irma Grese and Ilse Koch, may have stifled a more nuanced discussion of women's participation and culpability. Trials generated sensationalistic stories of female sadism, further fuelled by a post-war trend in Nazi-style pornography. Meanwhile, the ordinary German woman was depicted popularly as the heroine who had to clean up the mess of Germany's shameful past, the victim of marauding Red Army rapists, or the flirtatious doll who entertained American GIs. Emerging feminist views stressed the victimisation of women, not their criminal agency. This sympathetic image, despite the popularity of such novels as Bernhard Schlink's *The Reader,* has largely remained. In the cities of Germany today, one finds statues and plaques dedicated to the 'rubble women'. In Berlin alone, an estimated sixty thousand women shovelled and hauled away the ruins of the capital, discarding the past for the future. They were celebrated for inspiring the West German economic miracle and the East German workers' movement.

Among the myths of the post-war period was that of the apolitical woman. After the war many women testified in court or explained in oral histories that they were 'just' organising things in the office or attending to the social aspects of daily life by managing the care or duties of other Germans stationed in the East. They failed to see – or perhaps preferred not to see – how the social became political, and how their seemingly small contribution to everyday operations in the government, military and Nazi Party organisations added up to a genocidal system. Female fascists – in Nazi Party headquarters in Kiev, in military and SS and police offices in Minsk, and in gated villas in Lublin – were not simply doing 'women's work'. As long as German women are consigned to another sphere or their political influence is minimised, half the population of a genocidal society is, in the historian Ann Taylor Allen's words, 'endowed with innocence of the crimes of the modern state', and they are placed 'outside of history itself'.

The entire population of German women (almost forty million in 1939) cannot be considered a victim group. One-third of the female population, thirteen million women, were actively engaged in a Nazi Party organisation, and female membership in the Nazi Party increased steadily until the end of the war. Just as the agency of women in history more generally is under-appreciated, here too – and perhaps even more problematically, given the moral and legal implications – the agency of women in the crimes of the Third Reich has not been fully elaborated and explained. Vast numbers of ordinary German women were not victims, and routine forms of female participation in the Holocaust have not yet been disclosed.

Generalisations about *all* German women should certainly be avoided. But how do we begin to get some sense of women's roles vis-à-vis the Holocaust, from rescuer to bystander to killer, and all the grey areas in between? How can we more accurately place women in the regime's genocidal machinery? Assigning people to criminal categories such as *accomplice* and *perpetrator* does not by itself explain how the system worked and how ordinary women witnessed and participated in the Holocaust. It is more revealing to look at the wider distribution of power in the Nazi system and to identify more precisely who was doing what to whom, and where. For example, a female chief detective in the Reich Security Main Office directly determined the fates of thousands of children, and did so with the assistance of almost two hundred female agents scattered across the Reich. These female detectives collected evidence of 'racially degenerate' youths whom they branded future criminals. They devised a colour-coding system in their pursuit of some two thousand Jewish children 'gypsy' children and other 'delinquents' incarcerated in special internment camps. Such organisational, clerical skills were considered female, and well suited to the modern, bureaucratic approach to 'fighting crime'.

The female witnesses, accomplices and perpetrators featured here are based on research in wartime German documents, Soviet war-crimes investigations, East German secret police files and trial records, West German and Austrian investigative and trial records, documentation from Simon Wiesenthal's archive in Vienna, published memoirs, private wartime correspondence and diaries, and interviews with witnesses in Germany and Ukraine. The official wartime documentation – the SS marriage applications, personnel records of the civil administration, Red Cross records and Nazi Party agency reports – proved valuable for establishing the presence of women in various positions, detailing their biographical data and elucidating the ideological training of the organisations to which they belonged. But such records, while written and typed by individuals, are all but devoid of personality or motive.

Biographical portraits that delve into personal experiences and outlooks over time require a greater reliance on what German scholars aptly refer to as 'ego documents'. These are self-representations created by the subject: testimonies, letters, memoirs and interviews. These mostly post-war accounts pose many serious problems, but as historical sources they are not to be dismissed. Over time one learns how to read and hear them, how to detect techniques of evasion, exaggerated storytelling and conformism to literary tropes and clichés. And one tries to corroborate them to test their veracity. Yet it is the subjectivity of these sources that makes them especially valuable.

There are significant differences between the testimony given to a prosecutor, an oral history or interview given to a journalist or historian and a memoir. The narrator tailors her story to meet the expectations of the listener, and that story may change over time as the narrator learns more about her past from other sources and as the questions of the audience change. Oral histories published in the 1980s, for example, do not show the same sensitivity to the events of the Holocaust as memoirs published in the early twenty-first century. The more recent memoirs often attempt to deal with the question of knowledge and participation, since the female witness anticipates that the reader or listener will ask her, 'What did you know about the persecution of the Jews? What did you see?' Furthermore, memoirs – usually penned by the elderly – are often a collaborative project shared by a parent and her descendants. The aged wartime witnesses wish to leave a legacy, to record a dramatic chapter in the family history; the knowledge that their memoirs will be read by future generations dissuades them from being candid or graphic in recounting their encounters with Jews, their enthusiasm for Nazism or their participation in mass crimes. Sometimes the language in these accounts is coded, or only hints are given. In several cases I benefited from direct contact with the memoirist and was able to ask for more details.

One should not assume that memoirists and witnesses intend to deceive or hide facts, and that some terrible truth waits to be uncovered. It is natural to repress what is painful as a form of coping. The women who published memoirs wished to be understood and to have their lives affirmed; they did not want to be judged or condemned. As I waded through multiple accounts, it became clear which ones were more credible than others.

The consensus in Holocaust and genocide studies is that the

systems that make mass murder possible would not function without the broad participation of society, and yet nearly all histories of the Holocaust leave out half of those who populated that society, as if women's history happens somewhere else. It is an illogical approach and puzzling omission. The dramatic stories of these women reveal the darkest side of female activism. They show what can happen when women of varied backgrounds and professions are mobilised for war and acquiesce in genocide.

# 1

‖‖‖‖‖‖‖‖‖‖‖‖‖‖‖‖‖‖‖

# The Lost Generation of German Women

THE MEN AND WOMEN who established and ran the terror systems of the Third Reich were startlingly young. When the forty-three-year-old Hitler was appointed chancellor of Germany in January 1933, more than two-thirds of his followers were under forty. The future chief of the Reich Security Main Office, Reinhard Heydrich, was thirty-seven years old when he presided over the Wannsee Conference and unveiled Nazi plans for the mass murder of Jews in Europe. The legions of secretaries who kept the mass-murder machinery functioning were eighteen to twenty-five years old. The nurses who worked in the war zones, assisted in medical experiments and administered lethal injections were also young professionals. The lovers and wives of the SS elite, whose task was to ensure the future purity of the Aryan race with healthy offspring, were – as required – of fertile, childbearing age. The average age of a female concentration-camp guard was twenty-six; the youngest one was a mere fifteen years old when she was posted at the Gross-Rosen camp in the German–Polish borderlands.

Terror regimes feed on the idealism and energy of young people, moulding them into the obedient cadres of mass movements, paramilitary forces and even perpetrators of genocide. Male Germans who had the bad fortune of maturing at the time of the First World War became a distinctive lot, deformed in ways that we are still trying to diagnose. One historian has identified this generation of young men as 'uncompromising', hard-core ideologues and self-convinced professionals who realised their ambitions in the SS elite as developers of the Holocaust machinery in Berlin. A generation of young women also played their part in the genocide, not at the helm, but as the machine's operatives. What distinguished the female cadre of young professionals and spouses who made the Holocaust possible – the women who went east during the Second World War and became direct witnesses, accomplices and perpetrators of murder there – was that they were the baby boomers of the First World War, conceived at the end of one era and the start of another.

In late 1918, the German empire collapsed in military defeat, soldiers mutinied and the Kaiser, declared a war criminal, fled to the Netherlands. The patriarchal world of the old regime collapsed, and in its ruins anything seemed politically possible.

For women, the new order – Germany's first experiment in democracy, modelled on the American and British examples – brought with it the chance for more individual freedom and power in a modernising West. German women voted for the first time in January 1919 and achieved formal equality, at least on paper, under the Weimar Constitution. This was an extraordinary change, given that until 1908 German women were banned from political activities and, as the 'inferior' sex in German society, held subordinate positions that most German women considered natural. While women had been forced by the First World War to enter into the public sphere of war-related work – in factories, trams and government offices – they had little experience in politics, and most were content to call themselves apolitical. With the implosion of the monarchy, the political arena, previously closed to them, suddenly opened.

The Weimar Republic saw an explosion of ragtag movements, vigilante groups and organised parties of all stripes. In Munich alone, the nascent Nazi Party was among forty such movements in the early 1920s. Most proudly called themselves *völkisch,* a term that suggests 'of the people', but in this case 'people' referred exclusively to Germans. These popular movements were unabashedly nationalistic, xenophobic and anti-Semitic. They sought unity through racism, and rejected liberalism and parliamentary democracy as foreign encroachments on an imagined Germanic way of life where peace and order reigned. Drawing on a romanticised view of the past, those who exalted the *Volk* prized the union of German blood and soil and the steely resolve of the warrior. In the post-war humiliation of a defeated Germany, myths of a national rebirth and the search for a saviour to restore the country's honour were especially appealing to the youth and rural poor who flocked to the numerous people's parties.

German women's involvement in the formation of right-wing movements was probably minimal. Men were unwilling to relinquish their traditional dominance in politics, and women's issues were seen as secondary, not national priorities. Weimar's *völkisch* parties drew their strength from the men's world of the battlefront and not the women's world of the home front. Women were better represented in the established, pre-war parties such as the Catholic Centre Party and the Social Democratic Party. Only a radical, mostly urban minority backed the communist movement (famously co-led by Rosa Luxemburg, who was brutally killed after a failed uprising in Berlin).

Feminism lacked a dedicated women's movement of the kind that would emerge in the 1960s and 1970s. In Weimar politics, culture and society, the 'Woman Question' appeared instead in more diffuse, contradictory forms – for instance, as organised campaigns about prostitution, contraception, sexual pleasure, welfare reforms, labour conditions and assistance for German refugees from territories lost under the terms of the Treaty of Versailles. The movement that had found unity around the struggle to obtain the vote now erupted in a plethora of campaigns. Some, such as those that dealt with sexual liberation and experimentation, were explosively innovative; often the source of controversy, these campaigns inflamed the right as much as they emboldened the left.

Women's organisations often claimed to be apolitical, but in fact their assertions of female or family values were far more than window dressing in the national parliament. Those values defined in the most intrusive, usually divisive manner what it meant to be German. The women's section of the German Colonial League had long fought against racial mixing of Germans abroad, and the German House-wives Association trained young women to run a proper German household, one that exploited domestic servants, was stocked with German goods and was scientifically managed by a staunchly patriotic housewife wearing a spotless apron. There were countervailing trends, such as the work of the Association for the Protection of Mothers and Sexual Reform, which assisted unwed mothers and managed homes for single women and their children. But even this radical pre-First World War movement contained a core of male and female medical professionals who increasingly turned to 'racial science' to deal with social problems that concerned women.

The 1920s brought ordinary Germans an expansion of individual liberties and a greater degree of political power. Freedom of expression, leisure time, mobility, trade, access to the civil service – all were available in more abundance than ever before. Meanwhile, radio, magazines and the motor car carried the tempo of the city, and often its tumult, to the countryside. It all turned out to be more than most Germans wanted, however. In the chaos and uncertainty of modernity and democracy, restoring order and tradition became more and more attractive. Counter-revolutionary movements besieged the fragile republic. Disgruntled patriots and disempowered monarchists refused to accept Germany's defeat and continued their stubborn trench warfare, now brought to the streets of Germany and aimed at new foes, the red spectre of communism and the Weimar 'November criminals' – the signers of the Armistice in November 1918 – who had 'stabbed Germany in the back'. The old and the new right blamed conditions on the home front, not the battlefront, for Germany's defeat in the Great War, and the home front was seen chiefly in terms of two figures – the female martyr, emaciated by the Allied blockade that cut off food supplies to Germany, and the Jewish civilian, stereotypically dressed as a capitalist swindler or politician. Such myths and prejudices contributed to the political polarisation and dysfunctional coalitions of the fragile republic. Deadlocks were broken by calling for new elections. Germans experienced near-constant campaigning and an exhausting political culture of agitprop with its crude fusion of mass advertising and bullying that sent them to the voting booths frequently. In the period between 1919 and 1932, twenty-one different coalition governments tried to rule. It was in this Germany – with the strife and insecurity of incessant electioneering, runaway inflation and all the bewildering and exciting prospects of modernity – that most of the women who would participate in Hitler's genocidal project grew to adulthood.

German women's extreme turn to the right did not start with the Nazi Party. Of the thirty different official political parties of the Weimar era, women voted in the conservative majority, but not disproportionately for the Nazi Party, even when the Party's popularity peaked at the voting booths in 1932. For female conservatives, the Nazi Party was actually the least attractive option, since the Nazis did not accept female members or place women on the ballot. Modern politicking, strategised in beer halls and taken to the streets, was men's work. Women could march in the demonstrations and in uniform in the late 1920s, but they could not parade by the Führer himself. In the Party's official history books, Red Swastika Sisters – as nurses who cared for the Stormtroopers were known – were memorialised sentimentally: there was a lot of blood spilled in those early days of the struggle, and many wounds had to be treated by those nurses of the movement. Idealised as nurturers, women who supported the Nazi movement of the 1920s were relegated to subordinate roles. All the same, some women were attracted to Hitler's movement and took their own initiative in forming ancillary organisations, such as the Women's Battle League (1926), which strove for the social and political integration of women in the national community. German women who followed Hitler's cause did their part in the voting booth, in Party offices and at home. One early female activist recounted the political awakening of women to the Nazi movement and their roles in the early clashes and elections:

> Women could not remain uninvolved in this struggle, for it involved their future too, and the future of their children . . . Then we heard the first National Socialist [Nazi] speaker. We listened. We went to more meetings. We heard the Führer . . . Men stood in the front ranks. The women quietly did their duty. Mothers listened anxiously in many a night hour for returning footsteps. Many a woman peered through Berlin's dark streets, looking for her man or her son who was risking his blood and his life in the struggle against subhumanity. Many a leaflet was folded so that SA [Stormtrooper] men could leave it in a mailbox. Many a valuable hour was spent in SA kitchens and rooms. Money was always being collected. The new faith was passed from mouth to mouth. No path was too long, no service for the party too small.

Though active supporters of the Nazi movement, German women cannot be blamed for actually voting Hitler into power. Hitler was not democratically elected; rather, he was appointed chancellor by a cabal of upper-class, older men who thought they could use the youthful upstart to crush the left and restore conservatism.

As soon as Hitler was in office, he and his supporters exploited every opportunity and legislative loophole to transform Germany into a one-party dictatorship and a racially exclusive nation. Civil rights were suspended in February 1933, less than one month into his rule, and political opponents were arrested and thrown into prisons and the newly established concentration camp at Dachau. Trade unions were dissolved, Jewish shops boycotted, books burned. The entire civil service was 'restored', forcing those who were not of Aryan descent into 'retirement'. Some eight thousand female communists, socialists, pacifists and 'asocial' women were among the persecuted. In March 1933, Minna Cammens, who had served in parliament as a representative of the Social Democrats, was arrested for distributing anti-Nazi leaflets. During her interrogation and detention she was murdered by the Gestapo. Female members of the Communist Party, too, were arrested and killed, or found hanging in their jail cells. The Moringen workhouse was transformed into the first camp in the Reich with female inmates, including Jehovah's Witnesses, who were anti-war and refused to accept Hitler as their supreme saviour. Lina Haag and other wives of prominent German Communist Party members were arrested with their husbands. When the Gestapo escorted Haag through the corridors of her apartment building at lunchtime, her neighbours all closed their doors 'very quietly and carefully'. Haag spent five years in prisons and camps. Languishing in an isolation cell in a Stuttgart jail, she heard the desperate whispers of an inmate who had been sentenced to death. Another time, screams pierced the prison walls while a drunken Nazi guard sang a hit song of the era with a chilling refrain, 'When you leave, quietly say goodbye'.

The increase in female prisoners meant an increase in female guards, who were recruited from the Nazi Party Women's Organisation. Female medical staff members were also deployed to camps; by war's end, about one-tenth of camp personnel was female. At least three and a half thousand women were trained as concentration-camp guards, mostly at Ravensbrück, from where they were deployed to the various camps, including Stutthof, Auschwitz-Birkenau and Majdanek. Those who volunteered for the gruesome work saw these mass-murder sites as places of employment and opportunity. The uniform was impressive, the pay was good and the prospect of wielding power was appealing. Some of the women who became guards had criminal records of their own or were prisoners in the Reich and transferred to guard duty as a way to rehabilitate themselves in the Nazi system. During the war many were pressed into this kind of service to fulfil compulsory labour duty.

Once the female recruits completed their training, took their oaths and entered the camp system, very few exhibited a humane attitude towards the prisoners in their purview. Female guards at Camp Neuengamme were known for their shrill screaming, slapping and beating.

To a prisoner, however, such 'disciplining' would have been better described as random acts of terror – acts that were especially disturbing because it was a woman who committed them.

Outside the camps, as well, women persecuted other women. Prisoner categories were left deliberately vague and elastic. Anyone could be denounced as a shirker, a saboteur, an outcast or an 'asocial'. Entering a bakery one day, a woman failed to greet her neighbours with the expected *Heil Hitler;* she was subsequently questioned by the Gestapo. 'Asocials' – vagrants, petty thieves, prostitutes, the 'riffraff' who sullied German streets and tarnished the dazzling image of Aryan beauty – were arrested, even sterilised and killed. A dictatorship does not require a massive secret police force when one's neighbours are willing to do the surveillance work of the regime, out of fear, conformity, fanaticism and spite. Personal and political scores can be settled. The most vulnerable members of society, those on the margins, are expendable.

Hitler proclaimed that a woman's place was in the home as well as in the movement. At the Nuremberg Nazi rally of 1934, he employed the typical martial rhetoric. 'What man offers in heroism on the field of battle, woman equals with unending perseverance and sacrifice, with unending pain and suffering,' he declared. 'Every child she brings into the world is a battle, a battle she wages for the existence of her people ... For the National Socialist Community of the *Volk* was established on a firm basis precisely because millions of women became our most loyal, fanatical fellow-combatants.' In 1935 and 1936 speeches to the Nazi Party Women's Organisation, Hitler proclaimed that a mother of five, six or seven children who were all healthy and well raised accomplished more than a female lawyer. He rejected equal rights for women as a Marxist demand, 'since it draws the woman into an area in which she will necessarily be inferior. It places the woman in situations that cannot strengthen her position – vis-à-vis both man and society – but only weaken it.' Women who sought degrees in higher education and political office were restricted by quotas. As Alfred Rosenberg, the Nazi Party ideologue, summed it up: 'Hence all possibilities for the development of a woman's energies should remain open to her. But there must be clarity on one point: only man must be and remain a judge, soldier and ruler of the state.'

In the Reich's battle for births, Hitler's female combatants had to fall in line, follow orders, sacrifice for the greater good, develop nerves of steel and suffer in silence. They had to give up control over their own bodies, now placed in service to the state. Victories were measured not by births, but by the number of healthy Aryan babies. The mass campaign of selective breeding mustered German women across generations and classes who ended up suffering from, as well as advancing, the Nazi racial war. Midwifery as a profession exploded. In keeping with the regime's exaltation of purity and nature, Caesareans were restricted and breastfeeding was rewarded. Not all women were considered suitable soldiers. Those with so-called genetic disorders (including alcoholics and the clinically depressed), prostitutes with venereal diseases, Roma and Sinti women and Jewish women were subjected to forced sterilisations and abortions. Of the four hundred thousand non-Jewish Germans who underwent forced sterilisation, women made up about half. According to the historian Gisela Bock, several thousand died because of botched medical procedures. Ordinary German women and girls were betrayed by midwives and nurses, who upon the arrival of a child reported alleged defects and upon routine gynaecological examinations recommended abortions and sterilisations. Thus, in the civil war for perfect Aryan babies that was under way even before the outbreak of the Second World War, women made cruel life-and-death decisions for other women, eroding moral sensibilities and implicating women in the regime's crimes.

Political conformity was required of Germany's women and even girls. Indoctrination began formally at age ten. As of 1936, membership in the girls' wing of the Hitler Youth, the League of German Girls (Bund deutscher Mädel, BdM), was compulsory. Eventually the Nazis shut down most other youth programmes or assimilated them into the Hitler Youth, with the exception of some Catholic youth groups protected by the Vatican. Since protective parents who attempted to shield their children from the movement lost their authority in the household and standing in the community, they usually yielded to the badgering of Nazi Party agitators, neighbours and colleagues. In towns such as Minden, local officials supplied the Nazi Party with lists of registered female births, which were used by Party volunteers to go door-to-door conscripting German girls into the movement.

The League satisfied the desire of many girls – political or not – for community and lasting friendships. For some it was a steppingstone to full Nazi Party membership and a career in the movement, a way to acquire appropriate skills. The local League leader in Minden was 'incredibly authoritarian'; she was 'notorious throughout Minden' for her shouting and screaming, 'almost vicious'. The most odious of local Nazi leaders could serve as role models to young girls coming of age in small towns.

The young women of the era looked forward, not backwards. They were not self-proclaimed feminists; in fact, most in their generation spurned the suffragettes as passé. When the Nazis called to abolish the female vote in 1933, German women did not go on a hunger strike. Their enemy was not 'the oppressive male'; for many, it became 'the Jew', 'the asocial', 'the Bolshevik', and 'the feminist'. It was the Jewish intellectual who spoke of the emancipation of women, Hitler declared in 1934. The Nazi movement would 'emancipate women from woman's emancipation'. In fact, German Jewish women had played a significant role in social reform and women's movements in the Weimar era. Thus Hitler's pronouncements served two ends – the removal of Jews from German politics, and the crushing of an independent women's movement in Germany. The experimental laboratory of the Weimar era had to be fully discredited and dismantled while introducing another emancipatory alternative in Nazism, one that prioritised discipline and conformity. German women who felt empowered by the Nazi movement experienced a sort of liberation in camaraderie – not as feminists who wished to challenge the patriarchy, but as agents of a conservative, racist revolution. As full-fledged Aryan members of Hitler's fascist society, they were political despite themselves. Indeed, the 'Woman Question' now took the form of women and girls heading out to the streets for rallies and parades; to farms for labour

Members of the League of German Girls shooting
rifles as part of their paramilitary training, 1936

assignments; to summer camps, marching exercises, domestic-science courses, medical examinations and flag-raising ceremonies.

The ideology of the *Volk* had its own female aesthetic. Beauty – according to this ideology – was a product of a healthy diet and athleticism, not of cosmetics. German girls and women were not supposed to paint their fingernails, pluck their eyebrows, wear lipstick, dye their hair or be too thin. Nazi leaders condemned the entire cosmetics boom of the 1920s as Jewish commerce, as a cheapening of German femininity that turned women into prostitutes and led to racial degeneration. German men should mate with the girl next door, not the urbanite or the Hollywood-style vamp. A young woman's natural glow should radiate from physical exertion, from being outdoors and, in its most celebrated form, from pregnancy.

Hitler aimed to raise ordinary Germans' racial consciousness, but for many women the racial awakening was also a political awakening. Women began to act on the ambitious notion, at times daunting but more often energising, that they should expect more from life. In their memoirs and interviews, each of Hitler's Furies expressed similar experiences in their youth: as they completed their basic schooling and reached young adulthood, they realised that they wanted to become something. This aspiration is a cliché now, of course, but at the time it was revolutionary. Young women of modest backgrounds asserted themselves by leaving their villages, enrolling in training programmes as typists or nurses and joining a political movement. The daughters of those first-time Weimar voters imagined possibilities in Germany and beyond.

. . .

A Nazi Party rally in Berlin, August 1935, with banners declaring, 'The Jews are our misfortune' and 'Women and girls, the Jews are your ruin'

Rarely do the women featured in this book describe, or even mention, pre-war Nazi policies concerning Jews. Indeed, Brigitte Erdmann, a female entertainer for the troops in Minsk, wrote to her mother in 1942 that she had her first encounter with a German Jew when she was in Belarus. Did German women realise the centrality of the 'Jewish Question' in Hitler's ideology and grasp what was happening to the Jews? German girls growing up in Germany of course saw the crude propaganda, the images of Jews as inferior, in posters and newspapers. In fiction and film representations the Jew was depicted as something dangerous – and, for girls in particular, lecherous. In this sexualised form, anti-Semitism struck at the most intimate, emotionally charged domain of intercourse between German Gentiles and German Jews. It was tailored to Germany's 'Aryan' female population, understood as vulnerable sexual objects who needed to be vigilant protectors of their own bodies vis-à-vis Jews. This form of anti-Semitism also incited German men's machismo: protecting their women from 'dangerous' Jews was a test of their honour and their manhood.

In childcare courses, women received 'racial hygiene' (health-care) instruction that identified the odious characteristics of 'sub-humans' in facial features and head shapes. In secondary schools, all children created elaborate genealogical charts, which served two purposes: children became aware of their German bloodline, and teachers discovered who was Aryan and who was not. In new editions of textbooks, anti-Semitic slogans and grotesque images of Jews were paired with Nazi symbols and uplifting quotations attributed to an attractive, airbrushed Führer. Public name-calling and bullying of Jews was tolerated on playgrounds, at bathhouses and at sporting events. A Mardi Gras parade in one Catholic region included an elaborate float and a procession of Germans dressed as Orthodox Jews going to Palestine. As part of the mockery, participants donned 'Jewish noses'.

During the interwar period German girls witnessed the violence of politics, both in the streets and at school. They learned not only how to tolerate it, but how to take action against select foes and vulnerable classmates. When a German girl at one school tried to beat up a former Jewish friend, the Jewish girl retaliated, to her surprise. The German declared, 'You're a Jew, you can't fight back.'

By the time of the November 1938 pogrom, the First World War baby boomers were reaching adulthood. They saw, heard and read about the destructive assaults on Jews across Germany. Hundreds of synagogues in cities and small towns were torched, shop windows smashed. Stormtroopers and SS men vandalised Jewish cemeteries, digging up and breaking gravestones. Thousands of Jewish men were beaten up, and thirty thousand were thrown into concentration camps. Official German sources reported the Jewish death toll as ninety-one. The historian Richard Evans, however, has estimated that there were between one and two thousand deaths, including three hundred suicides. More than three-quarters of some nine thousand Jewish businesses in Germany were looted and destroyed. Women and girls who did the shopping saw this destruction; many of them commented on the mess that needed to be cleaned up, or complained about the disorder and inconvenience. Ordinary Berliners euphemistically called the pogrom *Kristallnacht,* 'the night of broken glass', expressing the destruction in material rather than human terms. One of these Berliners, upon seeing the glass shards in the morning light, thought to herself, 'The Jews are the enemy of the new Germany. Last night they had a taste of what this means.'

In their roles as shoppers and sales clerks, German women had everyday encounters with Jews in the Reich's consumer society. They chose which shops to enter and which to shun during the earlier boycotts, and saw that local businesses were changing hands. Prior to 1933, Jews owned some of the largest department stores in Germany, such as the Tietz chain, which included the KaDeWe, the Harrods of Berlin. During the boycotts, Nazi Stormtroopers defaced store windows and tried to prevent women from entering the shops. Most of these were small Jewish family businesses, but in the larger department stores such as Tietz many German women worked as sales clerks. Nazi leaders and German financiers drove the Jews out of business, forcing them to sell below true value, while Jewish managers were removed from management boards. For most German female sales clerks, this 'Aryanisation' of Jewish retail could mean the loss of a job or a new boss. In any case, it was an event, a visible change that marked the victimisation and then departure of their Jewish neighbours and employers.

The waves of Nazi assaults in the 1930s became overwhelming for German Jews, and eventually most Jews who could leave did. By 1940, about half had left Germany, two-thirds of whom were children. From the German perspective, the Jews who remained were invisible as human beings, but ever-present as a phantom or evil force that threatened Germany. Thus the Minsk entertainer, Brigitte Erdmann, and other German women who were taken aback by the presence of Jews in the East believed that they had not seen an actual Jew before, when in fact many had had daily contact with Jewish people while growing up in Germany.

The societal norm of disregarding the plight of German Jews was allied with the expectation that German girls should embody a feminine brand of toughness. Among the sporting exercises for young women in the League of German Girls were marching drills and sharpshooting. Young women, indeed girls, were trained to fire in formation with air rifles. The long-standing tradition of Prussian militarism not only cultivated a culture of total wars and 'final solutions' but, in its twentieth-century fascist form, integrated women into a martial society as patriotic nurturers and combatants.

The physical activity was coupled with a dumbing-down of the population. German schoolgirls were not taught subjects such as Latin, since knowledge of this kind was not necessary for future mothers. Instead, the girls were given pamphlets with advice on how to pick a husband: the first question to ask a prospective mate was 'What is your racial background?' For nubile women, such guidance and social support was considered useful. The public affirmation of motherhood also had its appeal. 'In my state the mother is the most important citizen,' Hitler proclaimed. Never before had German mothers enjoyed such recognition and so many services, such as more baby-care stations, more healthcare ('racial hygiene') and celebrity status at ceremonies where mothers were awarded the Cross of Honour for having more than four children.

Certainly one must be wary of taking Nazi propaganda and the declarations of Nazi leaders as fact. The propaganda meant to push women back into the private realms of *Kinder, Küche, Kirche* – children, kitchen and church – and the financial incentives that were supposed to increase marriage and birthrates did not yield the results Nazi leaders had expected. After 1935, the birthrate declined and the divorce rate increased. Statistics show that most German women were not married, were not constantly pregnant and were not staying at home. As the Third Reich established its proliferating agencies and offices across Germany (and later in the occupied territories), women became a more visible part of the workforce than ever before in German history. A woman of this generational cohort summed it up by saying that the First World War had taught them that 'everyone had to have a profession. You couldn't at all be certain that you'd marry . . . Who knew what the future might bring?'

And yet it would be inaccurate to overstate the freedom of choice that German women had in Hitler's Germany. They certainly could not choose to marry a Jewish man, or raise a child with a disease considered genetic. They no longer had political options, since the Nazi Party was the only legal party. And the types of careers open to them were limited. Before the war, all Germans fresh out of school or planning to attend university were expected to fulfil a labour assignment for the Reich, a six-month stint usually in agriculture. At these Reich Labour Service camps, though the sexes were separated, all socioeconomic classes were thrown together to develop a sense of national camaraderie. By early 1938, as part of Hitler's preparations for war, every female student enrolled in an institution of higher learning or a trade school had completed basic training in three areas: air defence, first aid and communications.

The Nazi system did not tolerate nonconformists. Once placed in military and government offices, female employees could not be dismissed except for a health reason, including pregnancy, or for misconduct, in which case they were punished. The duty to serve the Reich had been drilled into the children in school and in youth programmes, and those branded 'work-shy' or 'shirkers' were sent to the proliferating concentration camps to be 're-educated'.

In the summer of 1941, as Hitler's armies conquered more territory in the East, the labour drive was expanded by more women being placed in war-related industries, offices and hospitals. Nazi leaders prepared for a total war and a total empire. Eventually all of Europe was to be an Aryan stronghold governed from Hitler's headquarters in Berlin. Such global ambitions required the creation of a new caste, a German imperial elite, composed of young men and women.

# 2

||||||||||||||||||||||||

# The East Needs You

## Teachers, Nurses, Secretaries, Wives

i

IN THE EARLY YEARS of the Nazi movement, Hitler and his associates developed their imperial ideology and staked out their territorial ambitions. Restoring Germany to its position as a Great Power in Europe would complete what the Kaiser had attempted. However, unlike the British approach of securing hegemony in sea power and overseas possessions, the German tactic would focus on continental Europe, and specifically on the fertile lands of eastern Europe. Hitler's doctrine was spelled out in the bible of the movement, *Mein Kampf*, published in 1925:

> Just as our ancestors . . . had to fight for [soil] at the risk of their lives, in the future no folkish grace will win soil for us and hence life for our people, but only the might of a victorious sword . . . For it is not in colonial acquisitions that we must see the solution of this problem, but exclusively in the acquisition of a territory for settlement, which will enhance the area of the mother country . . . And so we National Socialists consciously draw a line beneath the foreign policy tendency of our pre-War period. We take up where

we broke off six hundred years ago. We stop the endless German movement to the south and west, and turn our gaze toward the land in the east.

*Mein Kampf* tied the aims of the movement to Hitler's biography in an unusual blend of memoir, diatribe and doctrine. The explicit call to colonise eastern Europe seems brazen in hindsight. We know the genocidal outcome of what Hitler summoned from his followers. In the twilight of European hegemony, though, such imperial claims by a self-perceived Great Power were considered legitimate. Hitler presumed that these territories were his people's collective right and historically deserved. As he would later muse in his bunker in Ukraine:

> The German colonist ought to live on handsome, spacious farms. The German services will be lodged in marvelous buildings, the governors in palaces ... What India was for England the territories of Russia will be for us. If only I could make the German people understand what this space means for our future! Colonies are a precarious possession, but this ground is safely ours. Europe is not a geographic entity; it's a racial entity.

Expanding the circulation of *Mein Kampf* in the 1930s, the state required that the book be used in the classroom to teach the 'essence of blood purity'. And the Nazi ritual of marriage included a special gift from the Führer: wedding editions of *Mein Kampf* were given to each German couple.

Perhaps, at first, the newly married German women who received this book did not grasp – if they bothered to read it – the implications of Hitler's call to colonise the East. But Hitler's demand for a restoration, indeed expansion, of Germany's 1914 borders was not unpopular. Among Germans, the experience of the Great War – in particular the humiliating loss of territory – only broadened the feeling that they were a *Volk ohne Raum*, a people without adequate space, which was the title of a best-selling novel in the 1920s. Nazi propagandists and intellectuals recast German history in school textbooks and popular exhibits as the story of successive waves of eastern migration. As of 1938, German girls in the Hitler Youth (BdM) learned new songs with verses such as 'Into the east wind throw your banners / For the east wind makes them wide / Over yonder we shall start building / Which will defy the rules of time.' In 1942 Joseph Goebbels, the Reich propaganda minister, and his staff opened a major exhibit in Berlin, *The Soviet Paradise*, which had been under development since 1934 and would be seen by 1.3 million Germans. In it, Goebbels paired the horrors of Bolshevism with the German *Drang nach Osten*, the Drive to the East. The exhibit traced Germans in eastern Europe back to the medieval history of the crusading Teutonic Knights, industrious German merchants of the Hanseatic League and hard-working German peasants, who in successive attempts all sought to stem the tide of Asiatic hordes driving west. Germans were civilisation's great defenders and developers. Women figured in *The Soviet Paradise* as well, as adoring wives and robust mothers. These images and tales were supposed to inspire ordinary Germans to go east and to accept the crusade against Bolshevism, the subjugation of Poland in 1939 and the invasion of the Soviet Union in 1941 as historically legitimate and necessary.

German women who went east in the Third Reich were not the first generation of German imperialists. Female missionaries populated the Kaiser's colonial elite in sub-Saharan Africa, and in the interwar period women were mobilised closer to home in the borderlands movement to rescue Germans who resided in the territories lost under the terms of the Treaty of Versailles. After Poland was defeated in September 1939, several thousand German women were pressed into labour service and strongly encouraged to holiday in Poland. The propaganda of the Nazi Party women's movement reignited imperial fantasies, proclaiming in 1942 that 'the expanses in the East which our troops have traversed, fighting and winning, become ever greater, [and] ever greater are the numbers of Germans who go out into the East (*Ostraum*) with the civilian administration ... The fighting troops are always quickly followed by German women.'

Over time it was expected that any woman who desired a position in the Party's upper management would complete some training in the eastern territories. In 1943 more than three thousand young women went to Poland to prepare for their careers. They cared for and educated ethnic German refugees who streamed from Romania and Ukraine into special villages in Poland such as Zamosz, where the occupying German force had brutally ejected Poles from their homes, stealing their property along with their livestock and personal possessions. In the history of German imperial expansion in Europe and overseas, the Nazi chapter was the most extreme in its genocidal policies, social engineering schemes and deployment of female activists.

In the Nazi imagination, the eastern *Lebensraum,* an Aryan living space abroad, was a frontier where anything was possible – a place where mass-murder factories could be constructed alongside utopian, German-only colonies. 'The East' evoked all the violent, but also romantic, cowboys-and-Indians stereotypes in literature and film of the time. Third Reich popular culture projected the Wild East as a fertile terrain where Teutonic bounty-hunters, posses and pioneers tamed the terrain and its savages. Ethnic Germans appeared in Nazi photographs in wagon trains while local gendarmes and SS policemen crossed the plains straddling motorcycles like cowboys astride horses. A popular family board game of the 1930s depicted German settlers as pioneers in the East.

Hitler, among those fascinated with the American West, made the connection explicit, proclaiming the duty 'to Germanise [the East] by immigration of Germans, and to look upon the natives as Redskins'. Himmler, meanwhile, spoke of the Nazi mission in the East as Germany's Manifest Destiny. Many Germans grew up reading the adventure novels of Karl May, or saw the 1936 film *Der Kaiser von Kalifornien* (*The Kaiser of California*), or saw a bigger feature in 1941, *Carl Peters,* about a German brute in Africa who decks himself out in a white coat and black shiny boots to whip 'the blacks'. These cultural productions, like the earlier horror and gangster films of the German expressionists – *Nosferatu, The Cabinet of Dr Caligari* and *M* – reflected, in the words of a cultural critic of the time, Siegfried Kracauer, 'those deep layers of collective mentality' as well as the 'psychological dispositions' of this era and generation.

The notion of *Lebensraum* was supposed to galvanize Germans – functioning in much the same way as the idea of the *Volksgemeinschaft* within the Reich – to conquer, colonise and exploit eastern Europe. Reclaiming Germany's border regions and heritage abroad was presented as an act of national self-determination: with the Wehrmacht's march into Poland and the Soviet Union, millions of ordinary Germans were expected to follow as imperial rulers and settlers in the conquered territories. The reality of *Lebensraum* would fall far short of its democratic promise.

The German juggernaut consisted of a combined assault of military forces, the SS and police, civilian government agencies and development contractors. The most powerful man in the Reich after Hitler, Heinrich Himmler, Reich Leader of the SS and Police, controlled both the security apparatus and social engineering. According to his grand scheme, called the General Plan East (*Generalplan Ost*), thirty to fifty million Slavic 'subhumans' would be killed off and deported over twenty years to make room for German settlers, while the 'lucky' helots who remained would serve their new German masters. The Race and Resettlement Office and other agencies of Germanisation fanned out across the eastern occupied territories in search of racially acceptable ethnic Germans and suitable colonial enclaves. Himmler instructed his men to carry out state-sanctioned campaigns of kidnapping. One version was in sinister fashion called the 'Hay Harvest Action'. If an SS man spotted a nice-looking blond-haired, blue-eyed little boy or girl in a Ukrainian, Polish or Belarusian village, he could grab the child. SS racial examiners would determine if the child had enough German blood and, if so, the child was put up for adoption. German women who were infertile or had miscarried, and who were desperate to prove their racial merit by becoming mothers, were likely candidates for receiving and adopting stolen children. Children who were not racially valuable were sent to children's homes and forced-labour camps or, in some cases, used as guinea pigs in Nazi medical experiments.

Evaluating and redistributing children was thus another arena for German women's participation in the Reich's state-sponsored genocide. In their roles as resettlement administrators and racial examiners, women escorted racially cherry-picked children from the East to the Reich and arranged for their placement in foster homes and state-run nurseries. Germanisation meant the forced assimilation of these children, their 'civilisation' by German female welfare workers and mothers. In typically passive terms, official German reports referred to the children as 'orphaned' when in fact German SS and military forces in the course of anti-partisan and mass reprisal operations had shot the fathers and sent the mothers to concentration camps. The 105 children from Lidice – the Czech village that the Nazis destroyed in retaliation for the assassination of Himmler's deputy, Reinhard Heydrich – are probably the most famous victims, but there were many more: estimates of stolen children range from fifty thousand to two hundred thousand. After the war the Polish government and surviving relatives requested that the children be returned. Most of the children were not identified, however, and many German mothers refused to give up those who were. Thus many of the children grew to adulthood in German households, and few learned where they came from. This aspect of the Nazi genocide would not have been possible without the involvement of German female administrators and German mothers.

Himmler had the dual charge of securing and expanding the German race by destroying its enemies and promoting the breeding of Aryans. The Nazi movement sought to take European history in a new direction, into an era of German hegemony that in its core anti-Semitic *Weltanschauung* would be free from the racial-political influence of the Jews. The scapegoating of 'the Jew' in a time of severe crisis was, of course, nothing the Germans invented, though the centrality of this 'other' in Nazi ideology was distinctive.

In Nazi thinking, the eastern 'living space' took contradictory forms: it was not only Germany's future Garden of Eden, a place of opportunity, but also a hostile terrain. Imperial dreams were set on the lands between Germany and Russia, inhabited by – in the picture painted by the Nazis – inferior, threatening races and political opponents. Such a paranoid hatred incited radical population policies and heightened security measures – all of which became the rationale for mass shootings of non-combatants, Soviet POWs and especially Jewish men, women and children. Starting in late July 1941, when it seemed that German predictions of the Soviet Union's rapid demise were coming true, Himmler demanded the extermination of Jews residing in villages deemed partisan nests, prioritising the clearing of the marshlands in Belarus. The mass murder began under the cover of the war and, as the historian Christopher Browning aptly put it, in the 'euphoria of victory'.

What routes did German men and women take to the East, and how many Germans were involved? On the heels of the German army, the German government and Nazi organisations deployed at least thirty-five thousand colonising agents in the occupied territories of the former Soviet Union. Nazi-occupied Poland also attracted its share of carpetbaggers, entrepreneurs, dilettantes, careerists, social climbers and former convicts; in total, some fourteen thousand German men and women worked in this administration, known as the General Government. The historian Michael Kater has estimated that nineteen thousand young German women were sent to annexed territories of Poland to assist with the resettlement operations. More women staffed the German post offices and railways. These figures do not include Himmler's SS and police personnel, the German Red Cross, those at armed-forces headquarters and field offices and government contractors. Transfers, leaves, deaths in warfare and visits or relocation of family members for periods of time further complicate the task of arriving at good estimates. But the estimate given earlier for women in the East – half a million – is based on the total number of documented nurses, secretaries, teachers, wives, Nazi Party activists and resettlement advisers, and covers the territories of eastern and south-eastern Europe, including the areas of Poland that were annexed by Germany in 1939.

In this chapter we will meet women in the largest of these categories – teachers, nurses, secretaries and wives – as they accepted or seized the opportunity to go east.

## TEACHERS

One did not become a convert to the Nazi cause overnight; it required indoctrination and reinforcement pursued relentlessly in the Reich's schools. For Hitler, a proper education should 'burn the racial sense and racial feeling into the instinct and the intellect, the heart and brain of the youth entrusted to it'. The school, according to a 1934 reform, should educate the youth in the service of nationhood and in the National Socialist spirit, and teachers had to be trained to become conduits of that spirit. Two-thirds of all German teachers attended training camps where they were subjected to physical and ideological exercises.

History lessons in German schools focused on German military prowess, past empires and heroic pioneers. Hitler was placed within a pantheon of heroes, including Charlemagne, Frederick the Great and Bismarck. Language instruction explained speech patterns not as regional dialects, but as racial variants. In maths class, students calculated government welfare costs for the disabled in state asylums, implanting in young minds an economic justification for the mass-murder programme of the patients who were called 'useless eaters'. In one textbook, students were taught how to 'observe the Jew: his way of walking, his bearing, gestures and movements when talking'. As one teacher told her students, the Jews were ugly not only on the outside, but on the inside too. An interwoven theme in all subjects was the superiority of the German race. A Jewish student in a public school later recalled her teacher appearing in the classroom one day wearing a swastika, pointing to her and telling her, 'Go to the back of the class. You're not one of us any more.' Those who challenged these tenets, teachers and students alike, were removed from the system. Physical beating of children who did not conform or were disobedient was common in the 1930s.

To implement the 1933 Law for the Prevention of Genetically Diseased Offspring, teachers were expected to report children with disabilities. If a child could not properly button his coat, did poorly on exams or lacked coordination in sports or on the playground, he was reported for 'screening'. In the Bavarian village of Reichersbeuern, such a lethal selection occurred in the intimate setting of a one-room schoolhouse. In 2011 I interviewed one of the former students, Friedrich K., now a man in his seventies eager to recount what he had experienced as a boy during the war. We sat outside on his terrace enjoying the customary late-afternoon coffee and cake. When we were finished, I asked Friedrich K. and his wife, who had joined us, about the leading Nazis in his village. He recalled that there was the local teacher, Frau Ottnad, but she was dead. She had committed suicide. He gestured towards the nearby chapel where she was buried, and mentioned something about her grave site, the kind of local details that inhabitants of small villages notice. I asked what she had done. He paused and looked at his wife, who nodded approvingly. Well, he explained, there was a nice little girl in our village I liked to play with. We climbed trees. She sat next to me in class. But sometimes she had seizures. It was epilepsy. And Frau Ottnad could not tolerate this. Then the girl stopped coming to school; she had disappeared from the village. We children were curious and asked our teacher, Frau Ottnad, about the girl's whereabouts. Frau Ottnad explained that the child caused too much disruption in class and that she had to be sent away. The child never returned.

In the teaching profession, as in nursing and midwifery, what was traditionally valued as the female virtue of nurturing remained, but now it was selectively applied on the basis of 'racial' criteria – judgements of who was human or 'subhuman', German or non-German, worthy of full participation in the community or subject to expulsion. Teachers took students on field trips to psychiatric hospitals – called insane asylums at the time – so that the students could appreciate their own 'racial health' in the face of patients on display who were deformed and screaming. Children were coached not to feel pity for these 'inferiors'. As the historian Claudia Koonz has observed, these outings went against bourgeois mores of not staring at the less fortunate and at social outcasts. Nazi socialisation actually *encouraged* the gaze at the inferior as affirmation of one's own superiority. One learned how to witness suffering arrogantly. It was a pedagogical technique not limited to Germany; the gaze at the inferior extended to the 'subhumans' in the imperial lands of the East.

A quixotic dreamer, Ingelene Ivens was to become one of Hitler's female combatants fighting for proper German education in occupied Poland. Ivens completed her teachers' training in Hamburg and, as she prepared for the exams to become a certified teacher, thought about where she would like to teach. Only those with the best marks would be taken into the foreign service, so Ivens studied hard. As a child, she had visited the Netherlands with her father; she had fond memories of the city that served as the seat of the Dutch government, The Hague, and of one of its buildings in particular, the German School. Ivens awaited official word of her assignment from the Cultural Ministry for Science and Art in Berlin during the spring of 1942 as Hitler's armies dominated Europe. Where might she be posted? There were many possibilities. The Hague would be ideal, but what about elsewhere in the Netherlands, northern France, Bohemia, Poland, Latvia or Ukraine?

When a thin blue envelope with official stamps on it arrived, Ivens suddenly felt her heart beating faster. She slit open the envelope and read, 'You are hereby assigned to the administration of the public grammar school in Reichelsfelde, District Posen.' Ivens was shocked. Her father left the room and began to telephone friends. Did anyone know where this place was? He returned as informed as he could be. Reichelsfelde was a village in the annexed territories of Poland. There was no post office in the village, no train station, no electricity and no plumbing.

Ivens was disappointed, but there was nothing she could do. Orders were orders, and there was little time to become sentimental about Den Haag. She began to pack and plan for her journey. She was summoned to the district capital city of Poznań (Posen), where she was to make her way by foot or bike about fifteen miles to her schoolhouse in Reichelsfelde.

Ivens was one of several hundred teachers from Germany who were sent to the Warthegau region of Poland to run one-room schoolhouses in remote areas, and among thousands of teachers and teachers' aides sent to other parts of Poland, Ukraine, Lithuania, Latvia and Bohemia-Moravia (Nazi-annexed Czech territory). Though Nazi authorities were not keen on placing single women in these rural outposts, they saw no alternative. With the ongoing war, fewer men were available for civilian desk jobs and professions. Nazi leaders were determined to pursue their 'civilising mission' in the East, no matter what the risks to single women. Schools were central institutions for converting ethnic Germans to the Nazi cause, and for creating a racial hierarchy that pushed non-German children out of the schools while developing a new elite of female educators. By March 1940, about six months after the start of the war, the Reich Education Ministry in Berlin had already instructed its regional offices across Germany to send trained teachers immediately to the eastern territories to fulfil this mission. In one region of Poland alone, some two and a half thousand German women worked in the German-only schools, organising the establishment of more than five hundred kindergartens. Like Ivens, these teachers had little choice in their assignments; attempts to be released from postings in places like Reichelsfelde were routinely denied. To deter defections, the Nazi Party's Association for German Female Youths and the Women's Organisation promoted assignments in the East as a patriotic duty and adventure.

The teachers and childcare workers who ran schools and kinder-gartens in the Nazi East contributed to the development and implementation of the regime's genocidal campaigns in a few key ways: by excluding non-German children from the school system; by privileging and ideologically indoctrinating ethnic Germans in Poland, Ukraine and the Baltics; by plundering Jewish and Polish property and belongings for the schools and schoolchildren; and by abandoning their students, many of them orphans, when the Nazis evacuated the

East. Schools were often managed by German women sent from the Reich and local ethnic Germans who assisted them. One young Latvian ethnic German woman who worked as an assistant kindergarten teacher in Poland and Ukraine recalled her work as a 'Sisyphean task'. Local SS policemen kept dumping more 'racially valuable' children into the school – children whose parents they had shot. Traumatised and uprooted, the children here and elsewhere in the burgeoning Nazi school system in the East were expected to learn German, sing German songs and memorise Hitler's maxims about proper behaviour and the superiority of the German race.

## NURSES

Of all the professions, it was nursing that brought the largest number of German women directly into the war and the Nazi genocide, as nurses occupied a variety of traditional and new roles in the developing racial state. They counselled ordinary women about 'racial hygiene' and hereditary diseases. In Germany, they participated in selections of the mentally and physically disabled in asylums and escorted these victims to their deaths in gas chambers or administered lethal injections. In the eastern territories, they cared for German soldiers and witnessed the deprivation and murder of Soviet prisoners of war and Jews. They worked in the infirmaries of concentration camps. They consoled German SS policemen and soldiers who recoiled from the experience of shooting victims at close range. They visited ghettos on official health inspections, and they visited ghettos privately as well, out of curiosity or a desire to obtain some object or service. They stood on railway platforms while Jewish deportees locked in railway carriages begged for help. They were primary witnesses of the Holocaust in Europe, and some committed mass murder as the euthanasia programme expanded from Germany into Poland. Who were the Nazi regime's nurses, and under what circumstances did they go east?

As the profession of nursing developed into a noble calling in the second half of the nineteenth century, it was limited to middle- and upper-class women. In the militaristic culture of Germany, it was expected that the 'angel of the house' should spread her wings in wartime to bring order, hygiene and maternal care to ailing German soldiers in field hospitals. Indeed, soldiers dubbed these nurses in their long white dresses and winged caps, flying from bedside to bedside, the 'angels of the front'. By the mid-1930s, with the overall muting of class differences in German society thanks to the new racial hierarchy and the call for national unity, social standing no longer mattered, and Hitler's plans for global war made the mass mobilisation of nurses a necessity. 'Model' nurses arrived in villages to give home-care courses and to meet with and recruit young girls, especially those who were in the Hitler Youth. Recruiters enticed young women with patriotic slogans and propagandistic images of smiling nurses in exotic settings and dressed in clean white uniforms – images that presented war as an experience of healing and caring rather than one of bloodshed and violence. Many teenagers were receptive to the call to serve the Reich; they wanted to escape the village and had already been exposed to a heavy dose of hygiene and racial biology in childcare courses. Some fifteen thousand women turned out in the recruiting drives of late 1939 and early 1940, just after the Nazi conquest of Poland.

During the Nazi era, nursing took on an acutely nationalistic and ideological character. Tailored dresses and modest caps replaced the gowns of the First World War. The most important piece of the new uniform was the pin, a military-style stamp of honour and organisational affiliation. Under the leadership of the SS officer and medical doctor Ernst-Robert Grawitz, the German Red Cross held informal but important ties to Heinrich Himmler, whose wife was a proud nurse. The Nazi Party regulated the certification of Red Cross nurses while it developed its own cadres of 'brown nurses'. Jewish nurses were permitted to work only in Jewish hospitals, caring only for Jewish patients. To become fully certified – a status allowing for work in any hospital – a nurse had to show proof of her Aryan ancestry and political reliability.

Nursing as it was now conceived left little room for humanitarian ideals. A nurse who completed her training in Erfurt was shocked by an instructor's comment that 'hatred is noble'. The traditional virtues of the nurse – sacrifice, discipline and loyalty – were now to be used to

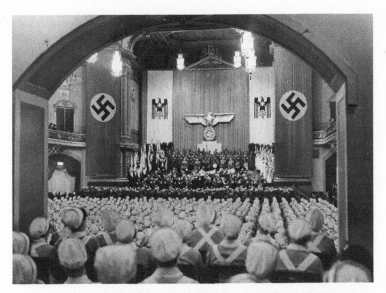

Red Cross nurses gathered in Berlin for a swearing-in ceremony

wage war. The nurse's mission, instructors stressed, was to strengthen the fighting power of the German military by caring for the soldiers, raising their morale and restoring their health. Like ordinary German soldiers, nurses had to take an oath to the Führer. A Red Cross nurse sent to Riga explained before a video camera recently that she had been taught about the 'evil people in Russia', the 'Bolshevik communists' who butchered and devoured children. It is apparent in the video that she had started to say 'Jews', but she quickly censored herself and used the words 'Bolshevik communists' instead. 'We all believed what we were told,' she said.

When nursing recruiters approached Erika Ohr, a sheep herder's daughter, in 1938, she was working as a domestic servant and nanny in the priest's house in Ruppertshofen, Swabia. She did not feel much at home there, especially since villagers looked askance at her – a young, single woman working alone in a priest's household? Local Nazi Party agitators spoke with the priest, recommending that Ohr join the

Party's League of German Girls. Feeling that she had little choice, Ohr joined. She attended few meetings, however, since many of them took place in the evening, when she was still at work in the priest's kitchen. She recalled nothing of the ideological content of the meetings she attended – or perhaps she suppressed those details in her recounting – but she did remember receiving the uniform, a crisp white blouse and dark blue skirt.

More decisive for her future was one event, probably also sponsored by the Nazi Party, at which Ohr met two Red Cross nurses. These nurses were also farm girls who, upon realising that their eldest brother would inherit the family business, had decided to seek an alternative and pursue a profession. Ohr found them inspiring in their Red Cross uniforms and lapel pins. They gave her a plan for escaping the life of a sheep herder or a domestic servant in the priest's household. As she put it, 'I wanted more.'

As soon as she turned eighteen, in 1939, Ohr registered for nursing college in the nearest city. First, though, she had to be released from compulsory labour duties in the Reich Labour Service, and then she had to secure a certificate attesting to her Aryan racial status. Once the bureaucratic documentation was done, Ohr had to convince her employer, the priest, to let her go. When the rumours of her departure circulated, neighbours could not believe that Ohr, the priest's cook, was to become a Red Cross nurse. Only when her large suitcase was packed and shipped to Stuttgart did they believe it.

With the outbreak of the war in 1939 came a growing need for nurses and female health aides. Ohr's application had arrived at an opportune time. But as she eagerly completed it she could not have imagined that so many young women like her would be sent across Germany and Europe to care for wounded military and SS policemen, and some to work in asylums and camp infirmaries murdering those deemed 'life unworthy of life'. In October 1940 she joined nineteen other young girls for the autumn training course. Her female superiors, the head nurses, were much older; one had served in the First World War. They were all extremely efficient, prizing correctness and cleanliness. Some clearly

Erika Ohr, 1941

enjoyed giving orders to the young recruits. One insisted that all nurses wear their hair parted down the middle for the proper matronly appearance. But Erika Ohr had her own preference. She parted her hair on the side, and when she returned home for a visit and was photographed in her uniform, that was how she proudly appeared.

After two years of intensive training in several clinics and hospitals in Stuttgart, Ohr was fully certified as a nurse and received her marching orders. All members of the German Red Cross – as well as nurses associated with an array of religious, Party and government organisations – could be called up for military service. This was official policy as of 1937, when, as part of Hitler's preparations for war, the Red Cross came under the command of the army. Ohr knew about the policy when she registered for nurses' training, but it was still alarming to receive those marching orders, which she could not refuse. Perhaps she had made a mistake.

Ohr had met German soldiers in a Stuttgart military hospital and had treated their injuries, but now she would have to work closer to the front and in a foreign land. She could be sent anywhere in Nazi-occupied Europe or northern Africa. Ohr had no experience abroad; she had never ventured more than a hundred miles from her home town in southern Germany. She was nervous when she reported to the district army office in Stuttgart to pick up her official relocation papers, stamped 3 November 1942. She was being sent to Ukraine. Ohr had little time to think about her destination: she was expected to leave for Berlin a few days later. In a rush, she packed and informed her family of her assignment. When she boarded the train that would take her to Ukraine, she realised that she was the only woman among thousands of soldiers. No one waved goodbye to her at the station.

In the summer of 1941, Annette Schücking, a highly educated young woman with a distinguished pedigree, also donned a tailored Red Cross uniform. She hailed from a family of esteemed nineteenth-century literary figures. Her great-grandfather had been the companion of Annette von Droste-Hülshoff, a literary giant whose heroic protagonists and romantic musings on Westphalia fit the ideals of Nazi culture.

In the Hitlerian state, Schücking was valued for her ancestry but certainly not for her family's liberal politics. Her pacifist father, an active member of the Social Democratic Party of Germany (SPD) – the party that had founded the Weimar Republic – was barred from politics when the Nazis assumed power in 1933. At home in intellectual circles and dismayed by her father's fate, Schücking decided to pursue a law degree despite the highly competitive quota system that restricted women's access to higher education. A patriot and an idealist, Annette believed that she could dismantle the dictatorship in the courts.

Soon, though, Schücking realised that she was helpless to change the Nazi system and the men who dominated it. At the University of Münster she was one of two women in her class; she and the other woman were routinely mocked by patronising professors who found their presence in seminars an affront to tradition. Given Schücking's strong academic performance, however, her professors gave her a pass mark on her first state examinations in July 1941. No matter how well she did, she would not be able to practise law: Hitler had barred women from the judiciary and the legal profession.

In any case, before she could finish her degree, Schücking was called up to fulfil her wartime labour duty. What could she do? Schücking wanted to avoid a routine clerical job, and she was certainly too highly educated to work in a factory. She detested the Nazis and their repression of political rights and freedoms, and her own career dreams had been frustrated, but she was still a proud German with a sense of duty.

Annette Schücking in her nurse's uniform,
summer 1941

Her peers, young German men, were being sent into battle and needed to be cared for, and she could not stay at home. At this time a newsreel was being shown in German theatres – *Mothers in Mogilev*. It showed nurses doing their womanly duty at war in Belarus – greeting Hitler, caring for wounded soldiers, measuring drug doses and serving refreshments and cake to the young soldiers. After a few months of training, Schücking was assigned to a soldiers' home in Novgorod Volynsk, Ukraine, close to the destination of Erika Ohr, the sheep herder's daughter.

Ohr's ambition and Schücking's idealism both found expression in nursing. Their employment in Ukraine and Russia, like that of so many of their fellow nurses and army aides, was integral to Hitler's waging of a genocidal war. These nurses were agents of a criminal regime, culpable by association, but not by their individual deeds. Other nurses did commit mass murder themselves, however. Of all the female professions, nursing contained the highest concentration of documented crimes, in the euthanasia programme and the medical experiments in the camps.

The case of Pauline Kneissler is among the better-known ones of a German nurse-killer. Born in 1900, Kneissler grew up in a well-off ethnic German household in the Odessa region of Ukraine. Fleeing the Bolshevik revolution, the Kneissler family made their way to Westphalia, where Pauline's father started to work in agriculture, but ended up with a job in the German national railway. Kneissler obtained German citizenship in 1920 and studied nursing in Duisburg on the Rhine. In the early 1920s she completed her training at various institutions and then landed a secure position as a municipal nurse in an asylum in Berlin. In 1937 Kneissler joined the Nazi Party. She was also a member of the National Socialist Women's League, the National Socialist Welfare Association, the Reich Air Raid Protection League and the Reich Nurses' League. Besides her active role in Nazi associations and full-time work at the asylum, Kneissler enjoyed singing in a Protestant church choir.

In December 1939 she was summoned by the police to report to the

Ministry of the Interior early in the new year. The address given was in fact that of the Columbus House headquarters of the Nazi euthanasia operation. There, she and about twenty other nurses were briefed by Werner Blankenburg of the Führer's Chancellery. Kneissler later testified:

> The Führer developed a 'euthanasia' law, which in consideration of the war was not to be published. It was absolutely voluntary for those present to agree to participate. None of us had any objections to this program, and Blankenburg swore us in. We were sworn to secrecy and obedience, and Blankenburg called to our attention the fact that any violation of the oath would be punished by death.

The nurses were assigned to the medieval Grafeneck Castle, situated about forty miles from Stuttgart and near where Ohr had her nurses' training. The castle – the former summer home of the dukes of Württemberg – is several miles from the nearest town and sits perched on a hilltop. After the First World War it was converted into a home for the disabled.

Kneissler's task was to travel to surrounding institutions with a list of patients who had been selected for transport to Grafeneck. The man in charge of the transports, Mr Schwenninger of the Charitable Foundation for Institutional Care, had the list of deportees to be killed. This list had to be matched against the patient lists in the facilities they visited. According to Kneissler, the patients 'were not all particularly serious cases'; many were in 'good physical condition'. On a given day, transports with about seventy patients arrived at Grafeneck, and Kneissler was one of the accompanying nurses.

Once at Grafeneck, the patients were placed in barracks and superficially examined by two doctors. Based on a questionnaire, 'these two doctors gave the final word whether a patient should be gassed or not ... In most cases the patients were killed within twenty-four hours of their arrival.' The doctors injected the victims with 2 cc of morphine-scopolamine prior to their gassing; afterwards, the doctors dissected many of the bodies. Following cremation, ashes were mixed together and placed in individual urns that were sent to the victims' relatives with a form letter. To maintain secrecy and protect the perpetrators, the doctors' names on the condolence letters were fabricated and the cause of death was falsified.

Between January and December 1940, medical personnel murdered 9,839 people at Grafeneck. Kneissler, who witnessed the gassings, found them frightening but not really all that bad, since, as she and her colleagues reasoned, 'death by gas doesn't hurt'.

Kneissler became a career killer at Grafeneck, Hadamar and other 'euthanasia' sites in Germany, assisting with the gassing procedure, starving patients and administering lethal injections to the mentally and physically ill almost every day for five years. After the war her role as a perpetrator in Germany became well known. What is less well known is the fact that she was briefly posted in the East – a posting that would contribute to the transfer of mass-murder procedures from Germany to Poland and Belarus.

Pauline Kneissler's profession, perverted under the Nazis, trained her and called upon her to kill. She joined a special unit of killers approved by Hitler. In contrast, the documented killing done by other German women in the East was dictated less by their professional training than by simple opportunity, individual character and proximity to power and violent settings. Even female guards in the camp and prison system could choose how cruel and sadistic to be towards prisoners and patients. The Nazi regime trained thousands of women to be accomplices, to be heartless in their dealings with the enemies of the Reich, but did not aim to develop cadres of female killers. Particularly outside the terror system of the camps, prisons and asylums, it was not expected that women would be especially violent or would kill. Those who did kill exploited the 'opportunity' to do so within a fertile sociopolitical setting, with the expectation of rewards and affirmation, not ostracism. In the East, it was secretaries and wives, not teachers or even nurses, who were most likely to become direct killers. Those who were close to the crime scenes, and to the men who managed and implemented the mass murder, were unavoidably involved – and, as will become clear, participated more than they had to.

## SECRETARIES

Besides the nurses, the largest contributors to the day-to-day operations of Hitler's genocidal war were the German secretaries and office aides, such as the file clerks and telephone operators working in state and private concerns in the East. Prior to the Nazi seizure of power, another revolution was under way in Germany, one that would prove decisive for this generation of women: the rise of the modern workplace and the surge of single working women who occupied it. By 1925 the number of women in white-collar clerical positions had tripled from the decade before. Between 1933 and 1939, young women increasingly sought work outside the traditional occupations of agriculture and domestic labour. Women filled the ranks of the bureaucratic state and of corporations, the very machinery that sponsored, organised and implemented the Holocaust. The ordinary young woman of the Weimar era was not a free-spirited flapper, and in the Nazi era she was not a demure housewife in a dirndl. Rather, she was an overworked, poorly paid secretary. Modernity could be exhilarating and exhausting.

Though exploited in the Nazi system, young women found new opportunities in the administrative field. One could work in an office in the Reich or abroad. One could work for a government agency or in the armaments industry. Ilse Struwe was among at least ten thousand secretaries who left Germany to work in the offices of the East.

Ilse had been a lively child – too rambunctious, in fact, for her Prussian household, where, as she later recollected, the watchword was silence. Her bedridden mother insisted that she keep still, be seen and not heard. Her father, a fruit wholesaler and Nazi Party member, beat her when she disobeyed. She soon learned that to be loved and accepted, and to be a brave, good girl, it was best not to challenge authority. Instead, she quietly endured.

At fourteen, Struwe lost her mother. Later she remembered look-

Ilse Struwe, army staff secretary, at her desk, 1942

ing at her dead mother's peaceful face, which seemed to say, 'Thank God I am done with this life.' At her mother's funeral Struwe met three girls who impressed her from the League of German Girls. They invited her into the youth movement when she was alone and grieving. Struwe went to the meetings and enjoyed the acceptance of her peers. She befriended a local boy in the Nazi Party's paramilitary organisation (SA) who clowned around and made her laugh. Later, when he was parachuted into Poland during the Nazi invasion, he wrote home to his sweetheart Ilse, boasting that he had cut off the beard of an elderly Jew. Struwe grew to dislike him.

As Struwe matured, she realised there were ways out of her oppressive household and village. Her miserable mother, dependent for her entire life, had advised her daughter to gain some vocational training. Struwe relocated to Berlin to attend high school and complete secretarial training at a trade school. But why bother with such training when she would get married anyway, her father wondered. He insisted that she come home and help him with the business. Struwe was prepared to follow his orders, but her uncle in Berlin suggested that she seek a position in the military. New offices were opening in Paris, which the Germans had just occupied. She applied.

Struwe was sent to France in 1940, Serbia in 1941 and Ukraine in

1942, opening post, typing reports, editing publications and relaying communications in the operations office of a Wehrmacht sentry. She was to be among some five hundred thousand in the Reich's military auxiliary service, women occupying supportive roles in the army, air force and navy. Two hundred thousand of these women were, like Struwe, sent to the occupied territories. When Struwe was transferred to Ukraine, she did not give it much thought. She wanted an adventure and travel, and besides, she had to go wherever she was sent.

Liselotte Meier, in contrast, chose to go east. She grew up in the Saxon town of Reichenbach at the foothills of the Ore Mountains bordering Bohemia. Meier and one of her childhood friends prepared together for white-collar work. They dreamed of careers in the nearby cities of Leipzig, Dresden, Berlin. Both would end up in the same office in Lida, Belarus. Meier had completed two years of a trade school and another two years of a commercial apprenticeship. At nineteen, she had the choice between working at a car factory in Leipzig and joining the new occupation administration in the East as a secretary. She chose the second. Along with others poised to become the new occupation staff, she travelled to Pomerania in Poland for a month's orientation at Crössinsee Castle, mingling with the newly minted imperial governors and receiving both vaccinations and ideological training.

Like Liselotte Meier, Johanna Altvater volunteered for action in the East. Altvater was a working-class girl from Minden in western Germany, where her father was a foreman in a foundry. The Westphalian town was socially rigid, economically depressed and piously conservative. There were not many job prospects here in the 1930s. In the modernising state, marriage was still a primary route to social advancement. But women could also aim for a higher status as a civil servant and were swelling the ranks of Hitler's state apparatus.

Altvater attended a middle school for girls, and in the local Hitler Youth she developed into one of the 'strong, brave women' and 'champions of the National Socialist World View'. When the League of

Liselotte Meier, c. 1941

German Girls was first established in her hometown, Altvater joined before membership of the Hitler Youth was compulsory. With her female comrades she was put to the test ideologically and physically. Socialisation here did not come in the form of traditional female values, and the League was no finishing school. But Altvater – part tomboy, part wisecracking flirt valued for childbearing hips – came close to the Nazis' ideal type. She could hold her own alongside male comrades in the racial struggle.

Altvater soon set her sights beyond the stifling atmosphere of Minden. From 1935 to 1938 she trained as a business secretary at a machine-manufacturing firm. Her supervisor evaluated her as 'very punctual, hard-working, honest and eager to work'. With this recommendation she was able to obtain a position as a stenographer for the city administration of her home town. But soon she became restless in her desk job;

she wanted to get closer to the action of the war. Her boss in Minden tried to discourage her from leaving, but to no avail.

Realising that Nazi Party membership would open up opportunities, perhaps in the newly annexed territories of Poland, Altvater filed her application. She was accepted in January 1941. Her clerical experience, single status, ostensible devotion to the Party and desire to relocate made her an ideal candidate for service abroad. She was tapped by the new Reich Ministry for the Occupied Eastern Territories to relocate to Ukraine, and left immediately.

Sabine Dick, born as Gisela Sabine Herbst in 1915, was slightly older than Struwe, Meier and Altvater. She completed *Gymnasium*, the more competitive type of high-school programme in Germany, and her route to an eventual assignment in the East was more prestigious than that of the other secretaries. She was nineteen years old when she accepted a position in the recently established Gestapo station in Berlin. From there she was transferred to the Reich Security Main Office. It was a large organisation, with a staff that would reach some fifty thousand in 1944. Dick worked in the counter-espionage department, where enemies of the state, broadly conceived as 'those who endanger the existence of the People's Community or the vitality of the German *Volk*', were investigated and where their arrests, interrogations and incarceration were arranged.

The secretaries who worked in this most notorious office in the Nazi terror apparatus fit a certain profile. Most were Nazi Party members or were active in Party organisations prior to their employment in the East. They were serious, self-assured women who were not intimidated by the Gestapo building, a place to which Germans were summoned and from which many did not return home. These job seekers saw it instead as an attractive place to work. The pay was better, and perhaps being on the inside felt more secure than being on the outside.

The expansion of Germany into Austria brought more German women into the Nazi system. By the time Hitler annexed his homeland in March 1938, two young secretaries in Vienna had already opted for Nazism. Fanatics, they would later volunteer to work in Gestapo offices in Poland and Ukraine.

Gertrude Segel, born in 1920, was the daughter of an SS second lieutenant and therefore a member of the SS hereditary community (*SS-Sippengemeinschaft*). Like many of her generation, she completed eight years of grammar school and middle school, followed by a two-year trade school. After working for a few years as a typist in a private firm, she joined the newly established Gestapo office in 1938 and remained there until February 1941, when she requested a better position, working for the commander of the Security Police and Security Service (Sipo-SD) in Radom, Poland.

Described by SS racial examiners as possessing an 'open, honest character', Segel asserted that she was an orderly housekeeper, thrifty and maternal. But she did not appear to be Aryan. She was short, with brown eyes and thick, dark brown hair. An SS doctor determined that her looks manifested strains of the 'Dinaric' race, which was still considered valuable German stock of the south-eastern variant. For a photograph that would later accompany her application to marry the SS commander Felix Landau, Gertrude chose – oddly enough – to pose in an embroidered blouse, typically worn on special occasions by provincial Slavic women.

The scholar Michael Mann has argued that Nazis outside Germany – most notably in the borderlands of Poland, Bohemia and Alsace as well as in Austria – developed especially fanatical tendencies in the 1930s. Their desire to become part of a Greater German Reich meant redrawing central Europe's borders and revolutionising or even destroying their own countries. In 1933, spurred by Hitler's appointment and consolidation of Nazi power in Germany, Nazi activists in Vienna aggressively sought to expand their support base. They organised evening social events to lure young single men and women. One of these women was Josefine Krepp.

Josefine Krepp was a twenty-three-year-old typist living at home in an outer district of Vienna. Her family apartment on the Krausegasse was

Gertrude Segel, c. 1941

not the best place from which to pursue a career or find a husband. In March 1933 Krepp made the trek into the city to attend a Nazi Party gathering. She paid two schillings to learn more about the movement and to meet other curious young men and women. That two-schilling entry fee became her first payment of Party dues. Krepp applied to join; it would be her first formal association with a political party. But she would have to wait to receive her official Party identification, because after the Nazis launched a series of bomb attacks in Austria, their Party was banned in June 1933. In the meantime, Krepp found a better job in the central police department. After Germany annexed Austria in March 1938, Krepp, who was still considered a Party applicant, was at least allowed to wear her Nazi pin. Her dedication and ambition were recognised, and she was offered another new position, this one in the Gestapo station at Berggasse 43, near the Ringstrasse in the heart of Vienna.

Krepp's office was just down the street from Sigmund Freud's home, Berggasse 19, which had been raided in the days following the *Anschluss.* The elderly Freud fled a few months later to Paris. He was one of approximately one hundred and thirty thousand Jews who were able to escape a salvo of anti-Semitic decrees and pogroms that ostracised and pauperised the Viennese Jewish community and left their synagogues, cultural centres, schools and businesses in shambles. Hitler had a special hatred for Viennese Jews. Many Austrians cemented their future in the Party and the Reich by proving themselves in Vienna in 1938 and 1939. In August 1938 the Austrian SS captain Adolf Eichmann set up his Central Office for Emigration in the former Viennese palace of the Rothschilds. There, he and his staff zealously perfected a system of forced Jewish emigration and expropriation of Jewish property, a model later applied to the mass deportations of European Jews to the Nazi death camps in Poland and to mass-shooting sites in eastern Europe.

Josefine Krepp was a direct beneficiary of these historic changes. As a recognised early supporter of the Nazi Party and loyal administrator, she was promoted from the regular police bureau to the elite security agency, the Gestapo. Krepp married Hans Block, an SS officer, and in March 1940 the couple received a nice apartment. It had been vacant since October 1939, when the first fifteen hundred Jews from Vienna were deported to a reservation in Nisko, Poland. Josefine Block's new neighbour on the Apollogasse was Gertrude Segel.

Secretaries like Block and Segel were not ordinary office workers. If they passed the SS examiners' test in physical appearance, genealogy and character, these young women in Himmler's headquarters in Berlin and Vienna could fully envision themselves as members of an emerging elite. The route to success could involve service in the East, and many volunteered to be posted in Poland, the Baltics and Ukraine. Some were after a suitable partner to advance their social position, some sought to realise their new-found ideological goals and some sought a liberating adventure. Many wanted all of the above.

Women who worked as secretaries in the Gestapo or the Reich Security Main Office typically remained in these organisations. As part of the hiring procedure, they took a vow of secrecy. Once they showed that they could be trusted, they were occasionally moved to different stations, wherever a pressing need for stenographers and typists arose. This was to be Sabine Dick's path. After the war she claimed that she had not been interested in relocating outside Germany, until her boss lured her with the promise of occupying the coveted front office for the chief of the secret police in Minsk. It was an influential position that paid better than her job in Berlin.

The tremendous growth of Nazi Germany, its proliferating state and Party offices, and its economic and military rearmament depended upon a young, female secretarial force of clerks, stenographers, telephone operators and receptionists. At the time there was some ambivalence among men and women about this group of emerging female professionals. On the one hand, they were necessary to keep government and businesses running and, since most were underpaid, they were a cheap source of labour. On the other hand, these working women were becoming careerists with a potentially 'boundless egoism'. Cantankerous critics complained that they were stealing jobs from men, weakening family traditions and 'failing to meet their obligations as mothers of the nation'. Yet such fears and prejudices had to be put aside once women were needed in the office to take the place of men called into battle. Thus this female contribution to the Nazi system was enormous, but it was publicly minimised. In Nazi ideology and propaganda, the mother remained the heroine of the German race.

## WIVES

Thousands of Gestapo secretaries were direct witnesses and administrative accomplices to massive crimes. However, while employed as secretaries, they were not likely to become violent and perpetrate crimes themselves. Paradoxically, some of the worst female perpetrators were women without an official role in assisting with crimes – women who acted out their hatred and expressed their power in informal settings. These were wives who joined their husbands – high-ranking officials in the Nazi Party, the SS and police and the occupation administration – in the East. Such women demonstrated two understandings of marriage. On the one hand, they epitomised the dutiful wife, subordinate to her husband and seemingly content with domestic work and child-rearing. On the other hand, when the Führer and the *Volksgemeinschaft* required it, their marriages became essentially partnerships in crime. In the Nazi power hierarchy, the fact of shared race between husband and wife could trump the inequities of gender. German women mimicked men doing the dirty work of the regime – the work that was necessary to the future existence of the Reich – because they were racial equals.

As SS brides, some two hundred and forty thousand German women were accepted into society's new racial nobility. According to Heinrich Himmler's 'Engagement and Marriage Decree', Germany's existence depended on the consolidation and reproduction of a superior racial stock of German Nordic men and women with staunch National Socialist convictions. The racial elite would be concentrated in the SS. Heinrich Himmler, whom Hitler appointed Reich Commissioner for the Strengthening of Germanness in 1939, was the chief regulator of German and non-German blood. The numerous organisations under his control, such as the SS Race and Resettlement Office, strove to identify and promote those with pure German blood (which of course could never be medically classified as a type) and a paranoid rejection of its pollutants. Racial mixing between Germans and Jews, or between Germans and 'Gypsies, Negroes, or their bastards', was a crime. Official policy now included forced sterilisations to avoid supposed threats to pure German blood, the criminalisation of abortions, and strict regulation of marriage to promote fertile unions.

Looking back on the madness of this ideology, we struggle to grasp how a generation became consumed by it, and with such urgency and seriousness. For those who had to turn Nazi racial ideology into practice, there were inherent contradictions to overcome and fuzzy notions to clarify. To that end, jurists, scientists, doctors and bureaucrats developed systems, laws and procedures, such as the Law for the Protection of German Blood and Honour, and the Reich Citizenship Law, otherwise known as the Nuremberg Laws. Sexual intercourse became a form of racial mating that had to be approved by the nation-state. The exacting administrator Heinrich Himmler named himself the sole authority for certifying marriages of SS men, concentrating on the files of his senior officers and the cases of questionable ancestry. From each marriage applicant – the SS man and his proposed wife – Himmler demanded extensive documentation certifying Aryan ancestry (detailed genealogical histories dating back to the 1750s, and often earlier), ideological loyalty, physical fitness, acceptable racial features (height, weight, hair colour, nose shape, head measurements, profile) and fertility. Hundreds of thousands of prospective SS brides were subjected to invasive gynaecological exams and tested on their domestic skills and maternal instincts. One of the applications for marriage that landed on Himmler's desk in 1942 was that of Vera Stähli and Julius Wohlauf.

Vera Stähli, soon to become Vera Wohlauf, was already cunning and attention-seeking, perhaps traits acquired in her difficult youth. Her father, a machine engineer, died when she was five years old. Vera and her mother moved from Hamburg to Switzerland to live with relatives, but later moved back to Hamburg, where in 1929, at seventeen, Vera completed her education in a trade school. Even with the onset of the Depression she managed to secure clerical jobs in various firms, but it was not possible to achieve her goal of living on her own.

After her mother died suddenly Vera navigated her own path. She left for England for six months. When she returned to Germany, the Nazis were on the rise. Vera had not been politically active before, but participation in some Nazi Party organisation now seemed advantageous. Moreover, the growth of the Party meant that more positions were opening up. From 1933 to 1935 Vera was employed by the Nazis' German Labour Front, which systematically dismantled and absorbed

Photos of Vera Stähli in her SS marriage application, 1942

the trade unions and forced out Jews, socialists and communists. She became an active member of the Reich Trade Association. Vera was not shy about her accomplishments. On her CV she claimed responsibility for expanding commerce in the German restaurant industry.

Vera fit the Nazi ideal of womanhood: five foot nine, 160 pounds, 'round-headed, blue-eyed, blond-haired, [and] straight-nosed'. She knew how to convince SS examiners that she was a thrifty, resource-ful woman who could manage a household. She liked order, had good taste and was clever. She completed the requisite courses in household management and childcare and was awarded athletic medals.

Vera's proposed marriage to Julius Wohlauf would be her second. In the mid-1930s in Hamburg she had managed to move up the social ladder, just as many young secretaries fantasised, through an office encounter and then marriage to a wealthy merchant. But to Vera's disappointment, her marriage remained childless, despite her 'most private wishes' to have children. This, she said to examiners in the divorce court, was due to 'the behaviour of her husband', who was drafted in May 1940 after several years of marriage. She claimed that he could easily have fulfilled her desperate wish to have a child, since he was often stationed close to Hamburg and home on leave. But he declined. Vera demanded a divorce, and after some time he agreed. In order to expedite the proceedings, Vera accepted all guilt. When she later revealed in court that she had not had intercourse with her husband for the past eight months, the judge questioned her fidelity and asked whether she had embarked on another relationship, which Vera denied. The divorce was made official in June 1942. In fact, a few weeks earlier, she and Julius Wohlauf had filed their marriage application in the SS Race and Resettlement Office.

Vera and Julius were in a rush to marry because Captain Wohlauf, a 'take-charge' unit commander of Order Police Battalion 101, was scheduled to leave for duty in Lublin, Poland. Wohlauf was one of Himmler's trusted field commanders and had just received the prized SS death's-head ring for his service in the East. The ink of Himmler's initials on their application was barely dry when the two lovebirds fi-nalised plans to spend their honeymoon together in Poland. They were euphoric. Julius Wohlauf had a beautiful, adoring wife with a large dowry of cash and other assets that more than tripled his own. Vera Wohlauf had been accepted into the new elite of the SS. Racial examiners noted on the marriage application that Vera displayed a Na-tional Socialist outlook and championed the movement with courage and vigour. But Vera was not one to stay home. She wanted to be with

Photos of Liesel Riedel in her SS marriage application, 1935

Wohlauf, who was at the centre of the struggle. She decided to join her betrothed in Poland at the end of July.

Liesel Riedel and her SS fiancé, Gustav Willhaus, were also eager to get married and enjoy the benefits of a raised social status. They submitted their marriage application in 1935. In her handwritten CV Liesel noted that she grew up around the ironworks of Neunkirchen and identified herself as the daughter of a senior foreman. With a year-ten education from a Catholic school, she went to work at a large chicken farm. For three seasons she helped in the household and did occasional odd jobs in the farm manager's office. Liesel was dissatisfied with menial work on the farm, however, so she enrolled in an eight-month course at a trade school. She developed her skills in household management and cooking. This was enough for her to secure a training position as a cook at an eatery in her home town, but she did not last there very long, either. She jumped from job to job. As a clerk in a trust office, her wages kept her below the poverty line, so she decided to apply for a position sponsored by the Nazi Party at the local newspaper, *NSZ-Rheinfront.*

It was in Nazi press circles, where she worked beginning in 1934, that Liesel became strongly affiliated with the movement and met Gustav Willhaus, a mechanic and the son of a maître d'. Gustav had joined the Nazi Stormtroopers in 1924 and the SS in 1932. He was a street brawler, and by the time he met Liesel he had the scars to prove it. Although Willhaus could barely spell and was assessed by his peers as illiterate, he was appointed sales manager of the Nazi newspaper *Westmark,* located in Saarbrücken, about twelve miles from Liesel's newspaper office. During their courtship, Liesel joined the Nazi women's organisation and did her share of expected charitable work in the Nazi Party's welfare and relief organisations.

What these young lovers saw in each other is hard to imagine from the official documentation on the couple. In their terse letters to SS headquarters in Berlin, they made demands, while not delivering what was requested of them. More than anything, the two come across as small-town swindlers out to exploit the system. Hitler wanted the movement to unify all racially valuable Germans, including working-class *Volk* like Liesel and Gustav. The Party prided itself on being anti-intellectual and anti-establishment, an attitude that suited these two perfectly. The fact that they came from the politically volatile region of Saarland may have helped them advance in the SS and the Party, or at least persuade Berlin examiners to overlook their shortcomings and dubious characters.

A territorial entity created by the Treaty of Versailles, the Saarland was historically a contested borderland between France and Germany, with a rich repository of iron ore useful for rearmament. At Versailles the Allies had intended to contain the German war machine, end the perpetual Franco-Prussian conflict and stabilise the region ethnically. The fact that the French occupied the Saarland to carry out the League of Nations mandate, though, fuelled the German campaign to undo the victors' peace. Hitler and Goebbels ramped up Nazi propaganda and political agitation in the Saarland to prepare for the region's annexation. In January of 1935, the year when the League of Nations mandate was due to run out, a plebiscite was held. Ninety-one per cent of the population voted to join the Third Reich. Liesel Riedel and Gustav Willhaus worked at the centre of this Nazi agitprop campaign, which escalated into a civil war. Riedel did her part in the press office, while Willhaus was among the uniformed thugs who beat up communists and socialists. In his victory speech in Saarbrücken, Hitler declared, 'In the end, blood is stronger than any documents of mere paper. What ink has written will one day be blotted out by blood.' Versailles, the Locarno Treaty, anti-aggression pacts – these were all just scraps of paper to Hitler. *The Volk,* war and imperial expansion were all that mattered.

On 30 October 1935, amid the national hysteria over Hitler's first big political triumph in Europe, Liesel and Gustav got married. But this brazen pair wed without the official approval of the SS, which could have been grounds for Gustav's dismissal. Gustav could not obtain the proper documentation to complete his genealogical chart. Part of his family was from East Prussia, another part from France, which complicated the process. But the couple's application was delayed by another issue: Gustav was Protestant and Liesel was Catholic. Liesel's family pressed for a wedding ceremony in a Catholic church and wanted the two to raise their children as Catholics. At first Gustav agreed to this, but SS examiners in Berlin strongly advised him to reconsider. Gustav had a duty to raise his children as Nazis, they insisted. The Nazi position was that the Catholic Church was more than an institution of faith. It was a 'political organisation that was intent on undermining the Nazi cause and German nationhood'. Gustav was 'losing his grip over the ideological direction of his family' if he allowed the children to be Catholic. Gustav and Liesel complied. They had found a common future as members of an emerging elite; family expectations and religious faith could be cast aside. Now their allegiance was to the Party and the SS.

As dutiful members of the Community of the *Volk*, Gustav and Liesel Willhaus tried for a few years to have a child. Finally, in May 1939, their daughter arrived, a few months before the outbreak of war in September. Gustav completed his combat training in Himmler's army, the Waffen-SS, the military wing of the SS. After filling a desk job in the economics and administrative main office of the SS in Berlin, he was called into action – not on the military front, but in the Nazis' 'war against the Jews' in the occupied territories.

In March 1942 Gustav was assigned to manage Jewish prisoners working in the armaments industry in western Ukraine, in Lviv (called Lemberg in German). He must have impressed his superiors with his ruthlessness, because he was later promoted to commandant of Janowska, the biggest labour and transit camp in Ukraine. At the perimeter of Janowska he received special housing, a villa large enough for his family. Liesel Willhaus and the couple's daughter, now three years old, joined him there in the summer of 1942.

Erna Kürbs grew up a farmer's daughter in Germany's agricultural heartland of Thuringia. Her family had lived in the village of Herressen for centuries. The community was small, just a few hundred hard-working people who were proud of their sixteenth-century mill, seventeenth-century church and nineteenth-century promenade.

Herressen lay on the side of a hill above a river valley, surrounded by fields of wheat, beet and barley. Seemingly isolated, it was only ten miles from Weimar, the birthplace of Germany's failed experiment in democracy.

If Germany developed a split personality during the 1920s of Erna's youth, then Weimar was its nerve centre, radiating electrifying pulses of modernity and shocking backlashes. Already in 1925 the right-wing *völkisch* parties had begun to take over the Thuringian state parliament, and a Nazi Party district chief was calling for the racial screening of all representatives. Much has been written about Hitler's failed 'beer hall' coup in 1923 and his showmanship in the subsequent trial, which served as his first national stage. But few know that after his conviction for treason the courts banned him from public speaking throughout Germany, with the exception of Erna's Thuringia. The reason for this exception was not that Weimar politicians were determined to uphold free speech in their budding democracy; rather, it was that Nazi Party activists had so effectively infiltrated that state that Thuringia could provide a haven for Hitler and a platform for his annual Party rally, moved in 1926 from Munich to Weimar. For Hitler, Thuringia provided a model of how the system of democracy could be destroyed legally from within, by swamping the parliament with Nazi delegates and cultivating the movement in the countryside with aggressive electioneering. In fact, when the Nazi Party reached its peak of popularity in free elections, capturing 37.4 per cent of the national vote in the Reichstag election of 31 July 1932, Nazi Party delegates in Erna's region garnered even more of the vote, 42.5 per cent. The Party's biggest supporters, here and elsewhere, were people like Erna – lower-middle-class Protestants and farmers.

In the German countryside, young women of Erna's generation were expected to keep the family farm running, labouring sun-up to sundown. The new cinema and mass advertising that tantalised young women with images of dazzling cities and rags-to-riches love stories made such drudgery all the more frustrating. And yet few women – who made up more than 54 per cent of the agricultural workforce in 1939 – were able to escape the farm. Like Erna, these young single women (and widows), though not formally recognised or paid, were essential to family businesses. The assumption was that this female workforce did not need much of an education to keep the traditional household economy intact. In Herressen, Erna went to a public school for seven years, followed by one year as a household servant in a neighbouring town. This was the extent of her experience beyond the village – until, in 1936, the 'sweet sixteen' Erna attended a local dance. There she met the man who would become her husband – Horst Petri, a rising star in the Nazi movement.

This encounter would change her life, as she wished, but in un-imaginable ways. The tall, handsome Horst was a local loud-mouthed Nazi Party agitator and SS man who enchanted Erna with his big plans. He spoke of restoring the honour of his heroic father, who died for the Fatherland in the Argonne Forest in the First World War, and of the renewal of a Greater German Reich. He had strong political views and romantic feelings for Erna, which she found irresistible.

Prior to establishing the Nazi Party cell in his small town in Thuringia in 1932, Horst Petri had become interested in agricultural science and economy. He was fascinated by the figure of the soldier-farmer, the romanticised, militarised notion of the Aryan peasant whose duty was to stem the tide of urbanisation. Petri read the bestseller *Volk ohne Raum* and started to believe that Germany's future was threatened by the lack of imperial lands – not territory overseas in Africa, but land to the east in continental Europe. His early commitment to the Nazi movement and his particular interest in its agricultural mission captured the attention of the Reich 'farmer leader' and first chief of Himmler's Race and Resettlement Office, Dr Richard Walther Darré, the 'blood and soil' expert, author of *Peasantry as Life-Source of the German Race* (1929), *New Nobility from Blood and Soil* (1930) and *Pig as Criterion for Nordic Peoples and Semites* (1933). Darré heavily recruited farmers to the Nazi Party, and he took Horst Petri under his wing. With Darré as his mentor, Horst completed a university degree in agriculture at Jena and SS training at Buchenwald and Dachau. His career path in the SS and as Darré's ideal of the soldier-farmer seemed limitless.

Erna Petri in Thuringia, late 1930s

After a year-long courtship Erna became pregnant. The two immediately submitted their marriage application to the SS Race and Resettlement Office. At eighteen, Erna was a young prospective bride (most women at the time married between the ages of twenty-five and thirty). The couple received Himmler's blessing, but not that of Erna's own father, who disliked Horst. But it was too late. The two wed in July 1938. Erna was no longer the farmer's daughter; she was the wife of an SS officer and an official member of the SS family tribe, to which she would make her contribution as a racially prized mother. Horst junior was born in November 1938.

Sometime in the late 1930s Erna Petri was photographed in Thuringia sitting on what looks like a DKW (Dampf-Kraft-Wagen) motorcycle. The photograph was enlarged and glued into her personal album, among Nazi-era memorabilia that Erna treasured for many years after the war. It is a striking photo – the last snapshot in which Petri radiates youthful innocence. Wearing an apron, with her hands on the steering bar and feet on the pedals, she appears ready to take off on a whirlwind ride.

Look closely at that photo and you can see the budding Nazi perversion of womanhood. True to her generation, she enjoyed the modernity of motion. The National Socialist Motor Vehicle Corps had a large following among lower-middle-class members like the Petris, who could not afford a Volkswagen, but enjoyed the thrill of car racing and the motorcycle. In Erna Petri's Germany, the earlier 'unrestrained individualism' of the New Woman of the Weimar era – who would have straddled the motorcycle in shorts, sporting a bob and lighting a cigarette – was bridled by new forms of conformity and racial hierarchies. Interwar German desires for national unity, a Community of the *Volk*, were transformed in the Nazi era into the crudest, most exclusionary and criminal form of racial club, and Petri had become a proud and adventurous member.

Petri's patterned apron was no symbol of domestic placidity. On the contrary, in Hitler's Germany it was a female expression of German superiority, in the form of order and cleanliness. Even before the Nazi takeover, the Colonial Women's League in Germany had promoted the notion that efficient housekeeping was an expression of 'cultural and biological Germanness'. In the Nazi empire this was taken to an extreme. German women were expected to carry out a civilising mission that entailed bringing 'superior' methods of housekeeping and domestic order to the primitive lands of the East. Even the term 'cleansing' took on a violent meaning. It became a euphemism for pogroms, and for removing 'inferior' races through deportation and, ultimately, mass murder.

In the summer of 1942, under the auspices of Himmler's Race and Resettlement Office, Horst and Erna Petri were given the task of cultivating and defending a Polish plantation in eastern Galicia. Horst's ideological fantasies were materialising, and his dutiful, aproned wife was by his side to join him in the crusade.

• • •

Women like Erna Petri embodied the two extremes of German femininity – the liberated woman on the one hand, the traditional housewife on the other. They experienced childhood in the Weimar Republic, but adulthood in Hitler's Germany. Having grown up in a bewildering world of rapid urbanisation, see-sawing economic crises and tumultuous mass politics, this lost generation of women had to find its bearings in Hitler's Third Reich.

The Nazi movement did not turn the majority of German women into blind followers or subjugate them into baby-making machines for the Reich. Rather, its racial-utopian goals and nationalist agenda sparked a revolutionary consciousness among ordinary Germans and excited a new patriotic activism. Women learned how to navigate a system that had clear limits, but also granted them new benefits, opportunities and a raised status, especially as they went east, where they joined the governing elite. In other words, they were an odd – and often confused – amalgam of the two eras.

Hitler told them that the war was a fight for Germany's existence, the ultimate showdown between the Aryan and the Slav, between German fascism and Judaeo-Bolshevism. Even after years of schooling and indoctrination, after seeing the violent forces of radical politics on the streets of Germany, hearing about the terror regimen in action at camps such as Dachau and Buchenwald, being exposed to official and popular forms of anti-Semitism, these German women were still not prepared for what they saw and experienced when they crossed the borders of the Reich and entered Ukraine, Poland, Belarus and the Baltics. And no one could have imagined what some would do there.

# 3

||||||||||||||||||||||||||

# Witnesses

## Arrival in the East

THE RED CROSS NURSE Erika Ohr soon forgot about her lonely departure by train from Germany. It was mid-November 1942. Hitler's forces were spread unevenly along the eastern front, a major Soviet counter-offensive was about to explode and another Russian winter approached. The train crossed the border into Poland, and suddenly 'everything looked totally different: the countryside, the houses, the train stations, the script on the signs'. Ohr saw bombarded villages for the first time. Around her the soldiers whose destination was Stalingrad stopped carrying on as they had been; there was no more joking or singing. Ohr realised that, despite Nazi radio and newsreels touting German superiority, the war was dragging on longer than expected. Back home, Stuttgart would soon experience its heaviest aerial bombardment to date. The Nazi push for world hegemony was being decided on the eastern front, and that was where all eyes were turned, including Erika Ohr's.

To Ohr, the journey east seemed as endless as the horizon. The train passed slowly through Belarus on its way towards Ukraine. Out the window there was not much to see but the blur of grey plains interrupted by occasional patches of bare birch trees. The incessant turning and screeching of the train wheels added to the monotony. There appeared to be no life whatsoever in this foreign land, no people, hardly a bird. Inside the train carriage, soldiers were lying among their packs. Some had nodded off; others reread old newspapers.

When Ohr finally arrived in the provincial capital of Zhytomyr, about ninety miles west of Kiev, it was late in the day. She was pondering what to do next when she heard female voices speaking German. Ohr noticed and decided to approach two women, military aides in uniform. They arranged for a driver and carriage to bring her to the surgical hospital across town, her new workplace. Located in a former school, the hospital accommodated about one hundred patients. It was nothing like the soldiers' hospital near Stuttgart where she had trained. This Ukrainian outpost stank of blood, pus and urine. Frostbitten soldiers wailed in pain. Bullets, shrapnel and limbs had to be removed. There was no time for welcome or orientation.

Another idealistic nurse underwent an even more difficult entry. After completing a quick course in nursing in Weimar, she arrived in the summer of 1942 in Dnepropetrovsk, Ukraine, and went straight to work on her first day there. The wounded kept streaming in, and she had to assist with one operation after another. Some two hundred suffering soldiers called out for her help. She darted from one bed to the next administering injections, suppressing the senses of the combatants while hers exploded under the stress. Before the day ended she had abandoned her post and fled to her room. She crawled into her bed, curled up in a ball, wrapped her arms around her head and bit down on her index finger like a child. How could she have dreamed of the war as an adventure?

For Ohr as for so many others, crossing into the East was a Nazi rite of passage, a separation from the familiar, which brought with it a sense of isolation amid the unknown. In official bulletins and recruitment propaganda, the newly occupied parts of Poland and Ukraine were described as a proving ground, an environment where one's toughness and commitment to the movement were tested. Entering this realm marked the start of a deep transformation of these women's lives. Initial impressions became indelible memories. One nurse arriving in August 1942 in Vyazma, Russia, recorded her first encounter with 'the enemy'. The train station where she disembarked was located next to a large POW camp. Masses of emaciated Soviet prisoners peered at her 'like animals hanging on the barbed-wire fence'. Descriptions of the landscape as barren and the inhabitants as animal-like or even invisible were typical of German colonialist rhetoric in letters of the time and would persist in memoirs penned decades later.

Front cover of a recruitment brochure for resettlement advisers in Poland: 'German Woman! German Girl! The East Needs You!'

While many found going east disorienting and difficult, for others it was an exhilarating passage to adulthood, one that gave them freedom for self-realisation. Driving through the 'partisan-infested' forests of Minsk, the young entertainer Brigitte Erdmann took in the scenery with her 'eyes wide open', relishing the danger. She was now a true woman in her own eyes, having lost her virginity in Belarus, and noted that she was honoured with the title of *Frau,* not *Fräulein.* Erdmann asserted her femininity and sexuality in this new terrain while other women expressed their masculinity. After volunteering for the Patriotic Women's Association, training as a nurse and taking an oath to the Führer as a member of the German Red Cross, one woman decided to leave her unhappy marriage and a small daughter at home, and headed to Belarus and Ukraine. In letters she sent home from the front, she expressed her loyalty to the Nazi campaign as a 'manly' honour. She wrote enthusiastically about the chance she now had to stand guard with a weapon in her hand, just like the men. Her official role as a nurse was clearly women's work, but when she had the opportunity to be a soldier, she willingly took up that role as well. We do not know if she fired the weapon, or upon whom. But like many other women in uniform, she relished the pride of being a victorious occupier, and she described the East as her place of liberation.

Nurses, teachers and secretaries entered several zones of Nazi genocidal warfare near the front and behind the lines. Most women did not directly witness the mass shootings of Jews, but they encountered some aspect of it. Only in hindsight did they recognise (or admit) the massive scope of what was happening around them, along with their own contribution to the regime's criminal policies. At the time, the Holocaust was unfolding in different forms and at different stages across Europe; it was neither a foregone conclusion nor the comprehensive event that we perceive it as today. Working from within the machinery of the Holocaust, female functionaries often saw the parts, but did not grasp their sum. Stories about the mass shootings in September and October 1941 in Babi Yar, Ukraine, circulated among soldiers and other personnel moving to and from the front and were reported in official German newspapers and Soviet bulletins. German propaganda units filmed pogroms in Lviv (Lemberg), and this newsreel footage was shown in German theatres. Beginning in January 1942, the Allies sent out multiple warnings to the Germans and their collaborators that those engaging in such atrocities would be punished after the war. But credible information about the gassing operations such as those at Belzec, which started in March 1942, was almost non-existent. At any rate, back in the Reich most did not care about what was happening to the Jews who were deported east. They were more concerned about the fates of loved ones fighting against 'Judaeo-Bolshevism'.

If female functionaries, professionals or family members of the ruling elite in the eastern territories witnessed or heard about an atrocity against Jews, it was easy to downplay it as part of the general horror of war, or shrug it off as someone else's plight. Anti-Semitism had desensitised Germans to the plight of Jews, and especially to foreign ones. Initially shocked by the violence of the war and genocide, most adjusted to it and learned to cope with it. As long as Hitler's armies were victorious, many thrived. The most unpleasant images could be compartmentalised in one's mind, overshadowed by one's daily routine, repressed by other immediate needs. One had to endure, no matter what. Wasn't that expected of a virtuous woman, a loyal German patriot, a racially superior Aryan?

In the East, nurses like Erika Ohr in their Red Cross garb were the most visible and numerous German women – in military and SS hospitals and in soldiers' homes. One ubiquitous propaganda image of the time shows cheerful nurses at a railway station providing relief to soldiers and SS policemen in transit. There was no nurses' welcome, however, for POWs and Jews who passed through these stations in transports, such as an inadequately heated train carrying 1,007 Jews from Düsseldorf to the Riga ghetto in December 1941. The train had broken down more than once because it was so overloaded with human cargo, and had stopped at several stations. While stopped, Jewish deportees tried in every way possible to obtain water and to get out of the train. Having realised during the journey that whatever awaited them was not good, they tried to attract the attention of travellers

Nurses at a soldiers' relief station

standing on the platform and threw them postcards and letters in the hope of alerting loved ones and others to their fate. At one station stop in Latvia, as in many others across Nazi-occupied Europe, German Red Cross nurses appeared on the platform. The temperatures were below freezing, and it was after one in the morning. The nurses presented the German police guards with a warm beef and barley soup. While the Germans enjoyed their soup, Lithuanian railway personnel turned off the lights in the 'Judenwagen'.

The Red Cross nurse Annette Schücking would become a rare exception to the pattern of indifference and cruelty, documenting not only the horrors she heard about and saw, but also her own moral indignation. On the eve of her departure for Ukraine in the early autumn of 1941, a journalist friend warned her that Russia was no place for her, that they were 'killing all the Jews there'. At the time, unable to imagine that such a horrifying statement could possibly be true, she remained curious about the prospect of German expansion and was in favour of the 'civilising' mission in the East. Soon, however, her friend's words were to echo in her ears.

On her journey by train to her new position, two uniformed Germans entered Schücking's compartment at the station in Brest Litovsk. In the Nazi-occupied East, train compartments were Aryan-only spaces; the 'natives' travelled in cargo and third-class wagons. In the compartments candid conversations often took place among German strangers in transit. The uniformed men started to speak with Schücking and her female colleague, another nurse. 'All of a sudden, one of them told us how he had been ordered to shoot a Jewish woman in Brest,' Schücking later recalled. The soldier said that the Jewish woman had begged for mercy, pleading that she had to take care of her disabled sister. He summoned the sister, and then he shot them both. Schücking and her companion were 'horrified, but didn't say anything'. This was their introduction to the East.

It was not long before nurses, secretaries and teachers began to grasp that the war was, as Hitler wished, a campaign of annihilation. For individual women, this moment of realisation occurred during the journey eastwards, through overheard conversations in a train compartment, at border crossings or when they arrived. Nearing the genocide was jarring for most women, since they were not formally trained in violence, either in committing it or responding to it. For the men it was different. Young men in Germany were raised in the shadow of the Great War's graphic, often homoerotic imagery of brutal trench warfare. Hitler Youth exercises often focused on overcoming fear, shaming cowards, enduring pain and forging bonds of comradeship like those of a gang. Marching exercises, shooting drills, public flogging of nonconformists and regular military training prepared the young men to kill. German women, aside from the specially trained camp guards, did not receive this degree of military indoctrination, nor did they form gangs to commit atrocities.

Because very few of the women who arrived in the East had received any preparation for witnessing or assisting in the execution of mass murder, their varied reactions to the Holocaust reveal less about their pre-war training than about their character and ideological commitment to the regime. Their responses ranged from rescue at one extreme to direct killing at the other. But the number of ordinary women who contributed in various ways to the mass murder is countless times larger than the relative few who tried to impede it.

Mostly out of curiosity but also greed, many German women came face-to-face with the Holocaust in one of the thousands of ghettos in the East. These 'Jewish-only' districts were officially forbidden territory; those who entered did so against Nazi regulations. Despite official threats and bans (or perhaps because of them), ghettos became sites of German tourism. And there was a distinctly female feature of this emerging pastime: shopping trips and romantic outings.

One Red Cross nurse in Warsaw had nothing planned for her day off. Her friend greeted her with a surprise: 'Today we are going in the ghetto.' Everyone goes there to shop, her friend gushed. The Jews place all their personal items on the street, on planks and on tables – soap, toothbrushes, cosmetics, shoelaces, whatever you need. Some even offer the items from their own extended hands. The nurse was hesitant to defy German rules by entering the ghetto, but her friend reassured her that German doctors were going there also, to meet up with Jewish doctors who would advise them about treating typhus. The two women went on their shopping adventure, and afterwards the nurse recorded that she'd seen poverty and filth much worse than in the Polish population. The 'ghetto smell' of 'those people' stayed with her for a long time.

The Nazi policy of ghettoising Jews began in Poland in October 1939, a month after the start of the war. Over time, the ghetto took on many forms and uses. In the villages the ghettos could consist of a few streets behind the main road, demarcated by some barbed wire. Viewing the Jews as a racial threat and an enemy, the Germans incarcerated them as a segregationist and security measure. Any facility could serve this purpose. German military commanders and SS and police officers would arrive in a small town such as Narodichi, Ukraine, announce that a ghetto would be formed and demand that the Jewish population report for registration. In Narodichi, Jews were brought to a local club; elsewhere they were brought to a school, factory barracks or synagogue, or even locked in abandoned railway carriages, while plans for the mass shooting or deportation to a camp were made. It could be days, weeks or months before these plans were carried out, depending on available SS and police forces, the whims of local officials and the orders of higher-ups such as Heinrich Himmler and his regional deputies. In the interim, local German officials, Poles, Ukrainians, Lithuanians and others 'traded' with the trapped Jews, who were forced to give up their personal possessions – everything from houses to coats and boots – for a loaf of bread or some firewood. Skilled Jewish labourers were selected from the ghetto population and assigned to heavy labour, such as road construction, and to war-related industries in mining, textile, carpentry and metalworking. Though these Jewish-only incarceration sites were often referred to as ghettos, they were in fact way stations to sites of mass murder, as well as 'death crates', in Goebbels's term, since famine, typhus and suicide took the lives of hundreds of thousands who were boxed into them.

The German showgirl Brigitte Erdmann also had her 'ghetto' experience in Minsk. Among the male admirers who attended her performances was a senior commander in the Organization Todt, a militarised construction agency that was a primary exploiter of Jewish labour. The German commander promised the showgirl that on their next date they would go to the ghetto. In Minsk, the ghetto was fenced in with barbed wire six feet high and guarded by two watch-towers. With some seventy-five thousand registered Jewish inhabitants at the outset, the ghetto was less than a square mile in size, spanning thirty-four streets lined with one- and two-storey wooden structures and bounded by the Svisloch River and the old Jewish cemetery. An additional thirty thousand German and Austrian Jews were housed separately in a special section of the ghetto. Waves of mass shootings and executions in poison-gas vans reduced the ghetto population by two-thirds. In the autumn of 1942 there were some nine thousand Jews left, mostly labourers, but still some non-working women, children, elderly and the infirm. Close to eight thousand of them would also be killed in 1943 as the Minsk ghetto was transformed into a labour camp.

Showing off his authority, appealing to the showgirl's desire for danger, the commander assumed that it would be impressive to 'slum it' in this forbidden part of town. And Erdmann fell for it, writing home to her mother how she looked forward to the date. A similar courtship that occurred on the grounds of the Cracow ghetto was captured in a series of photographs showing a smiling young secretary and an SS man in a picturesque carriage touring the ghetto.

A young teacher in Poland on a Hitler Youth training programme wrote home about what she witnessed in the Plöhnen ghetto in July 1942. Though the two hundred young women on the tour had been taught about Poland as a place of 'filth, laziness, primitiveness, fleas, lice and scabies', she was not prepared for what she saw. Just imagine this, she wrote to her parents – you go along the street and come across houses with the windows and doors boarded up, but inside is the noise of people constantly moving and murmuring. A large fence surrounds the houses, but the fence does not reach the ground. You look down and see feet shuffling below, some bare, some with slippers, some in sandals, others in shoes. It smells like a mass of unclean people. If you stand on your toes and peek over the fence, you see bald heads. Then suddenly you realise that it is a ghetto, and that all those people penned up in there must be Jews. One Jewish tailor at his work 'who smiled sadly' made her anxious and confused. She was relieved when she and the other girls left town. That disturbing ghetto scene was behind them. She could put the 'disappearing' Jews out of her mind.

Peering into the ghetto was more than a gesture of curiosity. It was an act of voyeurism that affirmed German superiority and the 'new order' in the East. To a German observer, the world of the eastern Jew was that of an exotic, distasteful native. In the confines of the ghetto, the threatening 'other' had been defeated and was being eradicated. In German thinking, Jews were a species verging on extinction, and their inevitable demise evoked a cruel fascination and pride. A female journalist reported on the Lodz ghetto as an 'unreal city' of Jews in 'greasy kaftans', while a student wrote home that the 'streets and squares swarm with Jews roaming around, many of them criminal types. What are we to do with this vermin?' Leaving the ghetto was likened to a return to civilisation, a regaining of one's control and place among the powerful. The daughter of the Nazi district chief of Warthegau, Poland, wrote to her fiancé about her adventures in the Lodz ghetto:

> It's really fantastic. A whole city district totally sealed off by a barbed-wire fence . . . You mostly see just riff-raff loafing about. On their clothes, they have a yellow Star of David both behind and in front (Daddy's invention, he speaks only about the starry sky of Lodz) . . . You know, one really can't have any sympathy for these people. I think that they feel very differently from us and therefore don't feel this humiliation and everything.

For the young women who were assigned to the East or who volunteered to go – to fulfil their ambitions and the regime's expectations, to experience something new and to further the Nazi cause – witnessing the realities of the Holocaust had usually several effects: it hardened their determination; it confused or eroded their sense of morality (as is clear in the assertion that the Jews in the ghetto 'don't feel this humiliation'); and it triggered the search for outlets to escape what was unpleasant or repulsive, for opiates such as sexual pleasure and alcohol. Vodka flowed in nightly parties with, as one secretary recalled, the 'nice lads in the office'. Moral transgressions seemed to go unnoticed, or at least unpunished. Scenes of unfettered greed and violence were common. Those who tried to stay away from what was happening around them found few places untouched by the war's devastation, and little solace.

Interaction with Jews and mass murder entered into these women's everyday lives in unexpected but recurring ways. Ingelene Ivens, the young teacher posted near Poznań, Poland, was shocked when she looked out from her one-room schoolhouse at the playground one day. Two emaciated Jewish labourers who had fled from a nearby camp were standing there, frightened and seeking some refuge at her school. Perhaps they assumed that children would be sympathetic. Instead the children shouted at them, and one boy threw rocks. Ivens intervened and scolded the rock-thrower while the Jewish men fled. A German

Red Cross nurse recalled a day in Lviv when she and other nurses were walking around town and decided to go to the old Jewish cemetery. Suddenly the nurse realised that she was treading on a fresh mass grave only loosely covered. Her foot had sunk into the earth – 'it stuck on me, that was unpleasant'. When a group of secretaries picnicked in the woods near Riga, they smelled the stench of the fresh mass graves. They decided to choose another spot. In the town of Buczacz, Ukraine, an agricultural overseer's wife noticed that the water tasted strange and realised that Jewish corpses had polluted the ground water.

Mass murder transforms the people who witness it and the physical environment where it occurs. What were rolling hills and sylvan glades in Ukraine became rough craters, death mounds and scorched patches. Hillsides held graves dug several yards deep (embankments absorbed bullets); riverbanks, too, served as shooting sites (blood flowed into waterways); and ravines like Babi Yar were filled with corpses and lime chloride, then dynamited shut. Personal effects and human remains could be seen on the sandy patches and barren spots between towns. The sites of mass murder were not in out-of-the-way places; rather, they often encroached on the shortcuts and paths that connected towns. Peasants, labourers and schoolchildren traversed them on foot and with carts. They were places of curiosity and of pillaging. The sites of genocide were also the very spots where German men and women went for recreation – the meadows for picnics, the forests for hunting, the swimming holes for cooling off and sunbathing.

In the rural settings of the Holocaust, resources for the Nazis' grandiose imperial endeavours were scarce. The few buildings in a town had to serve multiple purposes. A cinema could be a place of entertainment on one day, and on another a gathering place for victims prior to their murder. As one German teacher in Romanov, Ukraine, recalled, many Jews who survived the mass shootings were hiding in the forests, and her husband, the local forester, was aware of their presence. She and her husband did not help these Jews, or at least she did not mention to post-war investigators that they had done so. In her statement she described the mass graves she had often walked by in the woods. There were two large pits in an area 'as big as our house, about ten meters wide'. Before being killed, the Jews were gathered in the local school, the school where she worked. In the wake of the massacre, women in the National Socialist Welfare Association did their traditional charity work – collecting, organising, mending and distributing the clothing and bedding of the dead Jews who had been hastily buried in the woods near the teacher's house.

The urban scenery was also altered in ways visible daily. It was common to see bodies hanging from balconies and poles in Kharkiv, Kiev, Minsk and Zhytomyr. To avoid seeing them, and fearing that they might fall down on her from their precarious perch, the nurse Erika Ohr walked along the inside of the walkway near the doorways and away from the street in Zhytomyr. In Buczacz, a German boy came home from school and reported to his mother that there was a dead Jewish woman in a pool of blood near the pavement. The next morning on his way to school, the dead woman was still lying on the street. When he returned home for lunch, he saw the body again. Agitated, his mother went to the local gendarme and complained. Did she disapprove of the murder of the Jewish woman, or of the bloody 'mess' on the street that no one had cleaned up and that had upset her son? She does not make this clear in her post-war recollection.

The various cases of women who suddenly found themselves face-to-face with unexpected horror reveal moments of individual realisation followed by some adaptation to it. In the summer of 1942, Ilse Struwe, the young secretary who had been trained as a child to be seen and not heard, was stationed with fifteen other young women as a clerk in an army operations office in Rivne, Ukraine. A Jewish girl named Klebka worked in the office. One day Struwe decided to visit Klebka in the 'fenced, miserable ghetto, where the Jews were forced to live . . . It was horrible, ramshackle, dirty houses . . . "Filthy Jewish nest" was the term often spoken around Rivne.'

It was clear to Struwe from the sight of the ghetto that the Jews

German civilians and officials viewing the bodies of hanged men
on a street in Minsk, 1942 or 1943

were in a desperate situation. She was disturbed by this, but all the
same she carried on with her work and enjoyed the company of her
female colleagues in the special dormitory where they lived together.
But there were limits to distancing oneself in the East. The house
for the German female staff where Struwe lived was situated across
the street from the cinema. German SS men used this cinema as a
gathering point for Jews during their relocation from the ghetto to the
mass-shooting site at the outskirts of town. Ilse Struwe's room faced
the cinema:

> One night I was awakened by the hubbub of voices, banging tin
> cups, and soldier commandos ... I stood up and went to the win-
> dow, and looked out onto the street ... A crowd of people stepped
> out of the open door of the cinema onto the street, and under the
> guard they were led away. It was between three and four in the
> morning. I could clearly recognise men, women, children, elderly
> and youths. On their clothing I could see that they came from the

ghetto. Since September 1941 it was mandatory for all Jews to wear the star. At first I did not understand what was happening there. What are they doing? Why are they throwing pots and pans on the pavement, one after the other, with such rage? Then suddenly it came to me. They are trying to draw attention to themselves: See here what is happening to us! Do not allow this! Help us!

I stood behind the window and wanted to cry out: Do something! That is not enough! Arm yourselves! You are in the majority! A few of you could save yourselves! These persons, according to my estimate, numbered about three hundred – later I learned that it was much more – and they were being led by a handful of soldiers. But the prisoners [the Jews] dragged their feet, muttered with their heads down, along the dim street, capitulated without a fight. And I had a good look until the entire column disappeared. Then I lay down again on my bed. These persons will be killed. I knew it . . . The next morning in the office it was made known that these Jews had been shot a few kilometers from Rivne. We never saw Klebka again.

Ilse Struwe picnicking with colleagues in Ukraine, 1942 or 1943

The female personnel in her office spoke about the massacre. Struwe recalled different reactions. Some objected, complaining about the loss of Jewish labour. One stated under her breath that the Germans would conquer to the death. Another whispered: How awful. Most were afraid to speak out against it and just blurted out that Germany would be victorious. No one was critical of the young security policemen who shot the Jews.

Struwe, like many others, had wanted to *see* what was happening: she rushed to her window, craning her neck for a better look. Yet German leaders tried to reduce the number of direct witnesses to their crimes. The Final Solution was an official secret – in Himmler's words, 'a page of glory never mentioned and never to be mentioned'. Witnesses like Struwe were not supposed to look, let alone record and tell. In a notice to deport the Jews from the Tarnów ghetto, the local German commander ordered all residents who lived on the street along which the Jews would be marched to close the shutters of their windows during the *Aktion*. But such events aroused curiosity at least and, for many onlookers, *Schadenfreude*. Those at the scene experienced the event in a sensory manner that comes across in their recountings of the cacophony of property destruction, the screaming of victims, the salvo of gunfire. Struwe was confused as an observer, sensing danger, but looking on from a comfortable distance. She was surprised that the Jews did nothing to save themselves, but then again, she reasoned naively, their failure to put up a fight surely absolved her of any responsibility to get involved. After they passed by, she returned to her bed and tried to sleep. She could close her eyes, but the images and noises still pervaded her mind.

The entire *Aktion*, of which Struwe saw a glimpse, was one of several successive regional waves of massacres in Nazi-occupied Ukraine carried out under the orders of Heinrich Himmler, who urged civilian occupation officials to implement the 'Final Solution of the Jewish Question' fully – 'one hundred per cent'. In Rivne and the surrounding towns in Volhynia, one hundred and sixty thousand Jews were massacred in ghetto liquidations and mass shootings in the second half of

1942. They were hastily buried in about two hundred mass graves in the region.

From Rivne, Struwe was transferred further east, to Poltava, in the autumn of 1942. Now her unease about what she had witnessed in Rivne added to her disillusionment about the war and her role in it. Reports about German casualties in the Sixth Army around Stalingrad were piling up on her desk. She had to say goodbye to her male office mates, who would no longer enjoy the security of an office job; they were being sent to Stalingrad as replacements. New female staff were brought in. As she typed up the secret casualty lists and radioed the figures to Berlin, Struwe realised that defeat at Stalingrad was likely. Conditions and the mood in her office deteriorated. She began to question the war: 'What am I doing here, who am I? What am I doing in this man's war? Men make war. Men kill. And they need women as handmaidens in their war.'

Since her time in Belgrade in 1941, Struwe had become accustomed to seeing gruesome photographs of public executions. German war correspondents in the military took snapshots of the victims before, during and after their death, and sent the photos to military headquarters for propaganda purposes. Struwe's job was to open the post for her bosses, so she saw and read routine correspondence and classified material. One day at work a folder was placed on her desk with photographs in it. She opened it and saw dead 'partisans', who sat 'crumpled down with their arms raised'. And she thought to herself: How can one photograph such atrocities? In Belgrade she had been incensed by the photographs because she felt the images could be used by the resistance – they would jeopardise German security. In Ukraine, she started to question the policy of mass murder.

Struwe put the photographs aside and moved on to the next file. She suppressed her emotions and these upsetting questions. She worked without feeling, like a machine. As she later articulated it, 'a part of me was outside of myself'. Another woman working in Minsk expressed a similar reaction, writing to her mother in January 1943: 'I have unlearned my *Todesangst* [fear of death], I live in the moment and in the work, and don't allow myself to think of tomorrow [or]

Annette Schücking's personal photograph of the soldiers'
home in Novgorod Volynsk

yesterday. When does one get used to this life? I just want to work,
work, work. Not think, not feel!'

But Ilse Struwe's emotions could not be completely contained,
and what she saw could not be totally erased from her memory. In her
memoir she remembered that she cried incessantly and, isolating herself, was unable to befriend anyone. Only when she was transferred to
Italy in 1943 did she break free of the depression she had experienced
in Ukraine.

A similar disillusionment would come to Annette Schücking, the former law student, whose first shocking encounter with soldiers on the
train in Brest paled in comparison with what she was to see and hear
when she arrived at her destination in Ukraine. On her first day in
Novgorod Volynsk, an old fortress town with about eighteen thousand inhabitants (about half of them Jews), Schücking was told that all
the Jews had been killed. A German officer stated this matter-of-factly
as they all dined. Local Ukrainians who worked in the soldiers' home

with Schücking told her that about ten thousand Jews in the town and nearby towns had been shot. This seemed incomprehensible to her.

Determined to see for herself, she went to the Jewish quarter and saw the ransacked houses. Hebrew texts were lying on the floor along with other personal belongings. Her German colleagues collected useful items such as candlesticks to use in their local quarters or to bring home as war booty. Her orientation in Novgorod Volynsk had included a tour of the fortress that lay on the bank of the Sluch River, where Jews had been shot the month before, in September 1941. The tour guide, a member of the engineering staff, pointed out the spot on the riverbank where four hundred and fifty Jewish men, women and children were buried.

Everyday life in the soldiers' home where Schücking was a relief worker meant constant contact with German soldiers; on some days thousands visited the retreat to enjoy German cooking and conversation. Nazi propagandists called these military retreats 'islands of home'. In these German-only canteens, soldiers spoke openly about the massacres they witnessed and carried out. 'Oftentimes conversations with soldiers got personal fast,' Schücking would later explain. 'They were all men who hadn't been around women for a long time. There were the Ukrainian women, of course, but they couldn't talk to them – and they all had an intense need to talk.'

One day she was riding in a lorry and the German soldier who was driving blurted out his story. He told of an incident not far from the soldiers' home, in Koziatyn, a village south-east of Kiev. He and his colleagues had locked up several hundred Jews and denied them food and water. Weakening them was a preparatory measure. After two days the Jews were shot to death by a special squad that was active in the region. Schücking, with her lawyer's training, collected precise details and recorded them in letters she wrote to her parents. German soldiers needed to tell her what they had heard, seen and done. And she needed to write it down.

A German Red Cross nurse in Warsaw in 1943 listened to a wounded soldier who could not sleep. His company had been assigned to a shooting commando unit. There was a large pit; civilians were led to its edge, where he and his men shot them in the back of the head. An elderly woman at the edge of the pit ran to him. She was terrified and desperate. She had a photograph of herself in her hand. She gave it to him and asked that he give the photograph to her husband. The soldier had kept the photograph in his pay book, and showed it to the nurse.

Such stories are everywhere; soldiers and SS men who bloodied their hands in the genocide often told female comrades of their deeds. One day two executioners entered the private quarters of the Minsk showgirl Brigitte Erdmann, 'their eyes burning with hate, the hate of a mortally wounded animal or of an abused child'. One placed his head on her shoulder, and she comforted him. She delighted in the attention of these desperate men, and preferred to console them rather than confront them.

Schücking's letters home reveal a woman more critical of the violent men she encountered. On 28 December 1941, while travelling in a car, she met a sergeant. He explained that he had volunteered to shoot Jews in an upcoming action near Vinnytsia, Ukraine. He wanted a promotion. Annette advised him not to participate because 'it would give him nightmares'. In mid-January she met the sergeant again, and he confirmed that he had taken part in the mass shootings in Khmilnyk, where, on 9 January 1942, German SS policemen, assisted by local army and indigenous auxiliaries, had killed six thousand Jews. According to a Jewish survivor, the German soldiers 'went on a rampage; they smashed windows, fired their guns ... Corpses were strewn everywhere, the snow was red with blood, the barbarians were running around and shouting like wild animals: "Beat the kikes! *Jude kaput!*"'

To make mass murder more economical, German SS and police leaders, regional military commanders and Nazi Party officials developed a programme to confiscate and redistribute the property of Jews. Tons of clothing were stored, cleaned, mended and given to ethnic German refugees who were colonising the newly occupied territories. At the end of 1941, Schücking saw clothing piled in a warehouse established by the National Socialist Welfare Association (NSV). She had gone there to find some items for the Ukrainian kitchen helpers in her workplace. Some of the German female colleagues who accompanied her enthusiastically thanked the German officials who opened up the warehouse to them, declaring 'Heil Hitler' when they saw all the booty. Schücking was struck by the children's clothing in the piles, and took nothing; some of her female colleagues were equally uneasy. Schücking wrote to her mother and told friends at home not to accept clothing from the NSV, since it was from murdered Jews.

Every week she drove sixty miles from Novgorod Volynsk to the capital city of Rivne to pick up supplies. It was here that Schücking had her 'ghetto' experience. She saw Jewish women and children being led away in July 1942, probably part of the same operation that Ilse Struwe witnessed. Although the two women may not actually have met in Rivne, their lives intersected there, and they responded to the events in a similar manner, despite their very different backgrounds. Like Ilse Struwe, Annette Schücking expressed feelings of helplessness, fear and frustration. But there were limits to their empathy. Both asked: What can one do, after all? They kept busy and sought amusements – picnics, concerts – with their colleagues. They were among the few German women surrounded by thousands of soldiers; they carefully avoided the rough ones in the crowd, SS men and other notorious occupation officials who brandished their whips and pistols. After a few weeks in Ukraine, seeing the evidence of mass murder in Rivne in early November 1941 and the deteriorating condition of the few Jewish labourers who remained and then were also killed while she was there, Schücking wrote home to her mother: 'What Papa says is true; people with no moral inhibitions exude a strange odor. I can now pick out these people, and many of them really do smell like blood. Oh Mama, what an enormous slaughterhouse the world is.'

Among the tens of thousands of single women working in the various military, administrative and private business offices of the eastern territories, Schücking and Struwe represented the largest category, the bystanders. They were not presented with the choice to participate directly in the violence, or, as some extremists would see it, the 'opportunity' to collaborate. They were German female patriots doing their civil service. They were curious; they sought adventure. Once they entered the eastern territories and witnessed the atrocities, such as the ghetto liquidations in Rivne, they articulated emotions of concern and shock.

A secretary in Slonim was awakened at four in the morning by the sound of shooting. For hours she watched from her window as thousands of Jews from Slonim were herded out of the ghetto under constant gunfire and lined up. The ghetto was in flames. The next day, when she was allowed to leave her quarters – the SS and police had declared a lockdown during the action – she saw on the streets at the edge of the ghetto two long rows of charred Jewish bodies. Like Schücking and Struwe, she could hardly avoid witnessing the mass murder. She did not condone it, but she could not stop it either.

# 4

||||||||||||||||||||||||||

# Accomplices

WOMEN LIKE ANNETTE SCHÜCKING, Ilse Struwe, Ingelene Ivens and Erika Ohr were not exceptional women during the war. They were exceptional *after* the war. Of the hundreds of thousands who did go east, few published or publicly spoke at length about the Jewish victims and atrocities they had seen, as these four women did. During the Nazi era, many women were happy to don a uniform and embrace their new-found adulthood and civic identity in the movement. Then, in 1945, they removed and hid their insignias, and tucked their uniforms into drawers and attic chests. They concealed the provenance of items that they had plundered from the East, including the personal belongings of Jewish victims.

The general silence of German women after the war is rooted in many things, including feelings of shame, grief and fear. It was certainly in the interest of many women who were in the eastern killing fields to hide the fact that they were near crime scenes. Even if they wanted to speak, there were few who wanted to listen. There is no social tradition that encourages women to tell war stories about the violence they saw, experienced or perpetrated. In contrast, German women could speak about their hardships and victimisation on the home front – about doing men's work, such as operating trams, policing market places and managing farms; about the devastating aerial bombings of their towns; about homelessness, flight and post-war famine. Audiences were quite receptive to recollections that affirmed traditional wartime roles for women as staunch defenders, maids-in-waiting and innocent martyrs.

Their youth explains how so many of these women got swept up in the moment and the movement. Or was this a later excuse? In memoirs and interviews, and even as defendants in the courtroom, German women explained shameful actions with the comment 'Oh, I was so young in those days.' As young women they were naive, and they were malleable. But during the war, as each came closer to the horrible reality of the nation's deeds, each had to make a personal choice. And while there might not be the option to leave one's post, nor could one avoid being a witness to genocide, there were choices concerning how one behaved during and after the war.

Many German women encountered what happened, in its various stages. They peered into ghettos out of curiosity, discovered mass graves and, like Annette Schücking, were invited to sort through Jewish clothing and personal belongings. Like Ingelene Ivens, they encountered Jewish refugees seeking aid on the school playground; like Ilse Struwe, they saw from windows that Jews were being led away to the edge of town, and they heard the mass shootings. To protect themselves, most who saw something chose to shut their eyes afterwards. But what about the women who were at the centre of the mass-murder machinery and could not turn a blind eye?

In Holocaust studies one type of perpetrator, fashioned after Adolf Eichmann and others who organised deportations of Jews from Berlin headquarters, is the male bureaucratic killer, or desk murderer. He commits genocide through giving or passing along written orders; thus his pen or typewriter keys become his weapon. This type of modern genocidaire assumes that the paper, like its administrator, remains clean and bloodless. The desk murderer does his official duty. He convinces himself as he orders the deaths of tens of thousands that he has remained decent, civilised and even innocent of the crime. What about the women who staffed those offices, the female assistants whose agile fingers pressed the keys on the typewriters, and whose clean hands distributed the orders to kill?

As Hitler's empire expanded and contracted, women had to take on more tasks, not only in managing households and farms, but also in running government systems and private businesses. In fact, the proportion of women in the Gestapo offices of Vienna and Berlin was unusually high, reaching 40 per cent by the war's end. Women were expected to stand by men as well as fill their positions to free them up for the front. The exigencies of war accelerated the labour trends of the interwar period and also reversed the educational policies of the 1930s: women's access to higher education improved for a time, women swelled the ranks of government offices and a new female hierarchy emerged, from regular aides to senior staff. But such social mobility came with a price – participation in operations of mass murder.

Women secretaries, file clerks, typists and telephone operators were attached to the bureaucratic tentacles of the Reich system of rule. Each office or outpost employed at least one German woman from the Reich. If on average there was one female assistant reporting to five male administrators, this would put the figure of female staff in the civilian governing offices of Nazi-occupied Poland at about five thousand, with at least twice as many in Ukraine, Belarus and the Baltics combined. As administrative accomplices in central offices where the Holocaust was organised and implemented – such as the district governor's office or the Department of Jewish Affairs of the security police – most claimed that they were 'just doing their job'. But their routine procedures generated unprecedented crimes. None could claim ignorance of the human impact of her work.

Little has been written about the internal workings of these offices, in part because of inattention to the revealing testimony of secretaries who were on the inside or to that of the Jewish survivors who interacted with these women and identified them as having been at crime scenes. Within the local hierarchy of German female administrators, the secretary to the district commissar (regional governor) was the person most often seen by his side. The commissars were not numerous (especially if one considers the vast size of the area they governed), but they were notoriously visible, mockingly described as pheasants for the uniforms they wore as they strutted about – a garish mustard-brown, decorated with colourful Nazi patches and pins. Their female assistants earned the label of smaller fowl, *Goldammern* or 'yellowhammers' – sparrow-sized, thick-billed birds that nest in patches of scrub or ditches. In small-town settings such as the Polish-Lithuanian town of Lida, German officials spent a good deal of time together: they and their families shared housing, schools, canteens and offices, and they swam and picnicked together at local lakes and streams.

Among the elite in Lida was Liselotte Meier, the young woman who chose office work in the East over factory work in Leipzig. Her month-long orientation at Crössinsee Castle in Pomerania, Poland, included training in shooting a pistol. One of the dignitaries at the orientation caught her eye, a handsome Stormtrooper named Hermann Hanweg. Almost twice her age, Hanweg had worked his way up in the Party administration and, like many 'old fighters', was rewarded with a sinecure in the empire. The two spent time together in Minsk and fell in love. Hanweg insisted that Liselotte join him when he was given the post of district commissar of Lida. When they arrived there in the early autumn of 1941, a mobile killing squad had already swept through town and massacred the Jewish intelligentsia and patients in local hospitals. Thousands of Jews remained, however, and it was Hanweg's duty to make the region *Judenfrei*, free of Jews.

The twenty-year-old Meier learned to stay close to Hanweg and to mix business with pleasure. She followed him everywhere. With her desk positioned in front of his office door, she controlled all access to her boss. She knew the Jewish council members; some twenty years after the war, she could still identify them by name. She was also close to Hanweg's family, though perhaps not by choice. Hanweg ordered Meier to escort his wife and three children when they relocated to

Lida. The children called Meier 'Vice-Mama'; the wife of the commissar named her 'Brutus'.

In Lida, the Hanweg children attended a special German school and played in the local parks and forests. They routinely accompanied their mother and father on tours of the ghetto workshops, where thousands of Jews tried desperately to stay alive by fulfilling every order and whim of the local Germans. To please the commissar, a team of Jewish craftsmen created an elaborate electric train set for his son's birthday. They also presented Hanweg with a set of rings, one for each member of the family. Today the commissar's ring remains a treasured family heirloom. Featuring a large amber stone set in silver, it is decorated with the Hanweg coat of arms – a tiny axe and mace finely carved by an artisan with a keen eye for the minute detail of filigree.

Mounting wartime deprivations in the Old Reich – food and housing shortages – made the riches of the East irresistible. Secretaries may have received letters and special personal items from back home, but by far the bulk of care packages in the postal system were sent not from Germany to the East, but rather the other way round. Personnel in the occupied territories shipped trainloads of plundered items to family in Germany and Austria – crates of eggs, flour, sugar, clothing and home furnishings. It was the biggest campaign of organised robbery and economic exploitation in history, and German women were among its prime agents and beneficiaries.

This indulgence was not condoned by the regime; Jewish belongings were officially Reich property and not meant for personal consumption. Some plunderers, women among them, were punished and even executed for stealing from the Reich. But it is clear that in this particular activity there was little regard for obeying the Führer, especially because the massive theft was part and parcel of the economy of the Third Reich. If one had to do the dirty work of mass murder, one expected to be compensated. The greed of German men and women who gained access to the plunder was seemingly insatiable. The wife of a policeman in Warsaw, for instance, stockpiled so much that she lacked the space to hide it; she simply piled up the booty outside, around her house. The enterprising wife of a police official in Lviv who decided to sell her plunder brazenly established a shop on the very street where her husband worked at police headquarters. Wives of top officials paraded around in stolen furs and demanded superior living quarters, ordering Jewish craftsmen to lay stolen porcelain tiles in lavish bathrooms and to erect custom-made balconies. The excesses were so blatant, in fact, that they generated a number of critical reports and investigations during the war.

The distribution and consumption of Jewish goods near the mass-murder sites was experienced as a triumph and cause for celebration. Operation (*Aktion*) Reinhard, the Nazi campaign to murder 1.7 to 2 million Polish Jews (along with Jews of other nationalities) who were sent to the gassing centres of Belzec, Sobibor and Treblinka, produced one of the biggest plunder depots in all of Nazi-occupied Europe. Sitting on this pile of booty near Lublin was the manager of this murder operation, SS Major General Odilo Globocnik, and surrounding him were his 'ladies'. According to a former aide, Globocnik's secretaries 'cheerfully' prepared lists of Jewish deportees to Treblinka, lists of Jews who died and lists of confiscated property.

Globocnik's lovers and secretaries were not direct perpetrators of the Holocaust, or at least no testimony or documentation has surfaced proving that they committed violent acts. But they were accomplices: they took dictation and typed up the orders facilitating the robbery, deportation and mass murder of Jews. They performed these duties with the knowledge that they were contributing to the goal of total extermination of the Jewish people. They transmitted Globocnik's reports to Himmler on the 'successful' operations of the Final Solution. As the creators of professional and private havens for the top managers, such as Globocnik, they contributed to the normalisation of the perverse.

One day when Hanweg's son went to the ghetto workshops, where he liked to play, he discovered that no Jews were there. Since Jews in Lida were regularly shot in town and in the neighbouring villages, he was not surprised when he overheard adults saying that nearly all the Jews had been killed. The first and largest massacre had occurred on 8 May

1942, just over a mile from town. About 5,670 Jews were driven to the outskirts, forced to undress and kneel before mass graves and shot. A Jewish work detail spread quicklime and earth over the bodies. Then Hanweg and his deputy forced the workers, who had just buried their loved ones, to bow down and say thank you for allowing them to live. In town, the corpses of the elderly and children littered the streets. These victims had been too frail or small to walk to their deaths on their own.

All the secretaries in the offices saw the commotion and heard the gunfire. But Liselotte Meier was more than a passive witness: she participated in the planning of the massacres and was present at more than one of the shootings that occurred in 1942–43. In fact, post-war statements about crimes committed by the commissar's office in Lida stressed that Meier was the most knowledgeable person, 'better informed than many of the officials in the station'.

A certified bookkeeper, Meier went with Hanweg to the Jewish workshops three or four times each week and kept careful tallies of German orders for goods and deliveries from the Jewish labourers. She discussed the orders with members of the Jewish council and the elder of the council, an engineer named Altmann. She placed orders of her own as well. A former Jewish labourer recalled:

> Commissariat officials, German officers, and their relatives took advantage of the workshops and flooded them with orders that were completed on time. A special department handled leather leftovers received from boot factories, and made leather items such as belts, wallets, purses, stripe-colored boxes, and leather jewelry that especially charmed female officials at the commissariat offices.

Jewish labourers catered to Meier's and Hanweg's every wish, constructing a swimming pool for their enjoyment, renovating a villa and serving them post-coital delicacies as they lay naked in bed. In hindsight, it may seem incomprehensible that intimate relationships developed within the maelstrom of genocidal violence. But the violent horrors of the Holocaust were no mere backdrop to Meier and Hanweg's love affair; they were a central drama igniting its passion. The two were intoxicated with their new-found power and 'place in the sun', a sensation known in German as the *Ostrausch* or 'eastern rush'. It was a euphoria that was expressed in sex and violence.

Hanweg's secretary-concubine became his confidante. He gave Meier special access to the office safe where the most secret orders were stored. She did not take simple dictation from the commissar, which was mainly the job of the stenographer, but was often told to write up orders and take care of clerical matters with other local German officials, including the gendarme leaders. When questioned after the war, Liselotte Meier could not recall if she had issued an order that authorised the shooting of sixteen Jews who appeared late for work, an order that others later accused her of writing. During secret planning meetings before a mass shooting, Meier took the meeting notes and coordinated the logistics with executioners from the security police (SD), the local gendarmerie, the indigenous mayor and the deputy commissar in charge of 'Jewish affairs'. She was careful about how much she committed to paper. 'There was little written traffic about Jewish actions, that was absolutely secret,' she later stated. Her boss simply told the local police chief and office staff when and where the pits were to be dug.

Meier kept the coveted office stamp in her desk drawer; that meant that she could sign on behalf of the commissar. The official stamp and special forms, such as the worker's identification card (the so-called Gold Card), were potentially lifesaving bureaucratic tools. For a Jewish person, the only way to escape the shooting pits, other than flight and suicide, was to secure a labour assignment. The commissar and his staff had the authority to certify who was and who was not a Jew. They could decide who would be killed, who could be spared. Secretaries who participated in the selection of Jewish labourers and issued the identification cards had their favourites; one of Meier's was the Jewish hairstylist who came to her private quarters. While this stylist was a useful Jew, most others were, as she put it, 'that *Dreck*' – rubbish. In Slonim (in what is Belarus today), another special assistant to the district commissar, the secretary Erna Reichmann, stood before

Jews forced to march through Lida before being killed, with German
guards – a female official or civilian among them – presumably selecting
labourers and appropriating Jewish belongings, March 1942

a column of two thousand Jews who were being marched to the mass
shooting site. Jewish labourers were pulled out of the line based on a
formal list that she and her colleagues had typed up, or they were selected spontaneously. Reichmann spotted a Jewish woman who 'had
not finished knitting a sweater for her', so she removed her from the
column.

Yet even these skilled Jewish labourers were, to the Nazi way of
thinking, ultimately dispensable. Deprived of any worth or dignity as
human beings, Jews became the slaves and playthings of their German overseers. Killing Jews became a source of amusement in Lida,
like hunting rabbits. As one Jewish survivor recalled:

On one Sunday all the Jews of Lida were called out to go into
the nearby forest to clear out the rabbits hiding in the bushes,
and chase them in the direction of the hunters. A group of several hundred men were recruited for this job, and a long line
of Jews marched down the road to the forest in the deep snow,

shaking from cold and fear of what they would encounter. Suddenly a group of winter carriages appeared, including the local commissar Hanweg and his staff, senior officials, and women wearing beautiful fur coats. They were all drunk, lying around their seats in the carriage hugging and shouting, their peals of laughter echoing in the distance. The carriages galloped between the rows of marchers, and the shouting grew louder. The wild Germans mocked the Jews, laughed at them, and struck those nearby with whips. One of the drunken officers aimed his hunting rifle and started shooting at the Jews to the raucous pleasure of his staff. The bullets struck some marchers who collapsed in pools of blood.

A 'Frau Apfelbaum' with a shotgun in the Lida woods

After the war Meier admitted that she joined her colleagues on these Sunday outings and hunting trips. Jews had become easy targets that brought instant gratification to inexperienced, often intoxicated marksmen. Exhausted and malnourished, Jewish labourers moved slowly in the snow. Their dark figures stood out against the white winter landscape. A lucky few dodged the German bullets and found refuge in the camouflage of the forest. 'Trees saved us,' a survivor from Lida would later say. 'We had so much confidence in bushes, they could not see us there.' Meier could not have imagined that, twenty years later, Lida's Jews would reappear to identify and accuse her.

Historians of the Holocaust have often focused on the first wave of massacres in the Soviet Union, perpetrated by the mobile security units known as the *Einsatzgruppen*. By the end of 1941 these elite killing squads had gunned down close to five hundred thousand Soviet Jews. So extensive was the documentation of their gruesome work that after the war American prosecutors conducted a special Nuremberg trial against leading *Einsatzgruppen* members. But little has been said about those who typed up this damning evidence of the Holocaust. There were at least thirteen female typists assigned to Einsatzgruppe A. One of them listened carefully to her boss, Walther Stahlecker, as he dictated numbers adding up to 135,567 Jews, communists and mentally ill who had been shot in Estonia, Latvia, Lithuania and Belarus in the late summer and autumn of 1941. She helped type, copy and officially certify the 143-page report to be sent to Berlin from the Einsatzgruppe A outpost in Riga. A special map accompanying Stahlecker's final report to Heydrich in January 1942 depicted the near-completion of the Final Solution in the Ostland. A coffin was drawn for each region, and a tally of the total number of Jews killed appeared beside each coffin on the map.

Recipients of the Stahlecker reports did not have to bother to read every statement. The tallies were impressive enough, and the visual aid of the coffins communicated clearly the scope of the killing. Women in SS field offices prepared thousands of pages of such reports, received them in Berlin headquarters and then distributed them across Reich agencies.

A coffin-decorated tally by Einsatzgruppe A of Jews
killed in each region in 1941

Himmler realised that women constituted a critical labour force
for carrying out his genocidal plans. Besides association with the SS
as camp guards and fertile brides, women were permitted to join the
elite terror organisation in a special auxiliary corps of administrators.
In early 1942 Himmler ordered the establishment of a female reporting and clerical unit of the SS, the SS-Frauenkorps. He had to convince his subordinates that women should be respected not only for
their biological contribution, but also for their organisational skills.
In a famous speech to SS generals in Poznań in October 1943, Himmler praised his colleagues for sending their daughters, sisters, brides
and girlfriends to the new elite training programme. Appealing to the
men's sense of chivalry and honour, he urged them to comply with this
integration of women in the workforce as necessary for the war effort.
As for the morale of his female recruits, Himmler visited the school

and reassured them that their office work in the SS would not degrade them; on the contrary, it would enhance their marriageability.

The presence and promotion of women in the SS workplace was not without its conflicts and tensions. The woman appointed first SS female superintendent of Birkenau, Johanna Langefeld, greeted Himmler when he visited Auschwitz on 18 July 1942. Her male colleague, the Auschwitz commandant Rudolf Höss, thought Langefeld was too assertive and questioned whether she was up to implementing plans for the large women's camp in Birkenau. Himmler insisted that a 'women's camp must be commanded by a woman'. He supported Langefeld's position as SS senior superintendent and warned that SS men were not to enter the female camp. Career tracks in camp and other bureaucracies opened up for women in the modern Nazi state, not in subordinate roles, but in a hierarchy that placed them in commanding positions with unprecedented power, with the revered status of a uniformed government official.

When female administrators and guards abusively managed the prisoner population at a major camp or typed orders to carry out massacres of Jews and of Polish, Ukrainian and Belarusian civilians who had been branded partisans, they helped make mass murder standard operating procedure. They lent their organisational know-how and individual skills to the machinery of destruction. In Warsaw, secret police secretaries handled the paperwork on reprisals against Polish political prisoners. What did this actually entail? As one clerk explained, 'In the hallway, there was then a bunch of files, say a hundred files or so, and when then only fifty were to be shot it was in the women's sole discretion to choose the files. Sometimes the head of the division would say, "This or that person must go, get rid of that piece of shit."' Usually, though, 'it was up to the receptionists to decide about who would be shot. Sometimes one of the women would ask her colleague: "How about this one? Yes or no?"' This inside look at the Warsaw police department captures essential features of the Nazi terror – the paperwork behind it, its magnitude, its ideological fury, its routine randomness – and its dependence on women office workers.

• • •

In Tarnopol (a town in present-day Ukraine, but in Nazi-occupied Poland during the war), a twenty-two-year-old typist in the Gestapo office noticed special meetings during August 1942, attended by all the SS men from the region. After such meetings, her boss informed her that the office would be empty the following day and that the women would have to 'hold down the fort'. When the male staff returned, they were in a festive mood and told stories about mass shootings, often in gruesome detail. The killing was done with a large plank, 'like a diving board', which was placed over the mass grave. Jews were made to walk the plank, and fell into the grave upon being shot by sharpshooters, who stood at a distance. SS policemen from the young typist's office carried out shootings in Tarnopol, Skalat and Brezhany. One of the men approached her after returning from a massacre. He extended his hand to her and asked her to shake it. She refused, telling him it was dirty. 'Yes,' he replied, laughing, and he made a gesture as if firing a gun. Then he pointed to his uniform and boots and said, 'Look, here is a drop of blood, and here still another, and another.'

Sabine Dick, the secretary who worked in the Reich Security Main Office in Berlin before deciding to take a position in the office of the secret police in Minsk, did extend her hand to her bloodstained boss. When she arrived in Belarus she was a seasoned Gestapo secretary who had been on the inside for almost a decade. She was looking to advance her position and to increase her pay cheque. She was promised the best assignment – she was to be personal secretary to Georg Heuser, a former law student, professional detective and seasoned killer from Einsatzgruppe A. He would later be convicted by a West German court for the murder of 11,103 people.

Georg Heuser and Sabine Dick ran an efficient office and became friends. According to Dick's later testimony, when Heuser needed to issue orders for an *Aktion* against Jews, he would rush to his assistant's desk: 'Sabine, quickly write this up!' Sabine Dick understood the code language of such orders: though Heuser might dictate to her something about the 'thorough destruction of a ghetto in some place', the subject line rarely referred explicitly to Jews. Usually he had her draw up three sets of orders, one for each commander of a shooting squad. She completed the paperwork, and it was Heuser who hand-delivered the orders to his unit commanders. Thus the orders were not widely circulated, and no duplicates were made for the files. Once such orders were issued, the atmosphere in the office was calm or sometimes even festive and relaxed. The men were relieved that they were not being called into real combat in anti-partisan warfare. Shooting defence-less Jews was easier.

Orders issued for waging an anti-partisan campaign were different. Many more details were committed to paper, including all the names of participants, the assignment of weapons and the allocation of food and other supplies. In the orders that Sabine Dick typed for Jewish executions, there was no mention of food supplies. Instead, schnapps was requisitioned and given to the shooters. Those who joined the execution squads often returned drunk from the *Aktion* and went to the women's dormitory. Under the pretence that there were more reports to be typed, they dragged women from their rooms and, as another secretary put it delicately, 'sought our company'.

Anti-partisan operations could last for weeks; mass shootings usually occurred on one day. All the SS policemen on staff were expected to carry out atrocities against civilians and partisans, but no one was punished if he refused to participate in an *Aktion* against the Jews or if he chose to stay in the office on the day of the massacres. Neither men nor women were required to carry out the genocide, and yet the Holocaust could not have been accomplished if a sense of duty had not prevailed over the sense of morality. In favouring perceived duty over morality, men and women were more alike than different.

Not long after Sabine Dick and her female colleagues arrived in the eastern territories at the end of 1941, they saw that Jews who lived there or who had been transported there from the Reich were being massacred. The Minsk Gestapo office, which employed at least ten female clerks, typists, bookkeepers and translators, was an epicentre of the Holocaust. Many of the more notorious perpetrators of the Holocaust spent some time there, including Heinrich Himmler, who liked to make decisions on the spot and used killing sites in Belarus to test out murderous experiments with explosives and carbon monoxide.

In Sabine Dick's office there were about a hundred Jewish workers who slept in the basement. The building also contained interrogation rooms and torture chambers. Some Jews were hanged in the court-yard; others were loaded onto gas vans in front of the office. This was the atmosphere of her workplace.

It is hardly surprising, then, that around the office Jewish deport-ees and prisoners were spoken of in non-human terms. In the culture of consumption, trade and profiteering, a culture often dominated by German women, Jews were seen as commodities. When transports of Jews arrived in Minsk, the Gestapo office staff enjoyed an abundance of delicacies – which they called *Judenwurst*, Jewish sausage – stolen from the deportees. Nothing was to go to waste except the 'human trash'. Often at the centre of organising and distributing Jewish goods and property, the secretaries in the office handled the plundered 'Jewish sausage'. Before or after the Jews were killed, the secretaries prepared it, served it and ate it with their male colleagues.

But Sabine Dick wanted more than Jewish food. Colleagues in the office spoke about a big farmhouse in Maly Trostenets, about eight miles outside Minsk, that was stuffed with Jewish clothes and other personal items. The estate in Maly Trostenets was a labour camp and major re-ceiving area where local Jews and Jews from the Netherlands, Austria, Czech lands, Germany and Poland were shot in pits, then flattened with tractors. The farm and nearby forests would soon hold the larg-est concentration of mass graves of the Holocaust on Belarusian terri-tory; estimates of Jews killed there range from sixty thousand to one hundred thousand. Many of those killed at Maly Trostenets were well-to-do and had brought their most valuable possessions with them from Hamburg, Frankfurt and Vienna. When Dick's brother was killed in the war and she needed a mourning dress, she naturally thought of the depot in Maly Trostenets as a place where she could find one. SS *Obersturmbannführer* Eduard Strauch – Heuser's boss – remarked that it would not be appropriate for her, a German woman in her position, to wear Jewish things. She agreed and abstained from taking the dress. Gold was different. Sabine secured a document from her dentist certi-fying that gold was needed for fillings in her teeth, and presented the certificate to Georg Heuser. He gave her three Jewish wedding rings from the stash of gold kept in the office safe. After the war Dick claimed that the rings were lost in the chaos of the Allied plundering of her family home. But investigators did not ask her to open her mouth.

The secretaries Liselotte Meier and Sabine Dick were at the very centre of the Nazi murder machinery, and they, like so many others, chose to benefit from their proximity to power, plundering in depraved ways. The complicity of teachers, nurses, social workers and resettlement advisers in the East was not as routine and widespread as that of secretaries (and, as we shall see, of wives). But it was significant nonetheless, and worth examining for the evidence it provides on how the genocide drew women into its operations, often in an ad hoc manner.

In mapping the presence of German women in the East, one can find them in large numbers in regions with high concentrations of ethnic Germans: in parts of Lithuania, Ukraine and eastern Poland, and in settlements of tsarist Russia where German farmers and craftsmen had lived since the eighteenth century. With Hitler and Himmler envisioning these colonies as future Aryan utopias and Reich strongholds, young German women were charged with building up these settlements as the Führer's missionaries, also known as 'culture bearers'.

One such ethnic German stronghold was wedged between Zhytomyr and Vinnytsia, where Hitler and Himmler established their top-secret headquarters in the summer of 1942. About one hundred women from the Reich arrived to transform local ethnic German youths into Hitler loyalists. As official representatives of the National Socialist Welfare Association, these colonial enthusiasts established forty-one kindergartens and several birthing centres and nursing stations. Midwives instructed young mothers about 'racial hygiene'. Social workers and educators taught ethnic Germans that the Jews had set out to destroy the German people, and that the war was being fought against Jews who had surrounded and threatened to starve the Germans. They advised youths to protect the German race by following the Führer's example in not smoking or drinking. They distributed photos of Hitler and swastika flags, and they taught young people Nazi songs. These ethnic Germans were often destitute, but also quite receptive to the concepts of anti-Semitic scapegoating and vengeance: they had experienced Bolshevik terror in the 1930s, and they connected Jews with Bolshevism. German women, as culture bearers who worked diligently to indoctrinate ethnic Germans, were deadly enablers of the vengeance.

We have seen that within German occupation society was another female group, the wives of SS men. What is especially striking about these wives is that, unlike the secretaries, teachers, nurses or 'culture bearers', they were not officially given any direct role in the division of labour that made the Holocaust possible. Yet their proximity to the murderers and their own ideological fanaticism made many of them into potential participants. Others served as enablers.

Nazi leaders tried various measures to keep marriages intact during the war, such as laws against adultery. Wherever possible, they also encouraged wives of officials to go east for brief visits with their husbands. To travel, one had to possess a special pass to enter the occupied territories, which was arranged by the invitee, usually a husband, relative or a boss in a government agency.

Vera Wohlauf, whose first marriage to a Hamburg merchant she had parlayed into a second one with an SS police officer, arrived in Poland in the summer of 1942. She and her new husband, Julius, had quickly made arrangements for a wedding ceremony during his leave in late June, and Vera wasted no time in joining him in the East afterwards.

Julius was scheduled to command one of three companies of Order Police Battalion 101 assigned to the liquidation of the Miedzyrzec-Podlaski ghetto on 25–26 August 1942. Over the course of these two days, more than eleven thousand Jews were gathered in the market place. Those who could not walk or who resisted deportation were beaten and shot. Many collapsed in the summer heat. The corpses of young and old, men, women and children, approximately 960 bodies, lay scattered and in piles on the streets. After being herded to the train station, where nearly sixty railway carriages stood ready, the surviving Jews were shoved into the freight wagons, as many as 140 people per wagon. Many were crushed and suffocated by the lack of space and air. Those who survived this deportation massacre were transported to Treblinka, where they were gassed upon arrival.

The morning of the massacre, Julius Wohlauf was late for duty. When his comrades arrived at their captain's residence, out strolled Vera, who jumped in the front seat of the lorry, which was part of the convoy headed to Miedzyrzec. Perhaps there was still a morning chill in the air, or perhaps Vera wanted to dress the part, but she wore a military coat over her summer dress, and a cap.

Vera was not the only woman present at the massacre. Other wives of German officials and German Red Cross nurses were also there. The nurses were not tracked down after the war when Order Police Battalion 101 was investigated. The wives of some of the order policemen were. Vera was asked about this massacre in Miedzyrzec. She described it as a 'peaceful, nearly idyllic resettlement to an eastern work camp'. There were, however, witnesses who eventually testified otherwise. Vera Wohlauf was unusually conspicuous at the market place where the Jews had been assembled for deportation. She did not stand aside, but circulated among the victims, demonstrating her power and humiliating them. Allegedly brandishing a whip, a status symbol for Nazi colonisers in the East, Wohlauf was also described in post-war testimony as being pregnant. Vera, a confirmed attention-seeker, placed herself at the centre of the bloodshed in town. From the perspective of the Jews who had already suffered violent beatings and wild shootings in the Nazi round-up, Vera appeared as a persecutor, as 'one of them'.

The history of this *Aktion* has been studied by the Holocaust scholars Christopher Browning, Gudrun Schwarz and Daniel Goldhagen. Each has analysed the events and drawn different conclusions about one unusual aspect of this horrific massacre – the presence of Vera Wohlauf. In Browning's analysis, the men felt uncomfortable about her female presence at the massacre, which conjured up feelings of shame. Goldhagen, in contrast, stresses that the men of Police Battalion 101 were proud of their acts against Jews; Vera's incongruous pregnant presence merely reminded them that the dirty deeds of genocide were 'man's work'. But Browning and Goldhagen both analyse Vera's presence and actions in relation to the German men, the killers, rather than examine her own agency at Miedzyrzec.

Two months before the massacre, Vera had the medical exam required for her to marry Julius. The doctor noted that Vera had menstruated in May 1942 and that she showed no signs of being pregnant. Vera gave birth in early February 1943, which means that during the August massacres she was in her first two months of pregnancy, with her first child. She would not have been visibly pregnant at this early stage, contrary to what was prominently featured in post-war recollections by Julius Wohlauf's comrades and recounted by the wife of another order policeman in the unit. The information of her 'condition' may have been revealed by Vera at the time of the massacre, or it may have been stressed in hindsight.

The wife of a lieutenant in the battalion testified after the war that the police commander held a 'public' meeting after the Miedzyrzec *Aktion* 'before a rather large gathering of officers and NCOs, and in the presence of various wives who were staying with their husbands as visitors, including also me'. The commander, Major Trapp, explained that killing actions were off-limits to women, since it was 'outrageous that women who are in a state of pregnancy should witness such a thing'. In Hitler's Germany, the female badge of honour was the pregnant belly. In the biologically driven culture of the Reich, German women were valued for their fertility. Women's bodies and health were not their own private business; they were the subject of public discussion.

Vera Wohlauf's pregnant presence was understood at the time and afterwards as a double affront to the gender roles of men and women. An upstanding German woman at the centre of the massacre was problematic enough for the men, who enjoyed the company of their wives on the front, but wanted to set certain boundaries concerning women's direct involvement in the bloodshed. Holocaust perpetrators and soldiers fought the war to defend Germany, epitomised in the image of the fertile mother. Embodying the home front, Vera crossed into a war zone and the genocidal violence of the Holocaust. The reaction of Wohlauf's comrades revealed confusion, perhaps a form of cognitive dissonance. The Jews as an abstraction, a phantom force, had to die so that Germans could live – so reasoned a Nazi perpetrator. Yet how could a habitual killer in a police unit in Poland rationalise the blood on his hands in the face of this young bride who mimicked his brutal actions? To uphold his honour and loyalty, he was supposed to carry out the grim task so that she could remain innocent.

Perhaps what disturbed Julius's comrades most of all was that Vera, by all appearances a woman, behaved like a man. Her presence in Poland, along with that of the multitude of other German women who joined their husbands or worked in the occupation administration, tested and reshaped standards of conduct and sexuality. What women learned to do abroad was unacceptable behaviour at home. This revolution was not a smooth process; it was fraught with tensions and conflicts, many of which continued to punctuate post-war testimonies and recollections of the genocide. While interesting to study on its own, the dissonance has also obscured the history of what Vera actually did as a direct participant in the Holocaust.

There were many German women who out of curiosity, cruelty or other motives went to the crime scenes. As accomplices, they incited their male mates to kill while acting out in their own abusive ways. They spurned Jews in the ghettos and at railway stations. They confiscated and consumed Jewish personal belongings. They hosted parties when Jews were forced to leave their homes to face certain death at the mass-shooting pits and extermination camps. Photographs from the ghetto liquidation at Hrubieszow show smiling German onlookers. As the Jews were marched to the train bound for Sobibor, the wives of overseeing SS policemen enjoyed coffee and cake. Photographs from a personal album of a member of Order Police Battalion 101 show Vera drinking beer with her husband and his colleagues. The photo was taken when she visited him in the summer of 1942. Was it taken on 25 or 26 August, after the massacres in Miedzyrzec?

Mundane everyday activities and social, often intimate interactions

Vera and Julius Wohlauf enjoying refreshments, summer 1942

were intermingled with the genocidal violence of the Holocaust. The fact that Vera and Julius spent their honeymoon in the settings of the ghettos, mass executions, and deportations around Miedzyrzec, or that coffee and cake were served to the executioners and their wives as they watched the beating and deportation of Jews, demonstrates how systems of mass murder can become embedded in everyday life. The embedding, and the normalisation that accompanies it, allows such crimes to occur unimpeded.

Female accomplices such as Liselotte Meier, Sabine Dick and Vera Wohlauf were more than witnesses to the mass murder; they contributed in some capacity just short of pulling the trigger. Professional relations between men and women who developed efficient systems in their offices; the intimate dynamics between colleagues; the unholy alliances between Nazis and their lovers and spouses; the ambitions and anti-Semitic ideas of female professionals and Nazi fanatics – these were all forces that turned the utterances and declarations of Hitler and the sinister policies of Himmler into the horrific, everyday realities of the Holocaust.

The large number of female collaborators – who stole from the Jews, administered the genocide, and participated at the crime scenes – is missing from our collective memory and official histories. The role of German women in Hitler's war can no longer be understood as their mobilisation and victimisation on the home front. Instead, Hitler's Germany produced another kind of female character at war, an expression of female activism and patriotism of the most violent and perverse kind.

# Perpetrators

THE FIRST NAZI MASS MURDERESS was not the concentration-camp guard, but the nurse. Of all the female professionals, she was the deadliest. Centrally planned mass-killing operations began neither in the gas chambers at Auschwitz-Birkenau nor in the mass-shooting sites of Ukraine; they began instead in the hospitals of the Reich. The first methods were the sleeping pill, the hypodermic needle and starvation. The first victims were children. During the war, nurses gave thousands of deformed babies and disabled adolescents overdoses of barbiturates, lethal injections of morphine and denied them food and water.

All of this was done in the name of progress and the health of the nation. In the late nineteenth century, the modern science of genetics spawned the international field of eugenics, a term defined in the subtitle of a 1910 book by an American leader in the field, Harvard-educated Charles Davenport – *Eugenics: The Science of Human Improvement by Better Breeding*. In German circles eugenics was also known as racial hygiene, and it was aimed more specifically at policies to increase the Aryan population. Inherited 'genetic' defects and traits were understood as racial or group manifestations that defined human-ity's different civilisations, some deemed more advanced than others, all of them competing for survival. Racism, like nationalism, was viewed positively. Progress, imagined in German ideals of beauty and conduct, could be achieved only by removing humanity's blights. In the hands of revolutionary zealots, Nazi men and women of action, this science of human inequality had to be taken as far as it could go. Biological manipulations and sterilisations were insufficient to achieve the goal of Aryan perfection through social engineering, and segrega-tion was not enough, either. The only total, 'final' solution to the problem of racial degeneration was to destroy the contaminant, starting with 'defective' Germans. Misleadingly termed 'euthanasia' or 'mercy killing', the top-secret programme was personally authorised by Adolf Hitler and carried out under the cover of war.

From its beginnings in the Reich before the Nazi invasion of Poland, the 'euthanasia' programme involved the recruitment of female midwives and of medical personnel, both doctors and nurses. These professionals would eventually murder more than two hundred thousand people in Germany, Austria and the annexed Reich border-lands of Poland, and the Czech lands. Close to four hundred medical institutions would become stationary murder operations of racial screening and selection, cruel experimentation, mass sterilisation, starvation and poisoning. In the weeks before the Nazi invasion of Poland, the Reich Ministry of the Interior demanded reports from physicians and midwives identifying newborn infants and children under the age of three with severe physical and mental disabilities. Mothers were pressured to hand over their 'diseased' children to so-called paediatric clinics, which became processing and killing centres. As many as eight thousand children were killed in Germany and Austria before the programme was expanded to target adults. The categories of 'incurable' illnesses and disabilities – including 'feeble-mindedness', 'criminal insanity' and 'dementia' – became ever more blurred.

Mass shootings of Polish psychiatric patients began in Kocborowo (in German, Konradstein) in September 1939. In October 1939 came the unprecedented mass gassing of patients from the asylum in

Owińska (Treskau), who were brought to Fort VII in Poznań, where a rudimentary stationary chamber had been sealed with clay – an experiment that Himmler himself would observe in December 1939. SS and police mobile killing units swept through Poland, and later through the Baltics, Ukraine and Belarus, shooting thousands of patients in asylums and hospitals and gassing others in mobile vans. Back in the Reich, in the asylums at Grafeneck and Hadamar, hospital clerical staff typed up death notices and, as we've seen, processed shipments of common ashes to the victims' families. With Hitler's backing, medical health professionals and their technical experts developed a new genocidal expertise, which they applied to ever-larger operations of mass murder in the more remote eastern territories. In late 1941 and early 1942, scientists, engineers, 'crematorium stokers', drivers and medical staff were transferred to Belarus and Poland to implement stationary gassing methods first tested on Soviet POWs and later used against Jews in Belzec, Sobibor and Treblinka, the Operation Reinhard killing centres. Human beings became cargo, guinea pigs and ashes.

Granting 'mercy' deaths to German soldiers on the eastern front may also have been part of these mass-murder operations. According to post-war testimony of a member of a top-secret mission, selected agents of the 'euthanasia' programme who had taken an oath of secrecy to the Führer were mobilised for eastern service and brought to field hospitals near Minsk, where they 'relieved the suffering' of German soldiers. In December 1941 and January 1942, Viktor Brack, an SS officer who made his mark in the Nazi system as a gassing and sterilisation expert, led a team of doctors, nurses and technicians on this eastern mission. It was suspected by informed Germans at the time, and has been suggested by historians since then, that medical teams killed critically wounded and mentally and physically disabled German soldiers who were casualties of the failed Moscow offensive. One of the first to mention this deployment was the nurse and career killer Pauline Kneissler, whom we met in chapter 2.

In a post-war court, Kneissler disclosed that she was sent to Minsk to care for the wounded, though in the same testimony she bemoaned the fact that she was not permitted to serve as a 'regular' nurse with the German Red Cross in a field hospital. This contradiction in her testimony lends credence to a statement that she is alleged to have made to a friend, not in the courtroom. While she was in the East she gave lethal injections to brain-damaged, blinded and mutilated troops. Those killed were 'our own', she told her friend, referring to Germans. Apparently when Kneissler shared this information, she justified the action by asserting, as she had about the gassings at Grafeneck Castle, that the patients died painlessly.

The possibility that German medical teams killed the Reich's own soldiers was – and still is – a taboo topic, and we do not know for certain that it happened. But if the regime was already killing adult German men who were disabled or diagnosed as insane, why would officials bother to transport severely disabled or shell-shocked German men from the eastern front back to the Reich? Under the cover of war in the East, these injured soldiers could be reported as combat casualties, granting them a hero's death that would be mourned, but not questioned by the family. Perhaps it was the ideological hard core of the nurses' corps, the Nazi Party's 'brown' nurses, who carried out such actions. With their aprons filled with morphine vials and needles, they were certainly equipped to give gravely injured and shell-shocked soldiers a 'mercy' death. In 1942, Hitler's physician Dr Karl Brandt, who co-led the euthanasia programme in the Reich, was promoted to the position of Commissioner General for Health and Sanitary Matters. In this capacity he oversaw an expansion of the killing of patients (known as Operation Brandt), targeting hospitals and similar nursing facilities that were needed for military purposes. By war's end the German victims of euthanasia who were transferred from hospitals and nursing homes to gassing centres included geriatric patients, people who had nervous disorders and other injuries from aerial bombings and traumatised soldiers.

After patients in asylums and hospitals in Ukraine, Belarus, the Baltics and Poland were killed by mobile units or medical personnel, the facilities were usually taken over by regional authorities and converted into Hitler Youth clubs, barracks for German soldiers, clubs for SS officers and dormitories for female staff. But a few of these emptied facilities in Poland were used as killing centres for new groups of victims. In 1942 Hitler's euthanasia staff organised deportations of patients from the Reich to an asylum in Meseritz-Obrawalde, a German-Polish border town. Transports from twenty-six German cities arrived there between 1942 and 1944, usually under cover of night. Those sent from Hamburg in late 1943 and early 1944 contained 407 handicapped patients – 213 men, 189 women and five children. Few survived. Meseritz was supposed to accommodate about nine hundred patients, but during the war the transports just kept coming and it 'became a place of immense misery', as the female head doctor later said. Two thousand were crammed into the building, subjected to daily sufferings similar to those in a concentration camp – a roll call, forced-labour assignments and regular selections. Doctors and nurses killed patients who, according to post-war prosecutors, 'caused extra work for the nurses, those who were deaf-mute, ill, obstructive, or undisciplined, and anyone else who was simply annoying', as well as those 'who had fled and were recaptured, and those engaging in undesirable sexual liaisons'. Estimates of the number killed at this one site range from six thousand to eighteen thousand.

The female nurses who later confessed to killing patients at Meseritz had not signed an oath of secrecy concerning the euthanasia programme, as Pauline Kneissler had. One explained that it took at least two nurses to kill a patient, since the victims resisted taking the large doses of medicine and shots. Meseritz-Obrawalde was one of several 'wild' euthanasia sites deliberately located on the Reich's eastern frontier, where larger transports could be received and the victims killed indiscriminately and disposed of out of view.

The Holocaust, including the euthanasia campaign, was a state-sponsored policy. The killing was organised and carried out by employees and contractors of the state and Nazi Party organisations, and it took place in state-run institutions – specially constructed killing centres, concentration camps, asylums and hospitals. Within these public institutions one finds many women working as clerks, detectives, overseers and guards, and one finds female nurses and doctors who did the murdering themselves. The examples of female killers to follow, however, move the crime scenes outside these official sites of terror and incarceration, to the perimeter of camps, to the rural ghettos of the East, to the households of SS policemen, to the gardens of private homes and estates and to the open market places and fields of small towns in eastern Europe.

The frontier, a European stage where Hitler and his supporters fulfilled their imperial fantasies, was also a space for them to carry out criminal policies with impunity. Several of the female perpetrators in this chapter did just this as well. They slipped into another role – a hybrid character that embodied the stiff Nazi patriot, brazen cowgirl and cold-blooded anti-Semite. They carried whips, they brandished pistols and rifles, they wore riding breeches, and they rode horses. The transformation was extreme.

Johanna Altvater, the ambitious business secretary from stifling Minden, was twenty-two years old when she arrived in the Ukrainian-Polish border town of Volodymyr-Volynsky. A county seat, with thirty thousand inhabitants, the town was surrounded by wheat fields and forests delineated by the marshy banks of two rivers, the Bug and the Luga, where Germans liked to go boating and picnicking. The town was also an important military-industrial juncture with soldiers' barracks, a radio station, an airport, fuel depots, a brick factory, a textile mill and a clothing factory. For the Jews in town, these installations were critical to their survival as labourers.

A few months before Altvater's September 1941 arrival, members of an SS and police special commando unit had already initiated the first anti-Jewish measures in Volodymyr-Volynsky. With the help of the local German military commander, they formed a Jewish council, then publicly humiliated its members and buried them alive. The Jewish council chief committed suicide with his family. On 30 September, Yom Kippur, a larger massacre occurred. Altvater's boss, a 'gimlet-eyed runt' named Wilhelm Westerheide, arrived to take over as regional commissar. It was immediately clear to the Jews who had survived the first wave of massacres that life would not improve under Commissar Westerheide. He started 'target shooting' of individual Jews who were loading fuel barrels at the railway station.

In April 1942 the ghetto was sealed off with barbed wire. Until then Jews had been required to wear badges and live in a designated quarter, but could move in and out of that area. Jews, Ukrainians and Poles interacted in the local 'black market' economy. Once the ghetto was closed, a Jewish police force was formed. Along with the Jewish council, the Jewish police were expected to fulfil all German demands. Westerheide and his staff forced Jews to give up their money, jewellery, furniture and other valuables in return for bogus promises of protection. Wood and coal, necessary for surviving the harsh winter, were confiscated as well. In June 1942 the ghetto was divided into two communities, as one survivor saw it: the 'dead' one of non-labouring Jews, mostly women, children and the elderly, and the much smaller 'living' one of skilled workers. Ukrainian police auxiliaries guarded the perimeter of the ghetto.

In the summer of 1942 and autumn of 1943, waves of German-led mass-shooting actions reduced the Jewish population in the entire region from about twenty thousand to four or five hundred. These massacres began at the end of August 1942, when Westerheide returned from the commissars' conference in Lutsk. There, he and the other district governors in Nazi-occupied Ukraine had learned that their bosses expected them to carry out the Final Solution 'one hundred per cent'.

Though the order was of course not issued directly to 'Fräulein Hanna', Johanna Altvater decided to do her part. She often accompanied her boss on routine trips to the ghetto; she was seen hitching their horses to the gate at the ghetto entrance. On 16 September 1942, Altvater entered the ghetto and approached two Jewish children, a six-year-old and a toddler who lived near the ghetto wall. She beckoned to them, gesturing as if she were going to give them a treat. The toddler came over to her. She lifted the child into her arms and held it so tightly that the child screamed and wriggled. Altvater grabbed the child by the legs, held it upside down and slammed its head against the ghetto wall as if she were banging the dust out of a small carpet. She threw the lifeless child at the feet of its father, who later testified, 'Such sadism from a woman I have never seen, I will never forget this.'

There were no other German officials present, the father recalled. Altvater murdered this child on her own.

During the liquidation of the ghetto, the German commander of the nearby POW camp saw Fräulein Hanna, in her riding breeches, prodding Jewish men, women and children into a truck. She circulated through the ghetto cracking her whip, trying to bring order to the chaos 'like a cattle herder', as this German observer put it. Altvater entered the building that served as a makeshift hospital. She burst into the children's ward and walked from bed to bed, eyeing each child. She stopped, picked one up, took it to the balcony and threw the child to the pavement below. She pushed the older children to the balcony of the ward – which was on the third floor – and shoved them over the rail. Not all of the children died on impact, but those who survived were seriously injured.

Altvater did not act alone in the infirmary: she was there with one of her friends, the German gendarme chief named Keller. Keller had the authority to order the Jewish nurse, Michal Geist, to go down to the pavement to verify that the children who lay motionless were actually dead. The wounded and other children in the infirmary were placed in a lorry. Their work nearly completed, Altvater and Keller drove off, presumably to the death pits at the edge of town.

Altvater's speciality – or, as one survivor put it, her 'nasty habit' – was killing children. One observer noted that Altvater often lured children with sweets. When they came to her and opened their mouths, she shot them in the mouth with the small silver pistol that she kept at her side. Some suggested that Altvater and Westerheide were lovers, but most derided her as Westerheide's 'she-man' companion (*Mannweib*). Altvater did not get along well with the other women stationed in town, including a German Red Cross nurse and another secretary in her office. She visited the soldiers' home to socialise, but the other women 'did not think highly of her since she was always strutting around in her brown Nazi Party uniform and behaved like a typical butch'. She had a large frame and a close-cropped 'man's haircut'. Jewish survivors and German character witnesses recalled her masculine features, which they linked to her aggressive behaviour. In these depictions of Nazi violence, Johanna Altvater is portrayed in an ambiguous, indeed repulsive, male-female form. Her exceptionally male appearance became a way to explain her horrifically violent acts, just as – via a different mechanism – Vera Wohlauf's ultra-feminine state of pregnancy made her violence especially repugnant. But in neither case does gender alone explain the extent of the violence committed.

From the Volodymyr-Volynsky ghetto, Jews were driven to the fields of Piatydny. There they discovered wide trenches shaped like crosses; Jewish labourers had been forced to dig their own mass graves. In the two weeks that followed, as many as fifteen thousand Jews were shot here. Westerheide, who later bragged about 'bumping off' so many Jews, was seen there on horseback, as was Altvater's colleague Keller, later identified as 'one of the worst'. Near the mass-shooting site, Westerheide and his deputies caroused at a banquet table with a few German women. Altvater was among the revellers, drinking and eating amid the bloodshed. Music playing in the background mixed with the sound of gunfire. From time to time, one of the German executioners would get up from the table, walk to the shooting site, kill a few people and then return to the party. Polish farmers who were working in the fields near the site, some picking pears, heard the screaming and shooting and warned Jews hiding in the forest not to return to the ghetto.

The three thousand Jews who survived were crammed into small huts behind rows of barbed-wire fencing. Sleeping several to a bed and on floors, without any heat, they received a daily ration of no more than 390 calories, or less than thirty-five ounces of bread (about three slices); it was not enough to fend off illnesses, and a typhoid epidemic raced through the ghetto. One of the children who entered the ruins was ten-year-old Leon Ginsburg. He searched for his family, but learned that the Germans and their collaborators had killed most of them. Jews in the ghetto explained to Leon what had happened. They described a 'Polish woman, the lover of the Commandant', named Anna, who had 'the first pick of women's shoes and clothing'. In the ravaged ghetto, black-and-white photographs lay scattered on the unpaved streets, smiling faces of Jews enjoying pre-war weddings, holidays, schools and birthdays. Now they were all dead and stared at him like ghosts. Realising that he had to leave, he planned his escape to the woods.

Had Leon stayed, he probably would not have survived in the ghetto. Westerheide, Keller, Fräulein Hanna and their colleagues in the SS were relentless. In the first half of 1943, they organised another mass shooting, in which twelve hundred Jews from the ghetto and surrounding area were murdered. One thousand craftsmen and their families were retained until the last days of the German occupation, when Westerheide's office evacuated in December 1943. In fact, the last known massacre of Jews in Nazi-occupied Ukraine occurred here on 13–14 December 1943.

Nazi leaders understood that they might lose the military campaign, but were determined to win the war against the Jews. Completing its final sweep westwards from Russia back to Germany with orders to kill all remaining Jewish populations, a special commando unit brought the last Jews to a 'wooded area after a motorised platoon of Gendarmerie and Ukrainian auxiliaries had cordoned off the area. The rails for a pyre to cremate the bodies had been prepared there in advance.'

At the end of 1943, before the Volodymyr-Volynsky office was shut down, Johanna Altvater was already back in the Reich. After serving as the personal secretary for the highest authority in the district, she was transferred to the regional capital of Lutsk. According to her record, she was reassigned for disciplinary reasons. Altvater explained after the war that the reason for her transfer to Lutsk was an incident; after a night of partying she and her carousers drove a 'cow' into the ghetto. It is not clear what sort of game they were playing. She went home for Christmas leave and did not return to Volodymyr-Volynsky. The Soviets reoccupied the region in January and February 1944. Still hopeful that she would have a future in the East, Altvater applied to enter a civil-service programme for training the colonial elite.

When Johanna Altvater postured as a Nazi official, and when she

Erna Petri at her Grzenda estate, with her son in the fields *(top)*
and riding in a carriage in front of the villa *(bottom)*

became violent, she took on a male appearance. Vera Wohlauf wore a
military coat and cap to go to the Miedzyrzec-Podlaski massacres and
deportations. Such mutations were not total and irreversible, but
they are illustrative of the malleable roles that women in the East
slipped into and out of. As individual women navigated the multiple war zones of the East, and as some became conditioned to do
what was considered man's work, traditional presentations and roles

became confused. Nowhere was this mutability more chillingly apparent than in the cases of the SS wives who became perpetrators. These women displayed a capacity to kill while also acting out a combination of roles: plantation mistress; prairie Madonna in apron-covered dress lording over slave labourers; infant-carrying, gun-wielding *Hausfrau*.

Himmler's SS officers and their wives stationed in Poland, Ukraine, Belarus and the Baltics enjoyed the freedom of the East, the sense of adventure, the riches of the fertile land, the plunder of items confiscated from the 'natives' and the power of the whip. By the end of 1942, the SS controlled nearly one and a half million acres of farmland between the Black Sea and the Baltic. Within the constellation of plantations requisitioned by the SS was Grzenda (Hriada), once the grand manor house, or *dwór*, of a Polish noble, outside today's Lviv.

In June 1942, Erna Petri, who had memorably sat astride her motorbike back home in Thuringia, arrived at Grzenda with her three-year-old son. Set amid rolling hills and meadows, the white-pillared manor overlooked the surrounding villages. Visitors passed through an ornamental wrought-iron gate onto a road leading to a circular drive and an array of stables, chicken coops and servants' quarters. A century before, craftsmen had carefully laid small black, white and terracotta tiles on the floor of the north portico and vestibule. Ornate balustrades decorated the staircase and the veranda. One can imagine the excitement and pride Erna Petri must have felt upon arriving in this impressive home, such a stark contrast to the oppressive family farm in Thuringia.

Within two days she saw her husband, Horst, beating his labourers. He sexually assaulted the female household servants. Local farmers called him a sadist who enjoyed violence; he laughed as he flogged Ukrainians, Poles and Jews. Horst did not see himself as such. Rather, he was establishing his authority. Even as the war dragged on and victory became unlikely, Horst and Erna became only more brutal as they sought to maintain their grip on the estate. In summer 1943 they hunted down Jews who had fled from ghetto liquidations and railway carriages headed to the gassing centres. Horst initiated raids in neighbouring villages. Erna – who lived at Grzenda from June 1942 until early 1944 – also started to beat the workers, including the blacksmith, whom she slapped in the face. Violence was woven into the everyday domestic setting of bucolic life on the plantation.

The Petris' new estate comprised lovely gardens and other places to stroll on Sunday afternoons. Many high-ranking officials from the nearby capital, Lviv, known in German as Lemberg, liked to visit. One Sunday, the wife of the most senior SS officer in the region arrived with two aides, a chauffeur and an assistant. While the Petris led their visitors through the garden, one of the aides suddenly appeared and reported that four Jews who had escaped from a train headed to a gassing centre near Lublin had been caught on the estate. The chauffeur and Horst discussed what to do with them. Horst told his wife and her female guest that this was men's work, nothing the women should be concerned about. As the women walked away from the garden back towards the house, they heard four pistol shots.

Several months later, in the summer of 1943, Erna Petri was returning home from Lviv. She had gone into town to pick up some supplies. It was a sunny day. She reclined in the horse-drawn carriage while her coachman handled the reins. She saw something in the distance. When the carriage drew closer, she saw that it was children crouching along the side of the road, dressed only in shreds of clothing. It occurred to her that 'these were the children who broke out of the boxcar at the train station Saschkow'. As she would go on to explain:

> At this time all remaining Jews who were in several camps were being transported to the extermination camp. In these transports often and especially at the train station at Saschkow Jews would break out and try to save themselves. These Jews were all naked, so that the Ukrainians and Poles living in the area could be distinguished from them; the Jews were easy to recognise.

The children were terrified and hungry. Petri beckoned to them and brought them home. She calmed them and gained their trust by bringing them food from her kitchen. All Jews who were roaming the countryside were supposed to be captured and shot; she understood that. Horst was not at home at the time. She waited, but Horst did not return, so she decided to shoot the six children herself. She led them to the same pit in the woods where other Jews had been shot and buried. She brought a pistol with her, one that her father had kept from the First World War and given to her as a parting gift as she left for the 'wild east' of Ukraine.

Erna Petri told the children to line up facing away from her, in front of the ditch. She held up the pistol about four inches from the first child's neck and shot the child, then moved on and did the same to the second. After she shot the first two, 'the others were at first shocked and began to cry. They did not cry loudly, they whimpered.' Erna would not allow herself 'to be swayed'; she shot 'until all of them lay in the gully. None of the children tried to run away since it appeared that they already had been in transit for several days and were totally exhausted.'

Erna was alone when she committed this crime, but she was far from alone at the estate. Besides her husband, her two small children lived at Grzenda – the son whom she brought with her to the estate in 1942, and a daughter born there in January 1943. Her mother-in-law and an uncle were visiting, trying to escape the bombing raids and rationing back in the Reich, and in addition she was surrounded by peasants working the fields. The best view of the area was from the hilltop villa's second-floor balcony, where Erna, the quintessential German *Hausfrau*-hostess, served *Kaffee und Kuchen* to Horst's colleagues in the military and the SS and police. While pouring coffee Erna had overheard the men speaking about the mass shootings of Jews. She had learned that the most effective way to kill was a single shot to the back of the neck. When she led those children to the mass grave on the estate, she knew exactly what to do.

Domestic violence took on another, expanded meaning in the Third Reich. Female killers carried out heinous acts in or near their homes. Most common was shooting from the balcony, and in the presence of family members and lovers.

In the spring of 1942, Liesel Willhaus, the Catholic steelworker's daughter from the Saarland, arrived with her daughter in Lviv. They went to the Janowska camp, where her husband, SS *Untersturmführer* Gustav Willhaus, was appointed commandant. Liesel and Gustav were still working their way up the Nazi system, still eager to shed their working-class heritage for a new life of riches and power in the East. Gustav's promotion was their big break. Liesel inspected their new home. The villa stood at the edge of the slave-labour and transit camp. A machine factory housed some selected Jewish labourers in the camp, while the railway lines brought most of the Jewish population of Lviv to the gassing facility of Belzec, which began receiving Jews from Lviv in March 1942, about the time that Gustav Willhaus arrived at Janowska. Some three hundred thousand Polish and Ukrainian Jews died in Janowska or passed through it, making Janowska the biggest Jewish labour and transit camp in Ukraine.

Not long after arriving at his post, Gustav Willhaus became known as the 'bloodthirsty camp commandant'. Holocaust survivors called him a 'natural-born killer' who murdered people without hesitation, but also without much enthusiasm. He slayed his victims like a 'chaff cutter'. His wife developed her own reputation. First Liesel insisted that their villa required renovations and demanded the construction of a second-floor balcony where the family could enjoy afternoon re-freshments. She found ample Jewish slaves to do whatever she needed at home, including the gardening work. Liesel kept a close eye on them from the balcony. She used this vantage point to shoot prisoners – for 'the sport of it', one Jewish eyewitness stated. 'Willhaus's wife . . . also had a pistol. When guests came to visit the Willhaus family, and sat on the spacious porch of their luxurious house, [she] would show off her marksmanship by shooting down camp inmates, to the delight of her guests. The little daughter of the family, Heike, would vigorously ap-plaud the sight.'

Liesel Willhaus's preferred weapon was a Flobert gun, a French parlour rifle that looked fancy, but was cheap to produce. Flobert rifles were in wide circulation at the time and typically used for target prac-tice. It was the classic example of a 'domesticated' weapon, displayed in stuffy Victorian sitting rooms and used in the garden to kill pests. Its range was limited (about a hundred feet), but the impact was powerful enough to result in lethal injuries. In Ukraine, the parlour rifle was fitting for the self-styled female pioneer.

Death was often not instant for those who fell victim to one of Willhaus's shooting sprees. One time she fired a single shot at a Jewish labourer who was walking by the house. Her husband was standing next to her on the balcony. On another occasion, a morning in September 1942, she appeared on the balcony with her husband and a few guests and shot into a group of Jewish prisoners who were about sixty feet away, picking up rubbish around the house. One of the prisoners killed was a thirty-year-old from the village of Sambor.

In April 1943, on a Sunday, Willhaus appeared again on the balcony. With her child at her side, she shot into a group of Jewish labourers in the garden. At least four Jews fell down on the spot, including Jakob Helfer from the village of Bobrka. One day that summer, she aimed at a group of labourers further away in the camp. They were huddled together, trying to trade. About five were killed. Not long after this incident, Willhaus shot Jews during roll call, aiming more precisely at their heads. According to post-war investigators, Willhaus also aimed at the hearts of Jews sick with typhus. She shot them at close range.

The entire atmosphere in and around the Willhaus villa was one of bizarre contradictions. The juxtaposition of a repressively well-appointed bourgeois German home contrasted with the gunfire and suffering of the Jewish inmates. The balcony 'shooting gallery' was actually one of the 'cleaner' methods practised by the Willhauses and their colleagues. Sadistic spectacles were more their speciality: public beatings, hangings, sexual organs severed, children's limbs torn off.

Wives of SS men, including the wife of a commandant of Auschwitz, claimed after the war that they did not know what was going on behind the walls and barbed wire of the camps. They insisted that their homes were completely separate sanctuaries of normality where their husbands could find refuge from their stressful work. But the camp and the home were not separate worlds; they overlapped. Wives visited their husbands at the office – Liesel Willhaus, for instance, was often seen entering the Janowska camp – and husbands brought callousness and techniques for killing Jews home with them. It is not possible to believe that SS wives saw nothing, and it is not possible to believe that some, like Erna Petri and Liesel Willhaus, did not choose to participate in the killing.

We have seen that in the madness of the East, sadistic violence, domestic routines and intimate relations intermingled. Both Liesel Wilhaus and Erna Petri came to the East as married women, but for unmarried women, the incestuous, tight-knit community served to make the German-only outposts into 'marriage markets' for ideologically attuned and often morally corrupt mates. Office romances were common, and marriage was not the only result. Many children were born out of wedlock. Such promiscuous behaviour was not frowned upon; on the contrary, propagation of the Aryan race was a patriotic duty. The children of the new elite in the East were not sheltered from the violence. There are a few documented cases of fathers involving their sons in the killing, and of mothers like Liesel Willhaus involving their daughters. The story of the growth of female violence during the Reich is intertwined with a sexual revolution that tested boundaries and definitions of matrimony, procreation, child-rearing, femininity and pleasure.

The stories of two additional women killers, onetime Viennese secretaries Gertrude Segel and Josefine Krepp, are further illustration of how violent partnerships were forged in formal office settings, but acted out in intimate ones. In these cases the women met their SS husbands as secretaries in the Gestapo offices that contained an Austrian Nazi network. Many had come to know one another in the aftermath of the *Anschluss,* when the Nazi Party and its supporters fully infiltrated and took over the Austrian state. As the Reich expanded eastwards, many of these Austrians ultimately felt at home occupying offices in the former Habsburg lands of Galicia and Yugoslavia.

About forty miles south of Lviv, in the small city of Drohobych, the Gestapo secretary Gertrude Segel also shot Jewish labourers in her garden. When Gertrude met Felix Landau, commander of the Sipo and SD in Radom, Poland, in February 1941, he was married with two small children. Within a few months they became lovers, and Gertrude called off her engagement to an Austrian soldier, away at the front, who was not an SS man. Felix Landau, too, was sent into combat – in the Nazi 'war against the Jews', in occupied western Ukraine.

While committing mass murder in Ukraine, Landau kept a diary revealing his swings from forlorn lover to cold-blooded killer. He composed his text in the form of letters to his 'Trude'. Addressing 'his lovely bunny' on 5 July 1941, Landau described his victims in gruesome detail, perhaps rationalising his actions by explaining that one Pole who was covered in blood motioned to the Germans to fire faster to end his suffering. Landau wanted to impress Gertrude; he stressed that this human slaughter was hard work. He also worried that she would leave him. In his entries of 12 and 13 July 1941, Landau referred again to the incessant demands of the mass shootings: 'I hardly got any sleep . . . Finally I managed to read all my post . . . Trude wrote that she doesn't know whether she can keep her vow to me [to be faithful]. Why does this have to happen to me with a person I love so much? I have to see her and talk to her, and then my little Trude will be strong again. She must come here [to Drohobych].'

Drohobych – populated in 1939 by roughly ten thousand Poles, the same number of Ukrainians and fifteen thousand Jews – was once a boom town in the late nineteenth century, its sudden wealth spurred by the discovery of nearby oil fields. Landau had set himself up in style, in a comfortable home, and he desperately wanted Gertrude to join him. He made arrangements for her transfer from Radom while he initiated a divorce against his wife, who was also a former secretary in his Gestapo office. His wife returned to the Reich, leaving Landau and their two toddlers in Drohobych. Segel took up a new secretarial job in his office in Drohobych and moved into his home, where they hoarded piles of valuables confiscated from the Jews, such as furs, paintings and china. They forced the talented Jewish artist Bruno Schulz to paint murals in the children's nursery. These were beautiful, fanciful paintings, the fairy-tale characters bearing the faces of members of the Jewish community in Drohobych, including Schulz himself, who was later shot by a rival of Landau's in the Gestapo office.

Like the Willhaus and Petri families, Gertrude Segel and Felix Landau had a balcony on their villa. According to the testimony of a Jewish witness, on the Sunday afternoon of 14 June 1942, Gertrude and Felix were playing cards on their balcony. The radio was turned up and the sun was shining. They reclined on upholstered chairs. Gertrude wore a bathing suit; Felix was dressed in a white suit. A small group of Jewish men and women were working in the garden below, spreading soil. Suddenly Felix stood up and grabbed the Flobert long gun. He started to shoot pigeons. Gertrude also gave it a try. At this point either Gertrude or Felix turned the rifle down onto the Jewish gardeners, and shot a worker named Fliegner. They laughed as they left the balcony and re-entered the house.

On the streets in town, Felix Landau was also known for his open shooting sprees. One of the largest was in November 1942, when he and his men killed more than two hundred Jews, among them leading intellectuals and professionals, such as a Jewish professor named Szulc and a Dr Loew, the personal dentist of another sergeant in the Gestapo office. In town Landau was the notorious 'Jew-General' who presided over massacres from the very first days of the occupation through 1942 and 1943, reducing the local Jewish population from more than fifteen thousand to a few hundred by war's end.

The hedonism of Felix and Gertrude also became well known, especially as it was expressed in raucous parties. The Jewish survivor Jacob Goldsztein testified that Landau and Segel hosted drunken fests with other German occupation officials at the local riding hall. One of these was probably their wedding party on 5 May 1943. Gertrude danced on the tables and slapped the hands of the SS men seated at the table. After a night of carousing, Landau returned to the hall because Segel's gold necklace was missing. Landau found Goldsztein and another Jewish man who were cleaning up, and accused them of theft. Landau ordered Goldsztein to report to him the next day, and pressed Goldsztein about the necklace, telling him calmly that he should give it over. Goldsztein pleaded that he did not have the necklace and that he would never do such a thing as stealing a necklace.

Segel was present during the interrogation, reclining on the office couch. 'Don't be such an idiot, you pig of a Jew, you took the necklace!' she yelled at Goldsztein. Now Landau became angrier. His 'Trude' was upset and expected him to act. He started to punch Goldsztein, then kicked him and trod on him. He ordered Goldsztein to get up. He preferred to beat him standing, which he explained was more convenient than bending down to the floor. Later Goldsztein learned that an SS man who was flirting with Gertrude had stolen the necklace. (The man would eventually return it.) The necklace had originally belonged to a Jewish woman; Landau had confiscated it during a massacre and presented it to Gertrude as a gift.

Jewish survivors also testified that Gertrude ordered the deaths of her household help – three maids – and that she trampled a Jewish child to death. But in the late 1950s West German and Austrian investigators did not bother to pursue these incriminating eyewitness statements against her.

Segel's Austrian friend Josefine Krepp, now Josefine Block, joined her husband in Ukraine in 1942. In Drohobych, Josefine Block was not officially an employee of the Gestapo, but she hung around the office. Her husband was happy to give his little 'Fini' her own projects, like overseeing the community garden and expanding the workshops with Jewish labourers. She became pregnant in the summer of 1942, but she wanted to do more than mother the small child the couple already had and the baby to come.

When two hundred 'gypsies' were gathered in town, Block was seen with her whip ordering the Ukrainian militiamen to hurry up and kill them. Night was falling and the 'prisoners' had to be shot before dark, she said. Another time Block appeared at the local garden market, summoned four Jewish girls who appeared too weak to work and told one of her husband's employees to shoot them in her presence. Block often came to the market to pick up vegetables, and her arrival always struck fear in the Jewish workers. When the ghetto was liquidated in June 1943, she appeared again, this time at the collection point where Jews were gathered for deportation. She had on a grey ladies' suit and wore her hair loose; she held her camera and a riding crop. Occasionally she lashed out at a Jewish prisoner with her riding crop; the terrified deportees were subjected to further humiliation when she photographed them. A seven-year-old Jewish girl approached her, crying and begging for her life. 'I will help you!' Block declared. At which point she grabbed the girl by the hair and beat her with her fists, then pushed her to the ground and stomped on her head. After Block walked away, the girl's mother lifted the lifeless child into her arms, trying unsuccessfully to revive her.

Desperate Jewish labourers often approached Block to ask for help. They assumed that, as a young woman and mother, she would be sympathetic. But Block kept a weapon within reach, and in an instant could change roles – from a calm, attractive mother to a Nazi brute. She was seen using her baby carriage to ram Jews whom she encountered on the streets of Drohobych; two witnesses would later state that she had actually killed a small Jewish child with the carriage. Locals complained about her, but her husband, the Gestapo chief, deferred to his wife, explaining that he could not make any decisions without her.

The wartime and post-war documentation placing wives in these Nazi outposts is scattered across archives and private papers. It is mostly through the testimonies of German, Ukrainian, Polish and Jewish witnesses that we have learned about the presence and violent behaviour of these women. Accustomed as we are to thinking of killing, war and the perpetration of genocide as male activities, in the absence of accessible evidence to the contrary we remain blind to the extent of women's participation. We know that Holocaust victims experienced humiliation, deprivation, pain and even death at the hands of German women, yet many minimise this fact by insisting on various conceptions of genocide that are historically inaccurate and biased.

Historically, most mass murder occurs in the open and is therefore not confined to particular state institutions. This was true for Germans in the Nazi killing fields, who were caught up in the killing themselves while also drawing others into it. Many individuals whose regular, everyday work had little to do with Nazi anti-Jewish policy, let alone the killing of Jews, were recruited and persuaded to kill. Commissar Westerheide, for example – Johanna Altvater's boss – approached fellow Germans as they walked down the street and simply asked whether they might be interested in assisting in an *Aktion*. An official invited a German colleague for some recreational shooting, expressing his pleasure at the prospect of using live Jews as targets. It was not only the men who were recruited; women and girls were approached to fulfil a variety of ad hoc tasks connected with killing. Ukrainian girls were routinely used at mass shootings to assist in the collection and mending of victims' clothes. As 'packers' in the pits, girls pressed down on corpses with their bare feet; as 'hemp collectors', they gathered hay and sunflower stalks to be used for hastening the burning of the corpses.

In the Nazi war against the Jews in eastern Europe, the spatial divide between the battlefront and the home front was non-existent. Crime scenes included the balconies of villas, the grounds of rural estates such as Grzenda and banquet tables near the killing fields. For women such as Erna Petri, Liesel Willhaus, Gertrude Segel, Johanna Altvater and Josefine Block, contributing to the war effort went beyond consoling, protecting and supporting a male mate or a fanatical boss. These female perpetrators were incredibly, indeed shockingly, adept at slipping in and out of roles, from the unbridled revolutionary to the meek, subservient wife. Many female murderers held positions in the professional world – secretaries and nurses, for example. Trained and socialised at a particular moment in time, in Hitler's Germany, they exploited their power as imperial overseers and careerists.

Will we ever know more precisely how many German women behaved so violently, even murdering with poison-filled needles, guns, attack dogs and other lethal weapons? Numbers alone cannot explain events, but they can be revealing. For example, scholars and lay persons have long assumed that the Nazi camp system amounted to a few hundred, perhaps a few thousand, internment sites. But researchers at the US Holocaust Memorial Museum have determined recently that there were more than forty thousand sites of detention in Nazi-dominated Europe. The camp and ghetto system, usually seen as a universe separate from the rest of society, can now be understood as merging into local communities. The concept of camp walls as a distancing barrier is eroding. Although the higher number of camps does not imply a significantly greater number of victims, since individual victims typically experienced several types of camps and ghettos, it does tell us that there was a significantly higher number of perpetrators, accomplices and witnesses who created, operated and visited these sites. More people participated than we thought; more people knew about the systematic persecution and killing of others. And 'more' applies across the board: more men, more women and more children were involved than we knew. The large number of camps, and their integration into local communities, underscores the social dimension of the history of the Holocaust.

Can we approximate how many German women became killers in the East? We might start by following methods applied to estimating male perpetrators. But the estimates we have for male German perpetrators are rough, and based mainly on records from institutions charged with implementing the Holocaust. Combining personnel lists that place men in criminal organisations with investigative records on particular individuals in separate units of those organisations, such as Order Police Battalion 101, historians have estimated that some two hundred thousand German (and Austrian) men were direct agents of the Nazi genocide in the open-air shootings, ghetto liquidations and gassing centres.

For women we do not have comparable sources. There exist incomplete lists of female camp guards in 1944 and 1945, but these records offer only snapshots of female involvement and provide information only on camps administered by one arm of Himmler's agencies (the Economic and Administrative Office of the RSHA). In any event, these records reveal that about three and a half thousand women (most of them trained at Ravensbrück) worked as camp guards during these years. Until now this figure was the one usually attached to estimates of female Holocaust perpetrators. But of course not all female camp guards were killers and, conversely, not all female killers were camp guards: a huge number of victims in the East were killed outside camp walls. The personnel list of female guards trained at Ravensbrück, or stationed at about a dozen main camps mostly in the Reich in 1944 and early 1945, is – like the list I found in Zhytomyr – the tip of the iceberg. Could a history of male perpetrators confine itself to guard records from Dachau? Over the past few decades the lens focused on male perpetrators has widened to include ordinary Germans and non-Germans, in police units, regular army units and civilian garb. My examination of women killers and of the situations in which they killed should similarly expand our view of female perpetration.

The documentation I surveyed on the deployment of female professionals and family members in the East accounts for several hundred thousand women. In a peaceful society, women commit on average about 14 per cent of all violent crime and about 10 per cent of murders. In peacetime, women killers act alone, and they act against individual victims (usually relatives and mates), not against entire groups. In a warring, genocidal society, the number of men as well as women engaged in violent acts is much higher, and each individual act may lead to a larger number of deaths. After rounding up Jewish children in the ghetto infirmary, for example, Johanna Altvater killed some herself on the spot; others she forced onto a vehicle that took them to a mass-murder site where they were shot by male police units. Statistically, if we took the percentage of homicides committed by women in peaceful society and applied it to a genocidal one, like the Third Reich, then the estimate of female killers would be in the thousands. In other words, we could multiply Erna Petri by several thousand. But if we assume, as is likely, that women in genocidal societies – women who are empowered by the state, with 'enemy' groups as their targets – are responsible for a greater percentage of murders than women in peacetime societies, then even a few thousand begins to look unrealistically small.

When it comes to killers like the secretaries, wives and lovers of SS men in this chapter, we will never have a precise number. But the evidence here does give us new insights about the Holocaust specifically and genocide more broadly. We have always known, of course, that women have the capacity to be violent, and even to kill, but we knew little about the circumstances and ideas that transform women into genocidaires, the varied roles they occupy inside and outside the system and the forms of behaviour they adopt. Now it is possible to imagine that the patterns of violent and murderous behaviours uncovered here occurred across wartime Ukraine, Poland, Belarus, Lithuania and other parts of Nazi-dominated Europe. German women who went east embodied what the expanding Nazi empire was becoming: ever more violent. Ordinary young women with typical pre-war biographies, not just a small group of Nazi fanatics, went east and became involved in the crimes of the Holocaust, including killing.

Fortunately, with the military defeat of Germany, the heyday of the perpetrators would come to an end; the Nazi machinery of destruction would stop. The lives of these German women did not end, however. They returned home to the rubble of the Reich and tried to bury their criminal pasts.

# 6

# Why Did They Kill?

## Their Post-War Explanations and Ours

ERMAN MYTHS OF FEMALE innocence and martyr-
dom were born in the Reich's collapse and surrender to the
Allies. The horrors of the regime had been experienced by
Poles and other majority populations in the occupied East since 1939,
and by Jews and other targeted political and racial victims in Nazi
Germany since 1933, but for ordinary German women the bad times
arrived with the unravelling of the Reich. In the immediate aftermath
came the physical ordeals and moral dilemmas of evacuations from
the East, the violence of the Soviet Army and the struggle to survive in
what remained of their German homeland and war-torn families under Allied occupation.

One young schoolteacher in Ukraine who faced the advancing Red
Army as it pushed towards the Dnieper River in the summer of 1943
recalled her evacuation. There were so many children in the school,
all of them orphans. She and her colleagues assumed that the children
would be killed by the Soviets, but they decided to abandon them
nevertheless. The children cried; fearing for their lives, they clung to
their teacher and would not let her go. But, she insisted, 'we had to do

it'. She left Ukraine with other female personnel and headed for the Polish-German border. When she was given her work-release papers by the Gestapo, she had to sign an oath that she would remain silent about all that she had done and seen in Ukraine. After the war this teacher learned that the Red Army occupation of Chernihiv was indeed a 'bloodbath'; she heard that all men, women and children who had had anything to do with the Germans were shot.

The entire staff of the hospital in Zhytomyr where Erika Ohr worked as a nurse was evacuated at the last minute in December 1943. The small convoy of trucks containing medical personnel and wounded soldiers steered through the mayhem of soldiers rushing eastwards and westwards, on foot, in lorries and overhead in loud planes. In the fields along the road German tanks rolled over the fresh graves of German soldiers, destroying the individual markers that bore their names and their unit numbers. Those unit numbers could have provided Soviet intelligence with useful information for tracking German troop movements.

After months of stopovers in western Ukraine and Poland, Ohr eventually arrived in Hungary, near Pécs. It was May 1944. She noticed that the locals there were not very friendly. Ohr and her colleagues later figured out that only a few days before their arrival, the Jewish population had been 'transported away'. But some Jews remained. There was a ghetto with women and children near the nurses' dorm. Intruders had entered their dorm and had stolen things. From the proximity of these two places, Ohr inferred that the intruders were ghetto residents. Some desperate Jews did steal, of course, since the Nazis had taken everything from them – but Ohr does not offer evidence for her assumption or seem aware of the Jews' possible reasons for such an action. It was common in the Nazis' anti-Semitic propaganda to conflate Jews and criminals, a theme that Hitler and Goebbels hammered to the bitter end. Perhaps it had made a lasting impression on Ohr.

By the end of the war, Ohr had become accustomed to treating and burying German soldiers. She was less prepared to deal with sick civilians. Ethnic German women, children and elderly, who were fleeing on foot from the East to Germany, were among the wounded and ill. They crowded into a hospital near Brünn (now Brno, Czech Republic), which was overcome by an outbreak of measles. German children were dying each night. Ohr was not sure what to do with their small corpses. They could not remain among the living, next to their ailing mothers and siblings. This makeshift hospital had been placed in an empty school. Next to the main hall where the German refugee families lay ill on the floor, Ohr discovered a room filled with hooks. It was the school coat room where, weeks before, students had hung up their jackets and removed their boots. Ohr decided to place the children's corpses here. As she left the coat room, she made sure to close the door behind her.

Ohr contracted measles and was unable to evacuate when her colleagues left in mid-April 1945. A special transport had to be arranged for her. She lay alone in the main hall with a high fever. She heard the air-raid sirens and feared that she had been forgotten. She did not want to be left behind.

Whether innocent or guilty of Nazi crimes, German women expected to be the targets of revenge and objects of sexual plunder. In Hitler's April 15 proclamation – his last – to all the soldiers on the eastern front, in which he referred to the recently deceased President Roosevelt as the 'greatest war criminal of all time', he argued that the final defence of Germany must be to protect the *Volk,* above all German women and girls:

> For the last time, the deadly Jewish-Bolshevik mortal enemy has set out with its masses on the attack. He is attempting to demolish Germany and to exterminate our people. You soldiers from the East know yourselves in large measure what fate threatens above all German women, girls, and children. While old men and children are murdered, women and girls are denigrated to barrackwhores. The rest are marched off to Siberia.

The Nazi propaganda minister Joseph Goebbels tried to mobilise the resolve (and fear) of the German masses with images of Red Army soldiers as 'Asiatic hordes' savagely raping German women. Those frightful pictures became reality. Reports of mass rape were confirmed by the millions of German evacuees who trudged westwards in a chaotic, humiliating about-face. Estimates of women who were raped – and certainly not all of them were German women – range from one hundred thousand to two million. Girls and the elderly were not spared.

The Nazi regime laid down its arms unconditionally on 8 May 1945, officially marking the end of an era in Europe. For women who came of age in the Third Reich – who experienced adolescence, professional training, first jobs, first relationships and birth of first children during it – the defeat meant that ambitions were thwarted, dreams dashed and the future uncertain. One could not completely erase what was witnessed and done. Some loyalists and fanatics could not imagine life without Hitler. A few German women, either fearing Allied retribution or deeply ashamed, saw no choice but to commit suicide. Women who returned from the East hoped that their pasts would remain there. One woman, a self-identified believer and patriot, lamented in her diary that her world had crashed down around her. Were these German women returning from the East able to find refuge within the masses of victimised German women, the aggrieved widows and mothers who had suffered the aerial bombings on the home front, the mass rape by Red Army soldiers and the hardships of their defeated country?

Allied leaders made it very clear in a number of speeches – such as the Moscow Declaration of 1943 – that those who committed crimes would be punished. Upon the liberation of the Nazi-occupied territories, military tribunals and kangaroo courts sprang up. German officials and their local collaborators were rounded up, subjected to quick proceedings and hanged. The trials began with the highly publicised one in Krasnodar, Russia, in July 1943 and culminated in the remarkably restrained and thorough proceedings at the international military tribunal at Nuremberg, where the chief US prosecutor, Justice Robert H. Jackson, recognised the victors for agreeing to 'stay the hand of vengeance' by submitting 'their captive enemies to the judgment of the law'.

American, British, French and Soviet forces established their military governments in zones of Germany and Austria and introduced new legislation for punishing war criminals and 'denazifying' German society under the common terms and decrees set forth by the Allied Control Council. Denazification was meant to punish Nazi criminals, and to re-educate by exorcising the evils of Nazi ideology from German society and institutions – that is, rooting out the bad seeds. There were significant variations in how the different Allied powers dealt with suspects. Within a decade most of those in the western zones of Germany were released. The highest-ranking female leader of the Nazi Party, Gertrud Scholtz-Klink, had cleverly escaped Soviet custody, but was later arrested by the French for forging her identity documents. Apparently she was not a sympathetic defendant, because the French kept her in jail for four years and imposed a ten-year ban on her journalistic, political and teaching activities. Not long after the ban was

German female prisoners detained in Kassel, Germany

lifted, this inveterate Nazi published a self-congratulatory account of German women in the Third Reich.

All women in uniform were swept up in the Allied dragnet and placed in internment camps. In the territories occupied by the Soviets, German women were dealt with harshly. Some twenty thousand were arrested in the East and deported to inner Russia; they were not among those sent back to Germany in the late 1950s during the political thaw of pardons and amnesties. They were executed or died in captivity.

Ilse Struwe was relatively lucky. This Wehrmacht secretary was interned by the Soviets until December 1946, but not deported to the Soviet Union. She was more useful as a secretary in the Soviet Military Occupation Administration. She did not speak about what she saw that night from her bedroom window in Rivne, and she did not talk with others about the photographs of atrocities she had seen. If she said anything to anyone about what she had witnessed, she reasoned, 'I might as well hang myself on the highest pole.' She waited until the 1990s to publish her memoir.

Erika Ohr was also swept up by the Allies and interned in the summer of 1945 – in her case, in an American camp. Here she allegedly saw German POWs being tortured; they were made to stand in dirt up to their necks. Ohr was not sure why they deserved such a punishment. The only explanation she could offer in her memoir was an anti-Semitic one. In Ohr's view, since many of the Americans running the internment camp spoke German, they must have been related to the Jews who had been forced to emigrate. Now they were taking revenge on these German soldiers.

Since German women were not in the leadership, other than in women's organisations of the Nazi Party and in some medical establishments as doctors, they did not sit in the dock with the most prominent Nazis, such as Hermann Goering, Rudolf Hess and Alfred Rosenberg, who were tried at the International Military Tribunal in Nuremberg. The Allies had bigger fish to fry; they devoted their scarce investigative resources to tracking down top Nazis. Some women were tried in the zonal courts. The Soviets (and later the East

Germans) convicted female guards from the largest women's camp in the Reich – Ravensbrück – and the British went after the 'Beasts of Bergen-Belsen', including the twenty-two-year-old Irma Grese, who was executed by a military court. There were two German women in the American Nuremberg zonal trials. The first was Dr Herta Oberheuser, who was sentenced to twenty years for her cruel medical experiments, but released after seven. (She resumed her medical practice as a paediatrician in Schleswig-Holstein, until she was discovered and stripped of her medical licence.) The other woman was a state-sponsored kidnapper named Inge Viermetz. A secretary who climbed the ranks within the SS Race and Resettlement Office to become a departmental chief, Viermetz stood trial for the deportation of hundreds of Polish and Yugoslav children. She pleaded not guilty and denied any wrongdoing. Viermetz's insistence that she had performed charitable welfare work was convincing to the judges. She was acquitted in 1948.

One of the more famous prosecutors at the Nuremberg trials was Robert Kempner. When he returned to Germany with the US Army (after having been forced to emigrate from Germany as a Jewish attorney in 1935), he looked up his old secretary in Berlin, Emmy Hoechtl. She had worked during the war in the Reich Security Main Office for the head of the criminal police, Einsatzgruppe B leader Arthur Nebe. Emmy Hoechtl helped Kempner find some of the most incriminating documents in the German files, contributing to the prosecution and conviction of fellow Germans. But when she was formally interrogated in 1961 as part of West German investigations into the deployment of gas vans in the East, Hoechtl claimed that she could not remember anything about the crimes themselves or about the criminal activity of her bosses.

Robert Kempner also collaborated with his wife, Ruth Kempner, on an official study, 'Women in Nazi Germany'. This research was commissioned by the US government as an information source for the denazification of German women. The Kempners warned US occupiers in Germany that German women were fanatical supporters who had been integrated into all aspects of the government, including being formed into police units to monitor market places in Germany and to manage the correct distribution of rations. They estimated that seven million German women and girls had been indoctrinated into the movement. Sixteen million had been mobilised by the Reich Labour Front. Placing the women in categories according to the degree of 'public danger' they posed, the Kempners determined that about six hundred thousand German women were still dangerous because they were politically active leaders and indoctrinators. The Kempners advised US authorities to pursue a thorough purging and reorganisation of the educational and administrative apparatus of the German state, which had been infiltrated by female Nazis. It was a tremendous task of ideological transformation, which they believed could only be undertaken with patience, and 'without illusions about the limitations of their [German women's] personality range'.

German women were indeed very active supporters of the Third Reich, as the Kempners discerned early on, and the passage of time revealed that more were involved in the crimes of the regime than the officials at Nuremberg and in the denazification courts realised, or cared to know. Illusions about the behaviour of female perpetrators persisted, as did confusion about their motives.

Probing the depths of individual motives demands more than the reconstruction of a biography or of a crime scene. The narratives of the women who had lived in the occupied eastern territories and who were confronted by post-war interrogators to divulge their experiences, or who later reflected on them, offer clues about their motives, but the narratives are far from transparent. While not all women intentionally deceived, the self-portraits in these memoirs and testimonies are intended to appeal to an audience, whether bureaucratic examiners, zealous prosecutors, supportive family members or curious historians. Naturally the self-representations exaggerate, mislead, self-glorify or mollify. Shameful or unlawful acts, indiscretions, embarrassing mistakes, regrettable affiliations and negative sentiments such as hate are usually glossed over or omitted.

Nurses' memoirs, a large portion of the total, contain valuable information about female experiences in the war, but they can be misleading. Reading them, I was not sure if the authors were genuinely naive or unobservant as youths, or if their innocence had been embellished for present-day readers. How could Erika Ohr describe in detail a toothache or a meal that she had in Poland in 1944, but only vaguely recall the sense behind a lone 'partisan' being shot in the cloister of a field hospital? 'It could not be established who he was and what he had planned,' Ohr wrote dismissively, continuing, 'In this war there were so many ambiguities on both sides.' Moral relativism and thoughtlessness reflect the thinking at the time and after the war.

How did nurse defendants explain their motives and violent acts? In Allied and German courtrooms they often fell back on their institutional affiliations and training as care-givers as a kind of proof of proper intentions. They repeated the assertion that they had to fulfil their duty. In the post-war investigation of the crimes at the Polish asylum of Meseritz-Obrawalde, a nurse explained to a German court that it was her superior, a doctor who was the director of the asylum, who demanded that she and the other junior nurses assist with the killing injections. The nurse claimed that at first she refused, but the director told her there was no point in refusing – that 'as a civil servant of many years standing', she had to perform her duty, 'especially in times of war'. Then he tried to appeal to her soft side, reassuring her that the injections would end the suffering of the patients. Isn't that what she wished, to relieve her patients? The nurse insisted when she testified that she was just doing what was expected of her. One nurse charged with poisoning patients in Poland explained:

> I would never have committed theft. I know that one is not supposed to do that. In the bad times [pre-war depression years] I was a saleswoman, and I had in those times easy opportunities to do that. But I never did such a thing, because I simply knew that it is not permitted. Even as a child I had learned: you are not allowed to steal. The administration of medication for the goal of killing a mentally ill person, I viewed as my duty, which I was not allowed to refuse.

In her mind, she was not a criminal. She had a good upbringing and learned that stealing was a crime. Doing her duty was not a crime, she believed, even if doing that duty meant killing another human being.

Besides sharing tools of violence (the hypodermic needle, the whip and the gun), a passionate commitment to an ideological cause, an immoral perception of duty and pacts of loyalty and secrecy, German male and female perpetrators exhibited similar psychologies of denial and repression. Those confronted with their misdeeds replied along standard lines. *I don't know; I know nothing about that. I can't remember; I had to follow orders; I was on leave. I heard from others about certain actions against Jews, but I did not see any Jews. When I arrived at my station, all the Jews were gone.* Female defendants were aware of male testimony, were well versed in the art of verbal self-defence and also developed their own strategies.

Of course anyone being questioned by a prosecutor or investigator for a major crime will be circumspect and will try to avoid punishment. In fear and desperation, to save oneself and to spare one's family added shame and burden, one might lie, especially if the crime was committed in a place and time far removed from that of the trial, and is thus hard to prove. Many did lie. Is it so surprising that, among the more than three hundred thousand Germans and Austrians investigated across Europe, very few confessed?

More complex than the basic strategy of outright denial was the defence of being the martyr or victim. As the nurse Pauline Kneissler put it, 'I never understood mercy killing as murder . . . My life was one of dedication and self-sacrifice . . . Never was I cruel to persons . . . and for this today I must suffer and suffer.' Perpetrators who deny their crimes do not see themselves as evildoers who deserve punishment. It is the victim and the prosecutors who believe otherwise. In his exploration of evil, the social psychologist Roy Baumeister argues that perpetrators 'may see something wrong in what they did, but they also see how they were affected by external factors, including some that were beyond their control. They see themselves as having acted in a way that was fully appropriate and justified.'

Erna Petri did not deny her killing or overtly assign herself victimhood, but she did attribute her deed to circumstances at the time, not least to the influence of her husband, who was certainly a brutal man. When she was pressed to explain why she herself shot Jewish men and children, she stated:

> In those times, as I carried out the shootings, I was barely 23 years old, still young and inexperienced. I lived among men who were in the SS and carried out shootings of Jewish persons. I seldom came into contact with other women, so that in the course of this time I became more hardened, desensitised. I did not want to stand behind the SS men. I wanted to show them that I, as a woman, could conduct myself like a man. So I shot 4 Jews and 6 Jewish children. I wanted to prove myself to the men. Besides, in those days in this region, everywhere one heard that Jewish persons and children were being shot, which also caused me to kill them.

If Erna stressed her role as an SS wife, should it not follow that her husband would shoulder some of the guilt associated with the initiative she took in carrying out the killings? In fact, after the Stasi forced Erna Petri to confess, she stated that she had denied her crimes during earlier interrogations because she had assumed that her husband would cover for her. But he did not.

One of the more difficult motives to document was paradoxically the most pervasive: anti-Semitism. In the Third Reich, anti-Semitism was an official state ideology, which added to its unassailability. It became a defining element of the Reich. It permeated everyday life, shaped professional and intimate relationships and generated criminal government policies. Was there a female form of anti-Semitic thinking and expression, specific to women's roles, their place in the Nazi system and society – as secretaries, wives of officials, nurses and teachers?

During the Nazi era, the emotional desires, material needs and professional ambitions of German women – such as trying to curry favour with a superior, compete with a colleague or mate, keep one's job, secure a comfortable villa or a 'new' dress – determined the life or death of a Jew. In retrospect, these concerns, desires and ambitions are easy to dismiss as petty and insignificant when placed against the consequences of premeditated anti-Semitic hate and sadism. But the mundane and the grandiose intermingled.

A driving force behind the radicalisation of violence in the Reich was expressed by Erna Petri, and it applied to men as well as women. When Erna Petri, Johanna Altvater and others callously killed Jewish children, they manifested a Nazi anti-Semitism so profound that it reduced the value of even an innocent child's life to nothing. When the interrogator asked Petri, as a mother herself of two children, how she could shoot innocent Jewish children, she replied:

> I am unable to grasp at this time how in those days that I was in
> such a state as to conduct myself so brutally and reprehensibly –
> shooting Jewish children. However earlier [before arriving at the
> estate in Ukraine] I had been so conditioned to fascism and the
> racial laws, which established a view toward the Jewish people. As
> was told to me, I had to destroy the Jews. It was from this mindset
> that I came to commit such a brutal act.

In a setting ever closer to the front, within the partisan warfare zone, and in the midst of the Holocaust, German officials with their wives and female assistants tried to uphold the Nazi racist, imperialist mission and relied on violence as the primary instrument of control. It may have been a 'man's world' in the East, but women were able to adapt to it and then fiercely rationalise their actions in it.

Petri's testimony is rare. There are few wartime and post-war records of ordinary German women expounding on their views of Jews and the Holocaust. More common was a colonialist discourse about how stupid, dirty and lazy 'the locals' were, referring to Poles, Ukrainians and Jews, or veiled references to the dark terrain infested with 'Bolsheviks', 'criminals' and 'partisans', or to the infantilised native who is clever but inferior, and thus dispensable. In their accounts (both in court and in memoirs), women tried to minimise the Holocaust and the extent to which it was fuelled by their own anti-Semitism; they referred to the Holocaust as 'that Jewish thing from the war', or said that 'it was just that some Jews were being shot' or explained that the 'Jews want to take revenge on us'. Josefine Block suggested that the Jews were guilty for not saving their own kin. Erika Raeder, the prominent, outspoken wife of the incarcerated admiral of the navy, who was desperate to get her ailing, elderly husband out of jail, went so far as to argue that 'the treatment we Germans have had to endure is worse than anything that has happened to the Jews'. Raeder's comparison was, and is, morally reprehensible and wrong. Yet Raeder gained the sympathy of British and American leaders and the West German press. Her husband, who had been serving a life sentence, was released with many other high-ranking Nazi criminals in 1955. Pardoning the perpetrators may have been an act of political expediency, helping to integrate West Germany into the Western alliance. For conservative Germans, Nazis and neo-Nazis, however, Allied amnesties affirmed their self-perceived victimisation and prejudices. Comparing German and Jewish suffering, and shifting the blame for the war to the Jews, were more than defence strategies to deny Nazi crimes and culpability. The Holocaust denial associated with these strategies did not originate in the post-war courtroom; it had its roots in the ideology of the Third Reich. Most Nazi perpetrators and their accomplices – and even many witnesses to the crimes who suppressed what they saw – could not empathise with the Jews, during the war or after.

How did observers at the time and afterwards account for the extremely violent, even sadistic behaviour of some women? The wartime witnesses who observed female perpetrators and the post-war prosecutors who questioned them were in fact dumbfounded by their cruelty. When survivors tried to articulate what a world turned upside down by genocide looks like, those who listened to their testimony found it almost beyond comprehension. Recall the survivor who witnessed Altvater's cruelty: 'Such sadism from a woman I have never seen, I will never forget this.' The female killers stood out in survivors' memories, in their actions and appearance. It was expected that the mass of uniformed, crew-cut German soldiers and police could and did kill – but women? How could women act this way? That a seemingly maternal, caring figure could in one instant console tenderly and in the next instant harm, even kill, was and is one of the most befuddling aspects of women's behaviour in this history. And yet such behaviours were often embodied in the nurses, mothers and wives who were accomplices and perpetrators.

To assume that violence is not a feminine characteristic and that women are not capable of mass murder has obvious appeal: it allows for hope that at least half the human race will not devour the other, that it will protect children and so safeguard the future. But minimising the violent behaviour of women creates a false shield against a more direct confrontation with genocide and its disconcerting realities.

How might some 'experts' explain what these women did? The nineteenth-century criminologist Cesare Lombroso, known for measuring the heads of his subjects to determine their behaviour, claimed that female killers had smaller brains and were unusually hairy, likening them to under-developed primates. Sigmund Freud presented the deviant behaviour of women as rooted in their desire to be men, a form of penis envy. Another dubious theory posits that women have committed more crimes than have been documented, given that women are 'naturally deceitful' and secretive. The 'evidence' provided is women's skill at concealing menstruation and faking orgasms.

But how extreme *are* the biological differences between men and women when it comes to violent behaviour? Recent studies of animal behaviour – mostly of primates – have shown that males are more violent. When threatened, females bond with other females for protection. Males dominate social hierarchies, but females are the source of mediation and reconciliation. They are key in bringing about a deescalation when relations among male primates become tense. Can we apply theories of animal behaviour to the Holocaust? When comparing Nazi perpetrators to animals, one is reminded of the eminent Holocaust historian Yehuda Bauer's comment that applying terms like *beastly* and *bestiality* to the Nazis is 'an insult to the animal kingdom . . . because animals do not do things like that; the behaviour of the perpetrators was all too human, not inhuman'. Genocide as an idea and an act is a human phenomenon. Perpetration of genocide requires human cognitive abilities, an ideology of hatred with all its mythic and emotional power and well-developed systems for organising and implementing it. Humans are the only animals that commit genocide. The work of Frans de Waal, a leading primatologist, supports the fact that the majority of women in the Third Reich were not instinctively violent. But they were also *not* the mediating, empathetic agents of de-escalation that are found among female primates.

In non-genocidal societies, men commit, on average, almost nine-tenths of all violent crimes. Women who commit violent acts do so usually in the form of domestic violence, and rarely against other women. Some theorists attribute the preponderance of male violence to character traits such as higher self-esteem among men, 'the arrogance of the "male ego"', as contrasted with 'female patterns of insecurity, lack of assertiveness, and depression'. If violent behaviour can be explained by such character traits and socially constructed expectations, then the devaluation of individual life in Nazi Germany changed these traits and expectations, encouraging women as well as men to be assertive or even arrogant and spreading an inherently violent ideology of racial superiority. The violence of Nazi Germany was not an aberration, an inexplicable departure from typical female behaviour or nature. On the contrary, as the political theorist Hannah Arendt stressed, totalitarian movements use violence as an instrument, applying it manipulatively to gain and hold on to power. The female perpetrators of the Holocaust employed guns, whips and lethal needles to achieve a mastery that was not otherwise available, to lord it over victims of the regime rendered powerless.

A recent study of female criminals (based on 103 inmates in a US jail) found that 'the callous and unemotional component of psychopathy is comparable in both males and females', but the manner in which this antisocial behaviour is exhibited differs. In other words, men and women may have an equal measure of the emotional traits that potentially cause violent behaviour, such as lack of empathy and impulsivity, but women are usually conditioned to be less socially aggressive. The expression of traits that may be predictive of violence is influenced by other sociocultural experiences of a particular time and place, such as education and upbringing. Thus Johanna Altvater's sadism in the ghetto of Volodymyr-Volynsky was a product of nature *and* nurture, of biological and situational factors.

Other studies, including Theodor Adorno's work on the authoritarian personality, suggest that empathy results from an upbringing of moral socialisation. If a child is taught the negative effects of her actions on others, this increases empathy. If, on the other hand, she is disciplined not through reasoning but through 'harsh authoritarian or power assertive parenting practices which rely on the use of punishment', then stereotypic thinking, submission to authority and aggression against outsiders or deviants may be the result. Moral socialisation is not developed in these cases, and therefore little empathy. Fear hinders empathy. Historians cannot put their subjects on the couch or into a laboratory, of course, but I think it is worth pointing out that most Germans of the Nazi era were raised in authoritarian households where regular beatings – certainly not inductive reasoning – were employed to discipline and motivate children.

The idea of the authoritarian personality has another application here. For many women of the Nazi era, the father, the husband and the Führer were all authoritarian figures that shaped their lives in different stages. Erna Petri's father disapproved of Horst, her Nazi husband, but eventually Erna chose to align herself with a brutish mate instead of a protective father. The post-war testimony of many female defendants exhibits a fear of authority and the belief that one must obey or fulfil one's duty.

During the Nuremberg trials some male defendants underwent a series of psychological tests fashionable at the time, such as the Rorschach inkblot test. A psychologist who studied SS *Gruppenführer* Otto Ohlendorf, the head of Einsatzgruppe D, who confessed to killing more than ninety thousand men, women and children, concluded that Ohlendorf must be a 'sadist, a pervert or a lunatic' because he spoke about his cruelties in such a matter-of-fact, unflinching manner. When asked by the judge whether he would kill his own sister if he were ordered to do so, Ohlendorf said he would. But he was no brainless automaton; he was a well-educated, fully informed follower of Hitler and Himmler. Another Nuremberg court psychologist subjected Nazi leaders to various tests and concluded that such persons are 'neither sick nor unusual; in fact they are like any other person we might encounter in other countries of the earth'.

Such psychological experiments were conducted largely on the Reich leadership and on SS men. If tests were done on women, they have not been published. And yet those who actually bloodied their hands were not the leadership and mostly not SS men; thus the psychological assessments are not historically representative of the diverse combination of perpetrators, male and female, German and non-German. I interviewed the senior prosecutor Hermann Weissing, who was chief of the Central Office for the Investigation of Nazi War Criminals in North Rhine-Westphalia and who questioned thousands of suspects between 1965 and 1985 (including Johanna Altvater Zelle). He explained that he did not encounter anyone who could be described as psychopathic. 'The individuals were not insane, it was the Nazi system that was crazy,' he told me. Weissing was convinced that many of the perpetrators whom he investigated, including Altvater, had committed the crimes, but he also concluded that they were no longer a threat to society. They were 'normal', law-abiding citizens in the new democratic Germany.

Studies of perpetrator motivation explain that those who incite acts of hate are seeking to rid themselves and the world around them of its unsettling, messy ambiguities and complexity. The perpetrator mentality is one of 'splitting' – that is, all-or-none, black-and-white thinking. Perpetrators often see themselves as enlightened, as holders of a greater truth, superior to their foes, above reproach and accountability, struggling to break free of a world of dichotomies. The interwar German generation experienced the glaring extremes of war and peace: unbridled capitalism and state-regulated communism; the individual and the collective; the past and the future. Germans sought to transcend these conflicts, and yearned for a superior, utopian existence founded on something that seemed tangible and essentialist – biological racism. From our perspective, the Holocaust's machinery of destruction was a bureaucratic jungle of competing factions, entangled agencies, and bloody, irrational madness. To the perpetrators it was 'smooth', determined, systematic, necessary, sophisticated, exact – unpleasant, perhaps, but humane. The enemies – the Jews and other so-called racial defectives – were to be removed with surgical precision once and for all. Threats to Germany's existence would be overcome, the struggle resolved. In the minds of Hitler, his followers and many German patriots, the Final Solution was a defensive act of liberation from the encroaching power of a globalising Jewry.

The crimes committed by female perpetrators occurred within a web of professional priorities and tasks, personal commitments and anxieties. The perpetrator who accepts the perceived necessity of killing could in the course of one day shoot Jewish children and then arrive home to coddle her son or daughter. There is no contradiction here in the mind of the perpetrator; there is, rather, a startling degree of clarity. Nurses and doctors rationalised their lethal injections as ending suffering; the 'patients' were unhealthy, incurable, in a physical state of limbo. The patient's ambivalent state had to be resolved through a 'merciful' death. Of course, the so-called Jewish threat was in reality non-existent. Yet naked Jewish boys seeking shelter on the Petris' estate or toddlers in the ghettos of Volodymyr-Volynsky were murdered because their mere presence was anathema to the German fantasy of a utopian *Lebensraum*. In the perpetrator's mind, Germans and Jews could not coexist. Female killers, like their male counterparts, developed this conviction after years of conditioning in the Reich, absorbed it from a general climate of popular and state-condoned anti-Semitism in Germany and across Europe.

There is general agreement among scientists that the environment is the most important factor in determining whether one will become a perpetrator of genocide. Without certain settings and experiences, individuals with the proclivity to commit crimes would not commit them. In the course of their lives, and even in the course of an hour, perpetrators like Erna Petri could dramatically change their behaviour, at one moment feeding Jewish children and reflexively taking on the role of mother, and shortly thereafter placing a gun to the children's heads as executioner. Johanna Altvater, who bashed a toddler's head against a ghetto wall and was described as 'masculine' and 'ice cold' – 'someone you would not want to encounter on a moonless night' – worked in a child-welfare office after the war. The callousness shown towards Jews who were trapped in cattle cars, then marched to the edge of town to be shot, is not evidence of a unique German predisposition to kill Jews. German men and women, and their collaborators, first had to learn how to adapt to mass murder, including all its methods and rationales. The varied experiences of German women and men in the eastern occupied territories as they became direct witnesses, accomplices and perpetrators of the Holocaust broadened and deepened their anti-Semitic behaviour. Anti-Semitism there took on many forms, more elaborate and extreme than in the Reich, where sustained, visible violence was not tolerated and the 'Bolshevik' threat was not directly encountered. Judaeo-Bolshevism was, as we have seen, a powerful mobilising ideology of the war. Yet most women who went east were not rabid anti-Semites; in fact, most identified with other convictions and ambitions. The eastern experience proved transformative. It was in the eastern territories that Nazi anti-Semitism found its fullest expression and most profound development, and for some the anti-Semitic ideas absorbed there were not discredited by the defeat of Hitler's Germany.

Can one apply the typology of male perpetrators in Holocaust studies to women? The research here on female witnesses, accomplices and perpetrators shows that women did exhibit the same behaviours and motivations as men. Though women were not organised into mobile killing units like the *Einsatzgruppen* or the Order Police battalions, some did undergo militarised training as camp guards with the sole purpose of inflicting terror or, as they saw it, disciplining enemies of the Reich. The focus here has been on women who became perpetrators in other professional and private capacities, in the field offices and hospitals of the Reich, and in their homes. Here, in these varied roles and settings, we find that immoral, violent behaviour was manifested in diverse forms.

There were women in the elite ranks of the scientific and medical professions, women who conducted 'research' in the ghettos and asylums where genocide occurred. The female version of the desk murderer was found in the routine but lethal work of the Minsk Gestapo chief's secretary, Sabine Dick, and the Lida governor's secretary, Liselotte Meier. In Josefine Block and Johanna Altvater we see the female version of the sadist. The female version of the sniper-murderer was revealed in Liesel Willhaus and Gertrude Segel; of the executioner, in Erna Petri. Like their male counterparts, Hitler's Furies came from several backgrounds: working class and well-to-do, educated and uneducated, Catholic and Protestant, urban and provincial. They were all ambitious and patriotic; to varying degrees they also shared the qualities of greed, anti-Semitism, racism and imperialistic arrogance. And they were all young.

In the typology of female killers, there is a final group to be considered. Earlier work presenting women through pornographic caricatures, like the sex maniac in the film *Ilsa: She Wolf of the SS*, were offensive distortions. But there is an element of reality in these exaggerated depictions. We must account for the dynamic of male-female relationships as a causative factor, whether the energy was purely sexual or conjugal. Even in the most basic mating ritual, males and females perform for each other, and as a pair their behaviour continues to be shaped in private and public settings by their relationship and sexual attraction. For many couples – the Petris, the Landaus, the Willhauses, the lovers Hanweg and Meier and many others – the violence of the Holocaust was part of the dynamic of their relationship. Of course these relationships did not cause the Holocaust, but they were an integral part of the everyday terror that individual Jews and their families faced in the ghettos, camps and even at mass-shooting sites. On top of the daily deprivation, loss of family members and

Commissar Hanweg (with a rifle) and an unidentified woman
forcing a young Jewish man out of hiding

physical torture they faced, Jews in the East had to cope with the be-
wilderment of what many survivors described as a world turned upside
down, where German rulers who professed a higher civilisation conducted themselves with the utmost depravity and barbarism. Women
were often at the centre of these puzzling scenes.

German amusements, 'recreation' and debauchery in the ghettos
and near the mass-shooting sites were part of that world turned upside
down, and again women were there. The hedonist does not act alone:
pleasure is often pursued in pairs and groups. The *Ostrausch* – intoxication of the East – was an imperial high that increased the violence
of the war and genocide. Hedonism and genocide went hand in hand,
and women and men were its agents, its partners in crime.

Many personality types and professions helped the Nazis' machinery of destruction operate and expand. It was a German invention, but one run by many non-Germans as well, and these non-German participants proved just as opportunistic and anti-Semitic. By its very definition, genocide is a mass crime perpetrated by a collective, by an entire society against another group, usually a vulnerable minority. Political systems and government institutions are its mechanisms and organisational frameworks, but its force originates in the will of the people, as Hitler recognised. Genocidal regimes undertake violent revolutions that pit one group against another in what both groups believe is an existential struggle for their existence. In this form of total war, all men and women participate, and traditional roles are perverted in the militarisation of society. Moral codes of conduct are retooled – a phenomenon that is empowering for those in control, but disturbing, horrifying and deadly for those who experience its force.

As we have seen, at least half a million women witnessed and contributed to the operations and terror of a genocidal war in the eastern territories. The Nazi regime mobilised a generation of young female revolutionaries who were conditioned to accept violence, to incite it, and to commit it, in defence of or as an assertion of Germany's superiority. This fact has been suppressed and denied by the very women who were swept up in the regime and of course by those who perpetrated the violence with impunity. Genocide is also women's business. When given the 'opportunity', women too will engage in it, even the bloodiest aspects of it. Minimising women's culpability to a few thousand brainwashed and misguided camp guards does not accurately represent the reality of the Holocaust.

# 7

||||||||||||||||||||||

# What Happened to Them?

AMERICAN PROSECUTORS AND their staff were under enormous pressure in the post-war period to narrow a list of about two million German offenders down to a few hundred major war criminals. Men and women in the Allied internment camps were waiting release; their detention was interfering with the reconstruction of Germany. Though the International Tribunal at Nuremberg had declared the SS a criminal organisation, it decided that clerks, secretaries, stenographers, cleaning staff and other low-level support staff working in the Gestapo and other SS offices would be exempt from indictment. These underlings, according to Allied leaders' calculations, made up 30–35 per cent of the SS staff, or 13,500 people. Female detectives across the Reich and in the East who examined Jewish women and children, searching their personal belongings on train platforms or as they entered camps, or the former secretaries who transmitted killing orders, selected labourers and plundered Jewish belongings – personnel in these categories would not automatically be investigated as war criminals. Despite the alarming data compiled by the Kempners, criminal investigators and denazification courts reasonably concluded that women in the white-collar state machinery were not threats to post-war German society. German defence lawyers argued convincingly that desk clerks in the Gestapo offices, including female stenographers, had little knowledge of the criminal policies, and that they lacked the authority to commit crimes and conspire with their superiors.

The record of justice against Nazi perpetrators, male and female, is rather poor. Most German women who participated in the Holocaust quietly resumed normal lives. We've seen that post-war literary constructions and imagery stressed the image of the burdened German *Hausfrau*, the 'rubble women' who were the backbone of West Germany's rapid economic recovery (*Wirtschaftswunder*) and who struggled to provide for fatherless families with little food and shelter. This idea of German women as martyrs was at odds with the evidence of women participating in the evil deeds of the Third Reich. Those who were confronted after the war by survivor witnesses and brought to trial were portrayed either as appalling freaks of nature, or as naturally innocent and incapable of such monstrous acts. Intentionally or not, female defendants could exploit the latter prejudice to their advantage. Interrogators and investigators judged women based on their emotional responses. Court officials noted when women cried during the questioning or proceedings. Such a display of emotion seemed to indicate humanity, sensitivity and presumably an empathy that was consistent with the nature or instinct of female innocence and caring. And indeed, since most women were not sadistic murderers, such a bias was not unfounded.

After the war, Annette Schücking, the Red Cross nurse with the law degree who documented the 'slaughterhouse' of Ukraine in letters to her parents, was able to put her education to good use. In 1948 she became a founding member of the reconstituted German female lawyers' league; the Nazis had disbanded the earlier league in 1933. A self-proclaimed feminist, she successfully advocated legal reforms to curb domestic violence. She served as a judge in the civil court of Detmold for several decades. One case that landed on her desk involved a man who mentioned in his CV that he had been a policeman in

Novgorod Volynsk during the war. Schücking presented herself to war-crimes investigators and shared detailed information about the perpetrators she had met in Ukraine. She urged prosecutors to track down Sergeant Frank, the man who told her about his shooting of Jews in Khmilnyk, but Frank could not be found. In her opinion, her attempt to help had been rebuffed: 'It was impossible to talk openly in the court system with any colleagues who had been in the East. Former Nazis were everywhere.' Nothing came of her attempt to assist war-crimes investigators. In 2010, haunted by the images of Jewish children she saw being 'led away' to their deaths, she asked again, 'But what could I have done?'

Comparing investigations and trials in post-war Austria and the two Germanys, historians have found that there were female defendants in various categories, though they were in the minority. During the high point of prosecution in Germany and Austria – that is, in the first decade after the war – twenty-six women were sentenced to death for crimes committed in medical facilities and concentration camps. With one highly publicised exception (the SS policewoman who placed Anne Frank and her family on the deportation list to Auschwitz), German women were not pursued after the war for their role as administrators of the Holocaust in Gestapo offices and regional outposts in the East or occupied territories. As for violence that occurred outside institutional settings, there were a handful of cases against women who brutalised forced labourers in their private homes, farms and businesses, and fewer than ten indictments of German women who committed murder or were accessories to murder in mass shootings and ghetto liquidations. A female Nazi trying to escape prosecution in Europe would have found Austria even safer than Germany. The largest number of German female Nazis tried for murder or accessory to murder was in East Germany, with 220 female defendants tried between 1945 and 1990. The Austrians have not tried and convicted a Nazi war criminal (male or female) since the 1970s, a sad irony given Simon Wiesenthal's prominence as a Nazi-hunter based in Vienna.

What do the post-war fates of the women featured in this book reveal about the prosecution of the crimes of genocide? As will be seen in this chapter, the accomplices and perpetrators featured in this book faced investigators after the war, but only one was judged guilty. Most who were working in places such as Belarus, where the killing was an open secret, where the thousands of fresh mass graves marked the landscape, claimed that they saw and knew nothing. Most investigators and prosecutors were not very aggressive in their pursuit of female Nazis; German witnesses were not anxious to provide more information than was necessary, especially anything self-incriminating; and the judiciary in West Germany and Austria was not thoroughly denazified.

Shared participation in the dirty work of mass murder cemented relationships that extended well beyond the wartime years. Wives remained loyal to husbands; often they were grateful just to *have* a husband, given the struggles of the many war widows with children to feed. Vera Eichmann registered a fake death certificate to hide her husband, SS Lieutenant Colonel Adolf Eichmann. This was more than an act of conjugal love: it was a cover-up concocted by mates who had something to hide and something in common. On the eve of his execution in Israel, Eichmann expressed no guilt or shame about his role in the Final Solution and credited his wife for upholding his self-perception of innocence. As mirrors, women have magnified men's feelings of power and superiority as well as deflected the face of evil. Blind to the immorality of the violence, or perhaps not wanting to see it, most wives focused on their Christian duty to uphold their marriage vow and continued to serve as accomplices. As they had first emboldened their husbands to commit crimes, they maintained the innocence of their men to the end.

In Bavaria, prison chaplains counselled the wives of incarcerated defendants to support their husbands unconditionally. If the men had sinned, they could nevertheless find forgiveness with God's grace. The loving, loyal wife might lead her man to redemption, or so the chaplains hoped; the pursuit of justice in the courts was almost an afterthought. Neither the prosecutors nor the chaplains were able to persuade perpetrators to publicly confess to their crimes. Who knows what husbands privately confessed to their wives, but most wives did not see many options beyond staying married, even if they felt betrayed or loathed their violent husbands. Bavarian pastors and ministers discouraged divorces on the grounds of war crimes; the person seen as the moral failure was the wife who initiated such a separation, not the criminal husband. In the words of one chaplain who refused to grant a wife's request for divorce, those guilty of war crimes had committed an 'act of fate that affects both marital partners equally . . . This act of fate must be shouldered by both marital partners together.' Wives refuted charges against their perpetrator husbands, insisting on the upright and kind characters of these men, the fathers of their children.

Male perpetrators who found new mates after the war hid their crimes until investigators came knocking. When I telephoned a member of a special mobile killing unit that rampaged across Ukraine and Russia, his wife answered the call and refused to allow me to speak to her husband. She described her own suffering, explaining that during the war she had been a nurse. Then she began to sob. She had met her husband, a brewer, immediately after the war and learned decades later that he had been in an *Einsatzgruppe*. But she could not leave him: they had already started a family.

Pacts of loyalty extended from the home to the workplace. The Third Reich was defeated and discredited as a criminal regime. But the perpetrators continued to value oaths of loyalty and secrecy, not to their dead Führer, but to one another. In the post-war era, loyalty was a pact of protection against prosecutors and Nazi-hunters. Such bonds developed within killing units like Order Police Battalion 101, as well as between secretaries and bosses, and among networks of female colleagues and acquaintances. When the secretary for the district commissar in Slonim was asked to provide testimony about the war crimes of her boss, she received a letter from her boss's wife, who begged the former secretary to stand back and not influence the proceedings. Of course, not everyone abided by this pact or succumbed to the peer pressure that was rooted in the wartime experience. Harsh interrogations and blackmailing, especially in the East German police state, yielded detailed accounts and confessions. Bonds of secrecy could be broken down under pressure or by expanding the search for witnesses.

Secretaries who covered for their bosses were both distancing themselves from the crimes and protecting themselves from being smeared as 'denouncers'. One of Adolf Eichmann's secretaries in his Berlin office (Department IVB4) had been contacted in the 1960s when German prosecutors launched an extensive investigation of the Reich Security Main Office. This secretary remained tight-lipped about her former colleagues, their escape routes from Berlin and Prague and their systematic destruction of top-secret documents. In 1967 her immediate boss, Fritz Woehrn, was indicted by a West German court, and later he was convicted as an accessory to murder for the incarceration and ultimate death of 'half-Jews' (those in mixed marriages), Jewish hospital patients and Jews arrested for violating Nazi anti-Semitic bans on such things as owning a bike, going to the cinema, or visiting an Aryan hairdresser. In a rare conviction of a 'desk murderer', the Berlin state court established that Woehrn's motive was anti-Semitic hate and that Woehrn was one of the most 'radical and notorious' functionaries in Eichmann's office.

I contacted Woehrn's secretary about her work and her former bosses in Department IVB4. She was determined to keep her vow of secrecy. She insisted that she was apolitical, that she applied for the job in Eichmann's office simply because she dreamed about things like new shoes and needed a job. When pressed about her actual work in the office, she blurted out one word repeatedly, '*Erledigt!*' (Done!), as if rubber-stamping a document.

For her, at eighty-four years of age, this history was finished, and she wanted no more to do with it. Perhaps she had inadvertently articulated a deeper memory of her experience in the Third Reich, an era when deported and killed Jews, at least half of them women, were euphemistically described as *erledigt,* or finished off. Listening to her, I imagined a young female clerk in a powerful office in Berlin, satisfied not to be working in a factory or on a farm, routinely typing and stamping deportation lists or case files concerning Jews, 'asocials' and other enemies of the Reich, daydreaming about her social plans after work and those pretty shoes that she had seen in a shop window that morning. She was just 'doing her job', and eyeing its material rewards.

Sabine Dick, the onetime career secretary in the Gestapo, was more forthcoming. To West German investigators she offered detailed information about ostensibly mundane administrative procedures, often revealing key pieces of information about the bureaucratic routines of genocide. But she refrained from negative portraits of her bosses, either praising them as decent, warm-hearted, paternal figures or describing them sympathetically as overworked officials. Suspects like Dick had reason to fear Nazi-hunters and prosecutors, and became skilled at stymieing investigations. Time was on their side. There was the statute of limitations on Nazi crimes other than murder, and even murder was harder to prove as the memories of witnesses faded and witnesses died.

Still, despite her best efforts to protect her boss, Georg Heuser, and her own reputation, Dick's testimony had the opposite effect. She was questioned several times between April and October 1960. First she tried to divert attention away from the crime scenes in Minsk. She named former colleagues and presented details about the Berlin headquarters, but said she could not remember much about Belarus. When she was asked who was in the shooting commando units in Minsk, first her memory failed; then she declared that she was no denouncer. She also claimed that she feared retribution. She speculated that the German democracy would collapse again, another dictatorship would emerge and she would be the target of vengeance. This seems rather far-fetched but, given her biography, perhaps not entirely outlandish. She had lived through 'the age of extremes'; she had suffered the rise and fall of Nazism, had witnessed the terror of Stalinism and was being interrogated at the height of the Cold War. But the prosecutors were neither convinced nor sympathetic; they were simply annoyed that she was less than helpful in their pursuit of her boss, who was indicted for the murder of more than ten thousand people. They noted that Dick was paranoid and emotional, that she broke out in tears during the questioning.

There was another issue. Dick's husband had been a noncommissioned officer in the Waffen-SS, and he too worked in the Minsk office. Dick and her husband had sworn that they would not incriminate each other by admitting that both worked in the Gestapo office with the defendant, Heuser. The prosecutors reminded her that perjury was a crime, that she could be sentenced to fifteen years in jail for committing it. Dick tried a different tack. On one occasion she brought her thirteen-year-old daughter to the police station where she was being questioned, perhaps hoping to display her maternal side to police investigators. But this also backfired: her daughter complained loudly about being 'dragged into this shit'. Dick was smarter than her husband, who boasted about having built up the police station in Minsk. But investigators did not seem to care that he was still a Nazi; they were just glad that he answered their questions. Sabine Dick, the erratic wife, annoyed them. In the end she did offer incriminating details about their main suspect, her boss, and she was not prosecuted.

Gender bias of many kinds crept into the entire judicial process, beginning with the pursuit of criminals, continuing with the questioning and concluding with the sentencing. Whereas male defendants were judged by their place in the hierarchy and administration, their political ideology and their personal motive – as Hitler's 'primary accomplices', as desk murderers, as excessive sadists – the female defendants were judged with other considerations in mind. The influence of the husband or other male figure was considered similar to the role of peer pressure experienced by men in police and military units. A male defendant was not asked: How much did your wife or lover influence your hatred of Jews or pressure you to commit violent acts? No Lady Macbeth, goading her husband to commit murder as a display of his manhood, emerged in the courtroom. The defence lawyers effectively played up the presumed apolitical development and outlook of the women, whose ideological motivation, anti-Semitism, and racism were – like men's – difficult to document. Typically the motives, whether for killing disabled or Jewish children or for denouncing neighbours to the Gestapo, were attributed to personal desires and emotions, such as jealousy, loneliness, greed, revenge, sex or being 'blinded by love'. A woman who behaved like a man, shooting with a pistol, cracking a whip, riding around the killing fields of Poland

and Ukraine on horseback and wearing trousers and a manly hair-cut – such a female figure was unimaginable to most, passed over by the courts, and not discussed in the testimony. Women like that were loathsome reminders of a failed regime and the descent into fascist barbarism. If Germany and Germans were going to pursue a path of normalisation and shed their Nazi past, then the traditional female figure with its moral, aesthetic ideals had to be restored, not redefined.

Liselotte Meier, the secretary in Lida who was seen with her boss, Hermann Hanweg, and other German officials as they shot Jews from their carriages, admitted after the war that she had joined Hanweg on winter hunts. They shot at prey in the snow, she testified, but she could not remember if their targets were animals or Jews. Hanweg could not corroborate or refute her testimony: the Soviets had already tried and executed him. But Hanweg's deputy was still in Mainz, living above a bicycle shop with his wife. He was arrested and, in a rare demonstration of justice, sentenced to life in prison in 1978. The prosecutor who interrogated Meier was persistent, more aggressive in his questioning than most in West Germany. Perhaps his zeal stemmed from his own wartime experience; as a soldier fighting near Leningrad he had witnessed mass shootings of civilians. The prosecutor travelled to North America and Israel to collect testimony from Jewish survivors. He personally arrested Hanweg's deputy, dragging the man from his home in the early morning while his wife screamed obscenities. The prosecutor questioned the Hanweg family, including Hanweg's wife and children, who tried their best to recount events in detail, drawing sketches of murder scenes and recollecting names of Jewish labourers and events in the ghetto. When the prosecutor confronted Liselotte Meier with survivor testimony that identified her as having been with other German shooters, Meier feigned only a faint recollection of the event. In an obvious attempt to evade the question, she offered a confused jumble of 'I cannot remember', 'I cannot recall the details' and 'I cannot say if the people who were shot were even Jews'; nor did she know 'if the people were targeted or if someone was shooting in the snow'. After the war Meier admitted that she went with Hanweg to the Jewish workshops three or four mornings a week, and that she regularly walked through the Jewish quarter. It is revealing that she tried to hide the love affair she had had with Hanweg, which seemed to haunt her more than her role in the Holocaust. She sobbed during the questioning when pressed on the subject of her lover. Observers of her tears would have been justified in suspecting that it was not the loss of Jewish lives in Lida but rather her own loss of Hermann Hanweg that she mourned.

In the history of the West German pursuit of Nazi war criminals, there was one publicised trial of a German secretary in the East accused of murder. This defendant was Johanna Altvater. During the 1960s, dozens of Holocaust survivors living in Israel, the United

Johanna Altvater Zelle *(upper left)* in an album used
by Israeli investigators to identify her

States and Canada presented their testimonies about a German woman they called Hanna. Non-Jewish witnesses came forward from East Germany, Poland and Ukraine. Seeking some form of justice for the mass murder of an estimated twenty thousand Jews in the town of Volodymyr-Volynsky, survivors identified four perpetrators by name, although of course there were dozens more who had had a direct hand in the population's destruction. 'Fräulein Hanna' was among those four. Twenty years after the events, survivors recounted her horrible deeds.

What happened to Altvater after she left Ukraine at Christmas of 1943? She returned to her boring job at the city administration in Minden. She was not seriously questioned after the war about her activities in the East. 'She can be usefully employed,' her denazification documents noted. In the Minden city administration, she was promoted to welfare caseworker for youth. After 1945, former members of the Nazi Youth in Minden had reunions and sang the old songs. Many had come of age there in the 1920s and 1930s; they did not accept the Nazi regime as a criminal one, and avoided any critical reckoning with their own pasts. Altvater was in that group. She married in 1953, taking the name Zelle (which, ironically, means 'prison cell'). Her husband was an intern in the district youth office in the neighbouring town of Detmold. While he rose in the ranks of the civil administration of Detmold, Frau Zelle took over the care of a six-year-old boy whose education at a boarding school she sponsored. When this boy, whom she adopted, was a young man, he regularly attended her trial.

During the public trial proceedings (18 September 1978–31 October 1979), both Johanna Zelle and her former boss, the district commissar Westerheide, smiled at the cameras and insisted that they were innocent. Westerheide began to brag about his authority in Ukraine, as if those times were the peak of his career. He consistently spoke about Volodymyr-Volynsky as 'his city' and referred to 'his Jews', whom he had to place in a ghetto because, as he explained, there was a military depot in town that had to be secured from those 'suspicious' ones. The defence lawyers warned him, 'Herr Westerheide, please remember that you no longer find yourself in the Nazi period. You were not as important as you present yourself. Were there not others with more power who carried out the actual tasks?' The judge also tried to rein him in, advising him to stick to the facts and not expound on Nazi ideology.

Both Zelle and Westerheide were charged with murder and complicity in the murder of nine thousand Jews during the ghetto liquidations and mass shootings of September and November 1942. Both defendants were seen as responsible, in their official roles, for implementing policies that brought about deprivation, loss of property and loss of life. By the time the trial occurred in West Germany in the state court in Bielefeld, the statute of limitations had run out for all crimes except murder, and aiding and abetting murder. According to German law, in order to obtain a murder conviction the prosecution had to present convincing evidence that the accused demonstrated excessive cruelty, deceitful behaviour and base motive (such as race hatred). In assessing the guilt of the accused, the court privileged documentary evidence over survivor witness accounts. Probably more decisive, however, was the general reluctance of judges of this immediate post-war generation to convict, let alone harshly punish, defendants accused of Nazi crimes. The testimony against Westerheide and Zelle was extensive, and wartime documentation placed them at the scenes of the crimes. Nevertheless, the two would be acquitted.

As the accused, Johanna Altvater Zelle presented herself as a sensitive woman who abhorred violence. She admitted that she had witnessed deportations, but said she had only heard about shootings. Trying to gain the sympathy of the court, she pleaded that during the war she was just a young woman, only a secretary who had been sent to the East. This image clashed with newspaper articles that described the grin on her face as she listened to courtroom testimony about the 'blonde murderess' with a whip who had forced Jews to their death. Excerpts from testimony about her luring children with sweets and shooting them, and throwing children over balconies and against walls, also made it into the press coverage.

The prosecutor argued for multiple life sentences for both defendants and a warrant for their immediate arrest, since the two were not incarcerated during the trial. Both requests were rejected. When the judge, Dr Paul Pieper, acquitted them, he cited 'insufficient evidence'. The verdict was announced in Bielefeld in November 1979, and a public protest ensued, organised mainly by the Association of the Victims of Nazism (VVN). Eight hundred demonstrated in the city centre. A University of Bielefeld professor gave a stirring speech that condemned the German justice system for avoiding the prosecution of Nazi war criminals, for discriminating against witnesses and for tolerating neo-Nazism. Referring to the *Brown Book,* an East German publication that sought to expose former Nazis in the West German government, the professor asserted that the justice system in Bielefeld was controlled by former Nazis.

In July 1980, the Federal Supreme Court (Criminal Appeals Chamber) decided that the case should be reopened. Judge Pieper, it was argued, had not weighed the evidence properly, discounting witness statements. Neither had he pressed the defendants – especially Johanna Altvater Zelle – about their alibis. Questioning the logic of the decision, the Supreme Court noted that if Zelle was seen at the ghetto liquidation, if she admitted being there and if the court accepted that she was there, then one must accept that she was at a crime scene. Yet the court had not sufficiently questioned her about why she was there or what she was doing.

The proceedings moved from Bielefeld to Dortmund, the location of a central office for the investigation of Nazi war crimes. The chief prosecutor in this office, Hermann Weissing, who had failed to obtain a life sentence in the court of Bielefeld, was under pressure to bring more evidence and witnesses to the new trial. Weissing sought help from Israeli police, Simon Wiesenthal in Vienna and the World Jewish Congress in New York. By March 1982, when the second trial started, Weissing had secured twenty additional witnesses, but some of their statements contradicted ones from the first trial or statements made decades earlier. At this point the process of collecting witness statements against Westerheide and Zelle had gone on for almost twenty years.

The proceedings ended in November when, to everyone's surprise, the prosecutor himself asked the court for an acquittal. 'Despite strong suspicion of criminal deeds,' Weissing reasoned, 'the believability of the surviving victims is in doubt.' In later reflections on the proceedings, Weissing commented that the cases against Nazi perpetrators were no different from any others. He believed that the survivors' stories were true, but 'their statements were not objective evidence', despite the large quantity of them. That Zelle and her colleagues were anti-Semitic was also indisputable, Weissing concluded, but there was still not enough evidence to convict them of murder.

In December 1982 Zelle and Westerheide were acquitted for the second time. Another protest took place, followed by a flurry of critical press commentaries in Germany and abroad. Zelle died in Detmold in 2003, about a week before her eighty-fifth birthday.

In the case of Johanna Altvater Zelle, a lack of written wartime evidence led to her acquittal, even though the prosecutor believed that she had brutally killed Jewish children in a ghetto in Ukraine, and even though she admitted that she had gone to the ghetto liquidation on her own initiative. Testimony from dozens of eyewitnesses was considered insufficient evidence. With such reasoning, few could be held accountable. An all-powerful genocidal regime of male and female perpetrators who acted as masters of life and death was vindicated by the totality of the system – or, as Hannah Arendt put it, by the 'rule of Nobody' (which became the 'responsibility of nobody' in the post-war courtroom). Zelle's victims, children whom Zelle shot in the mouth or bashed against the ghetto wall, did not die an 'ordinary' death; thus, logically speaking, Zelle was no 'ordinary' woman. According to German law, however, she was ordinary, and so were her alleged crimes.

There is another irony in the legal history. Men in the system could use their formal positions in the hierarchy as a defence that they were following orders, or claim putative duress (albeit mostly unsuccessfully). Female killers could not use this defence. In a genocidal system of shared perpetration, it is difficult to document and prove individual base motive. But women like 'Fräulein Hanna' displayed just this:

when they murdered, they overstepped their authority, thus showing individual initiative – a demonstration of the excessive behaviour that by German law constituted first-degree murder. But that is not how West German prosecutors made their case against such women, and ultimately not how judges crafted their verdicts.

Prosecutors could place secretaries at crime scenes in their official positions in the Nazi administration. It was more difficult for prosecutors to find hard evidence against the wives of SS men, women who made their way to the East outside formal channels. Usually SS wives came to the attention of prosecutors because their husbands had committed crimes and victims who survived came forward with statements incriminating the wives. What happened to the SS wives we've followed here – Gertrude Segel, Liesel Willhaus, Josefine Block, Vera Wohlauf and Erna Petri?

In Austria, criminal investigators first arrested Gertrude's husband, Felix Landau, and then opened a separate case against her. Gertrude Segel Landau was detained in 1947 and 1948. When questioned, she evaded, lied and denied. Pressed about events that occurred just five years earlier, she stated that so much had happened since then, it was hard to remember anything. Landau presented herself as the naive girlfriend of a Nazi SS officer – she was Felix's lover at the time, not yet his wife – and as a mere secretary, an insignificant cog in the machine.

Yes, she admitted, she and Felix were on their balcony on a summer Sunday in 1942, but it was only to shoot at birds. They were playing an innocent game, making fun of their neighbour across the street, who was a veterinarian and had pigeons on his roof. Gertrude still seemed amused by this game. She claimed that she scolded Felix when he turned his gun on the Jewish labourers in their garden, since, as she said, turning directly to the examiners as she spoke, 'it was not right to shoot human beings'. Then, according to Gertrude, Felix said to her, 'Come on, it is just a Flobert gun, nothing can really happen.' When questioned about the Flobert, which was seen in her hands, she protested that Felix had bought it for his four-year-old son. Trying now to remove herself from the murder scene, she claimed at first that she had gone inside the house before Felix shot the Jews in the garden. Then she admitted that she was on the balcony next to him. She drew a sketch of the scene and of the bullet for the prosecutors. The entire event, she told them, was Felix's fault.

As the Allied occupation authorities in Vienna began to scale back on the internment, investigation and prosecution of suspected war criminals, the Austrian judiciary felt little pressure to punish their 'own', including defendants such as Gertrude Segel Landau. In 1948, under examination, Gertrude found herself in a favourable climate. She and Felix had divorced in 1946, and now he was at large; he had escaped from an Austrian jail in 1947. Gertrude played up her post-war compliance with the authorities as a demonstration of her wartime innocence. She was no criminal; she was a good Austrian citizen. She pointed out that it was she who had dutifully appeared when summoned, she who had answered questions. If you are looking for evidence of guilt, she told prosecutors, look for my fugitive ex-husband, not me. It was an effective strategy on Gertrude's part; she was not prosecuted.

Austrian investigations revealed a Viennese web of perpetrators and accomplices in the SS and police offices in Galicia, the former Habsburg territory of Ukraine. This network included secretaries and wives of the SS chiefs. On 19 October 1946, Austrian police arrested Gertrude's neighbour, Josefine Block, in her apartment on the Apollogasse. These two female perpetrators in Drohobych lived on the same street in Vienna again. Josefine Block was charged with crimes against humanity, war crimes and murder. While searching her apartment, the police found wartime photographs. They also found old Nazi newspapers, an anti-Semitic diatribe by Joseph Goebbels (*Das Buch Isidor,* 1928), a bayonet and a sword.

When questioned, Block admitted to being present at the crime scenes. She said her husband gave her a free hand in making decisions and managing the market garden where she employed Jews, and that she established her own workshop with Jewish workers. Josefine insisted that she never hurt, beat or killed anyone. The Jewish witnesses who accused her were on a revenge mission, she claimed.

Fear of revenge was one of the wartime rationales for killing all Jews, including children, and it was typical for perpetrators to cite that fear when they were questioned or prosecuted. Himmler had warned his men that Jewish children and the Jewesses who begot them would rise up and avenge the death of Jewish men. To Josefine Block, the war was lost, and now she was being subjected to a victor's justice led by Jews. She argued that the Jews were going after her because her husband, the Gestapo man who was really in charge, had fallen in battle in 1944.

The desperate Block tried every angle. As a war widow, she tried to blame the crimes on her dead husband. She attempted to present herself as a rescuer, taking credit for saving the life of the survivor who denounced her. Like Vera Wohlauf, she brought up her pregnant condition as a mitigating factor. How could she parade around with a whip and beat a Jewish girl when she was in a late stage of pregnancy herself? None of the witnesses, neither former German colleagues nor Jewish victims, mentioned that she was pregnant. They did recall her taking her infant in a baby carriage down the main street and ramming Jewish labourers with the carriage.

In a final twist of morality and maternity, Block – the self-proclaimed 'friend of the Jews' – argued that her Jewish accuser, her former seamstress, was the real murderer: the seamstress had abandoned her own one-year-old child in the ghetto so that she could save herself, Block said. Astonishingly, this shameless 'blame the victim' defence was taken seriously in that Vienna courtroom in 1949, and Block was acquitted. Exhibiting little understanding for the survivor witnesses, lacking critical distance from the anti-Semitism of the defendants and favourably biased towards their fellow Austrian citizens, the male judiciary remained sceptical of the testimony of Jews, especially of statements that described atrocious female behaviour.

More than a decade later, in the 1960s, Vera Wohlauf was summoned for questioning about her husband's wartime activities. Before the interrogation began, she was informed that, as the wife of the accused, Julius Wohlauf, she was not legally obligated to testify and had the right to refuse to answer questions without providing an explanation. She understood the law, but asserted that she wanted to testify regardless.

She met with investigators on the morning of 19 November 1964. When asked about her time in Poland, Wohlauf explained that she arrived in Radzyń at the end of July 1942. She was driven there with the wife of another member of the Order Police, Lieutenant Boysen. Skipping over the period of the ghetto massacres in August 1942, Vera asserted that she returned to Hamburg in September. Though she claimed that during her stay in Poland she remained exclusively in Radzyń, the questioner was able to place her at Miedzyrzec, the site of the massacres. Vera admitted that a German family with whom she was acquainted was managing an agricultural estate at the edge of Miedzyrzec. Now and then she and her husband visited this family, the Doberauers, and stayed overnight. Vera did not want to reveal that she and Julius had gone to Miedzyrzec for another reason.

Question: Do you remember during your stay in Poland with your husband that you were driven to an *Einsatz* [operation]?

Vera Wohlauf: This question cannot be answered in one sentence, at any rate one cannot reply with a simple yes or no to this question.

Question: Frau Wohlauf, then I will now present to you more concretely which case I have in mind and ask you please to respond to me afterward in the most exact manner possible. Various witnesses, former subordinates of your husband, reported that on a day in autumn 1942 you accompanied your husband to M[iedzyrzec] to a Jewish expulsion. According to the witness statements, you and your husband were picked up by truck from your lodging in Radzyn. You supposedly wore a military coat. In M[iedzyrzec] you allegedly watched over the *Aktion* and when the *Aktion* was over that evening you were driven back to Radzyn.

Vera Wohlauf: In the first moment, it seems to me the claim that I wore a military coat is impossible. At any rate, I have no memory of that. I would rather not present my statements here too definitively because

I can imagine that one will draw any conclusions that do not correspond with the true facts of the case. On the other hand, I would like to avoid giving you the impression that I am not being truthful, if for example through several witness statements the opposite can be established. At any rate, I cannot remember whether I wore a military coat. It is worth considering that for any reasons it could have happened differently. I was pregnant at the time and my clothes did not fit me properly. For example it is possible that my husband put his coat over me for whatever reasons.

On the day before the execution in question we traveled to the Doberauer home [located near the crimes in Miedzyrzec]. I just wanted to visit the Family Doberauer, it was not known to me that the following day an *Aktion* would take place, and I assume that it was not known to my husband. I cannot give good reasons for this assumption; in any case the behavior of my husband did not indicate to me that he knew of the events that occurred the following day. I cannot remember whether we spent the night after the questionable *Aktion* at the Doberauers' or whether we returned to Radzyn. It is more likely that we returned to Radzyn.

After we spent the night at the Doberauers' my husband left early the following morning. I did not know what he would do. Around midday, Frau Doberauer and I went to town to do some shopping. Regarding that, please note that I personally went along because Frau Doberauer asked me to. We were totally surprised when we saw in town a crowd of persons. A lot of persons stood around, presumably Polish. As we got closer, we saw that people in brown uniforms and members of the SD got people out of their homes and organised them into columns on the street. Frau Doberauer and I did not know what was happening. I did not even know that the concerned people were Jews. From the discussions right there at the site, I pretty soon concluded that these were Jews. I was very shaken by these events, although I in no way was aware of the actual fate of the Jews. I presumed, and I was convinced that this was an evacuation of Jews who were to move to new apartments and lodgings elsewhere. I do not know what happened thereafter. In any case, my husband was suddenly there. I heard a shot and saw an old woman collapse. The shot was fired from a man in a brown uniform. Then my husband said:

'Have they gone mad, I will disarm them immediately.' Then I went away with Frau Doberauer. I do not remember whether my husband accompanied us or not.

Allegation: Frau Wohlauf, I must state again that witnesses reported that you drove with [the men] in the morning to the *Aktion* and returned that evening, and that the members of the [Order Police] Company were outraged that you were inspecting the *Aktion*.

Vera Wohlauf: I am sticking with my depiction. The contrary statements of witnesses are not correct. I never knew about all of these things. For the first time I learned of them after my husband was arrested and the attorney reported about these serious allegations levied against my husband. It is entirely illogical that my husband brought me from Radzyn to this *Aktion*, while I had absolutely no idea about these things and besides that I was pregnant.

It is clear from Wohlauf's testimony that her pregnant condition was useful to her after the war as evidence of her non-involvement in the massacre. Note that even years later both Wohlauf and the examiner preferred to use the euphemism *Aktion* and the word 'expulsion' (*Aussiedlung*) rather than more explicit terms. Wohlauf tried to minimise the mass killing to one 'execution in question' and downplayed her husband's role in it. We know from the historian Christopher Browning's extensive research on Julius that he was a seasoned killer and liked to flaunt his role as the unit commander; one of the policemen in the unit mocked him as 'the little Rommel'. Targeting eleven thousand Jews, the Miedzyrzec deportation was the largest operation that this unit of Order Police Battalion 101 carried out. Wohlauf expected that hundreds of Jews would be killed on the spot, and indeed 960 Jews were later buried by the survivors. This particular *Aktion* was unique, not only in its scale, but also in its open slaughter on the streets and in the market place. Julius and Vera knew what they were getting into.

Like most German defendants and witnesses who were questioned after the war about the massacres, Vera Wohlauf's evasive statements contain contradictions and clues. She admitted that she saw the clearing of the ghetto and the shooting of an elderly Jewish woman. She identified the shooter as a man in a brown uniform, the colour worn by leading Nazis and lcoal collaborators, attempting to vindicate her husband, who wore a green uniform, the colour worn by regular policemen. When asked directly if she had joined her husband at an *Aktion,* she replied that she could not answer with a simple yes or no. Instead she focused on the coat, perhaps not realizing that it was a potentially incriminating detail – that the coat linked her to the police uniform and her proximity to the executioners. In the end she admitted to wearing the coat, and explained that her husband gave it to her because she was pregnant, because she might have needed to cover herself. Would ill-fitting clothes warrant the wearing of a heavy military overcoat on a hot August day? Perhaps Vera and Julius were engaging in some form of role-playing, and the coat was his way of including her in his unit, as 'one of the boys'.

In any case, Vera Wohlauf was not herself investigated. There was no clear evidence that she killed or assisted in the killing. Julius Wohlauf, who had resumed his career in the Hamburg police after the war, was arrested in 1964 and later sentenced to eight years in prison for aiding and abetting in the murder of more than eight thousand Jews in Poland. Yet Vera claimed that she had 'absolutely no idea about these things' during the war or until her husband was arrested.

The crimes of Elisabeth 'Liesel' Willhaus did not go unnoticed after the war: she was one of sixteen people indicted for the mass murder of more than four hundred thousand Jews in the Lviv (Lemberg) region. She and 'Fräulein Hanna' were among the very few Nazi female perpetrators to be indicted in West Germany for murder.

In July 1943 Liesel's husband, Gustav, was sent into combat with a Waffen-SS unit. Liesel remained in Lemberg as long as she could: her industrial home town in the Saar was being heavily bombed. But the Red Army advanced into Galicia and recaptured Lemberg in July 1944, and Liesel returned home. Gustav was killed in action near Frankfurt in late March 1945. As a war widow with a small child, with no pension from her husband, Willhaus stayed with her family for a while. By 1948 she had married again, this time to a lawyer. She and her new husband started an Automat business. When war-crimes investigators found her in 1964, they also discovered that Liesel and her new husband had a record of petty crimes and violations in connection with their business.

In spite of her wartime and post-war history, investigators were unable to prosecute Elisabeth Riedel Willhaus. Since her place in the Nazi killing machinery was not formalised in an official position, there was no wartime documentation to corroborate witness testimony. She was at the crime scene and carried out mass murder publicly, but she was not held legally responsible.

German prosecutors noted that a remarkable number of people testified against Willhaus. Not all of them were Jewish survivors, whose memories and testimonies were considered less reliable by many German courts; indeed, some of those testifying against her were her husband's former SS colleagues. All those who testified, as well as the prosecutors who elicited the stories, were shocked by the behaviour of the commandant's wife, which 'went against all preconceived notions of "female character"'. Yet, for reasons that remain unclear, she was released.

At the end of the West German 'Lemberg Trial' the presiding judge asserted that it was not the task of the court to master Germany's past; it was the task of the entire nation, 'whose conscience cannot be released and all its stains wiped clean here in the court'. Several members of that nation, defendants with blood on their hands, were allowed to go home with their conscience cleared by their peers.

The fate of perpetrators tried in East Germany was radically different. Erna Petri was among the few German women – perhaps the only one – to be convicted for shooting Jews. She was one of 12,890 people to stand trial for Nazi-related war crimes and crimes against humanity in East Germany between 1945 and 1989. About 90 per cent of these cases were prosecuted by 1955, mostly before 1951. Her trial was among a dwindling few still taking place in the 1960s.

By the time Erna Petri was arrested, in August 1961, she was no stranger to the East German police system. The previous summer, her

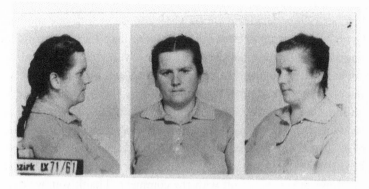

Arrest photographs of Erna Petri

husband, Horst, had been arrested for alleged anti-state activities. The Stasi had been reading the Petris' mail, in particular their correspondence with their son in West Germany. They suspected that Horst, a member of the local agricultural commune, was sabotaging the latest collectivisation drive; he had made critical comments about the government in a letter to his son. They also believed that Horst had denounced an East German agent to the West Germans. But when the police searched the Petri house, they did not find much evidence of anti-state activities, only some 'agitational literature', including a political pamphlet from West Germany. Their more significant finds were a guest book and photographs from Grzenda showing Horst Petri as an SS *Untersturmführer* lording over the SS agricultural estate with his wife. The guest book contained the names of senior SS and police and Wehrmacht officers, as well as the signature of the wife of the region's most notorious Nazi mass murderer, the chief of the SS and police for District Galicia, Friedrich Katzmann.

It is not clear if the uncovering of Horst's Nazi past was a coincidence. In any event, based on seventeen witness testimonies, mostly of former Polish and Ukrainian labourers on the estate, the state prosecutor in Erfurt determined that Horst and Erna Petri tortured, abused and killed forced labourers as well as Jews who sought refuge in the forests, fields and multiple barns and stables of the SS manor at Grzenda.

The confessions extracted under duress from Horst and Erna

Petri are rich in detail and on the whole consistent with one another. German prosecutors determined that Horst's post-war activity, which was the cause of his initial arrest, was relatively insignificant, certainly not as reprehensible as the clear record of his and his wife's 'most severe war crimes and crimes against humanity'. They were interrogated for three hours together on 31 August 1962; each of them was asked to confirm or deny the crimes of the other. Husband and wife also stood trial together on 10–15 September 1962. In the audio record of the trial, Erna is so forthcoming about the details of her criminal actions that the prosecutor cuts her off with the comment 'Thank you, we have heard enough.' Horst was less forthcoming. In the end, however, the court decided that Horst's crimes were worse than Erna's.

In his final judgement the judge wrote that their heinous deeds 'occurred 18 to 20 years ago, but it is in the interest of the establishment of a democratic people's justice and essential that these crimes be uncovered without regard for the passage of time'. Furthermore, he asserted, since the imperialist powers continued to plan crimes against peace and humanity, all peace-loving peoples had to be vigilant in preventing the recurrence of such crimes. In the interest of justice, he insisted, such crimes must be punished. The judge argued that in this particular case the terror system of Hitler's fascism came into clear expression, as his dictatorship controlled not only Germany, but also the occupied territories. In practice 'this terror was built on unscrupulous elements, to which these accused belong'. In typical East German Cold War rhetoric, the court asserted that Horst Petri was not only a fascist then and now, but also a demonstrated enemy of the socialist construction of 'our workers' and farmers' state'.

The Petri case offers a rare example of how gender factored into the treatment of war criminals in East Germany, as well as a glimpse into the psychology of a female perpetrator of the Holocaust. Although Erna tried to shield her husband from her own crimes, the judge was of the opinion that Horst Petri was responsible in part for his wife's behaviour. The court explained the sentencing by stating that 'between the two defendants there are differences' and that in Erna's case one must consider that she became a murderer because of her husband's profound influence. In addition, 'the constant interaction with the SS beasts in Grsenda [*sic*] was a considerable factor in causing her to commit crimes'. Above all, the court argued that her crimes were not as extensive as those perpetrated by Horst Petri, who routinely killed and abused on his own initiative, without direct orders. That warranted the death penalty, the court explained.

Erna gained the sympathies of some officials, who noted that 'from time to time she showed human emotions', but she was judged harshly by most. She confessed to murdering six Jewish children between six and twelve years of age. It is clear in the interrogations and judgement that what the lawyers, the interrogators and ultimately the court found so reprehensible, almost beyond imagining, was her capacity to kill children. As one interrogator asked in response to her confession, 'How could you do this with two of your own small children at the estate?'

When Erna Petri was arrested, she had denied committing any crimes. She admitted only that she had heard about Jews who were shot in the woods on their estate. About a month into her incarceration and questioning, however, she began to crack under the pressure. On 15 September 1961, she was subjected to an interrogation that began at eight A.M. and finished at one A.M. the next day, with a one-hour break for lunch and another for dinner. The chief interrogator, named Franke, began, 'Which crimes did you commit during your stay in Grzenda?' Petri replied that she was indeed at this estate from June 1942 until early 1944, and that she had beaten workers, including the blacksmith who was now serving as a witness against her. As the barrage of questions continued, she eventually admitted that she remembered the shooting of Jewish men who had been caught on the farm after they escaped from a train headed from Lviv to Lublin.

In his questioning, Franke referred to statements made by Polish eyewitnesses that Erna had single-handedly shot Jews with her own pistol. Franke extracted the details from Erna. Before ending the session he asked, 'Why have you denied shooting Jews yourself until this point?' Erna replied that she feared punishment and that she thought her husband would admit to those murders on her behalf.

At the trial, Erna and Horst told the judge that during the war they had decided to keep quiet about Erna's shooting of the Jewish children. Horst had reassured Erna that shooting them was the right thing to do, but he did not want everyone to know about it. There was a chance, since Erna was not officially authorised to kill Jews, that she might be questioned by an SS investigator. Plus, Horst said, he did not want his wife to be the subject of local rumours. A male sadist was acceptable, even effective, in 'keeping the natives down'. But a female sadist was potentially a problem, a target of revenge, even an embarrassment. Erna herself seemed unsure about how her actions would be received. She explained at length that she had fed the children before killing them, apparently expecting the court to be touched by her kindness and by her frank admission. Yet she also got caught up in her own lies and 'memory lapses'. The judge admonished her and branded her a liar. Erna laughed nervously. The verdict came as a shock: her husband would be guillotined, and she would spend the rest of her life in prison.

But Erna Petri did not resign herself to her fate. From her jail cell she retracted her earlier statements. Her pleas for release, and those of her children on her behalf, were roundly rejected. She wrote letters to the prosecutor's office, long, detailed reflections and explanations. Her colleagues and family reassured her that former Nazis received amnesties; surely she would be released too. She expressed no remorse about her wartime deeds, but instead began to spin a large web of stories and excuses. In numerous letters to lawyers, she complained that the court interpreter mistranslated testimony that implicated her. In one appeal of 18 September 1963, Erna insisted that she did not kill anyone and had never handled a gun. Out of love and fear – *aus Liebe und Angst* – she had falsely admitted to murdering the children, in the hope of protecting her husband's future.

Then she tried another tack. She had heard about Jews who were being deported to the Lublin district and gassed, she said, and it had shocked her at the time. She protested at the deportations, telling Horst that 'those people [the Jews] are human after all', but her brute of a husband silenced her and warned her that if she did not shut up, she would get in trouble. Erna was now desperate to establish herself in the eyes of the law as an anti-Nazi. In 1938, she said – alluding to *Kristallnacht* – she had made a critical comment about the unfair treatment of Jews. It was only because she was pregnant that she was not arrested right then and there.

In a politically riskier appeal, Erna described her unfair treatment by East German interrogators. She had been tricked during one session, she said. The ploy that was used was typical of Stasi methods. She was presented with a confession signed by her husband, which she later realised was a forgery. The confession stated, according to Erna's recollection of 1963, 'I admit that my wife shot Jewish children and persons'. When Erna saw this confession, she 'was full of indignation', since 'I never did such things that he accused me of'. But then, thinking it over, she realised that her husband did not wish to do her harm – 'he is in danger and needs my help'. Erna decided to accept the blame, to lie on his behalf. Or so she said now. But could she really have made up the details about how she shot the six Jewish children, the graphic account of where and how she did it and how the children responded, all for the sake of her husband?

In November 1989, the Berlin Wall, officially known in the former East Germany as the 'anti-fascist protection barrier', came down. Erna Petri, by then sixty-nine years old, sat in her cell at the notorious Hoheneck prison in Saxony. For decades Erna had been retelling her story with variations and contradictions. Would the West German lawyers who were to review her case upon the collapse of the German Democratic Republic see her in a more sympathetic light than the East German jurists who had convicted her? The beginning of her incarceration had coincided with the construction of the wall in August 1961, and now, with its collapse, Erna stood a chance of being released.

In a December 1989 letter seeking a review of her case, Erna wrote to West German lawyers about the unlawful interrogations of the Stasi and presented yet another version of what had happened in her time at Grzenda. No, she had not killed Jews, but she had taken regular trips to Lviv, where she went to pick up supplies. As part of her errands, she visited the Janowska camp to select Jewish labourers and brought them back to Grzenda. She remembered having Jewish female household help, but she did not know what had happened to them. (In her statements of 1961, she had described these Jewish women as troublemakers.) Insisting that she was innocent, Erna wrote, 'I sacrificed myself for my husband, the man my parents warned me about'. Horst was justifiably punished, she said. His execution was warranted because he did kill Jews.

In the next few months and years, German jurists, mostly from the former West German system, would begin to review Erna's case and others to determine their judicial integrity. Some East German political prisoners were released; others enjoyed reduced sentences. Families of deceased prisoners sought compensation and the rehabilitation of their family names. Erna's children lobbied for the release of their mother, who was among the few female prisoners serving a life sentence for Nazi war crimes. They wrote pleas to West German Chancellor Helmut Kohl, US President George Bush and Russian Premier Mikhail Gorbachev. They petitioned members of the German parliament. Their mother, they argued, was an innocent victim of Stasi methods of interrogation and torture. Her confessions had been extracted under duress. Hadn't she suffered enough for twenty-five years in the terror chambers of the medieval Hoheneck fortress, separated from her family and grieving the loss of her husband, guillotined by the East German state in 1962? The children's pleas mentioned nothing of their mother's wartime past in Nazi-occupied Poland. Nonetheless, the jurists decided to uphold the East German court's life sentence.

Erna Petri, although not rehabilitated or pardoned, was eventually released from prison. She came home in 1992, for health reasons. One account claims that an underground SS organisation, Stille Hilfe (Silent Aid), made a successful case to the district court in Stollberg, the location of the prison, to release Petri. Silent Aid may have paid for Petri's apartment when she was released, and may also have been responsible for her being invited to Bavaria, where she enjoyed the Alpine mountains and lakes with Gudrun Burwitz, the daughter of Heinrich Himmler and a prominent member of Silent Aid. Erna died in July 2000; she had celebrated her eightieth birthday a few months earlier. Two hundred people – everyone in the village and a number of others whom the family did not know – came to her funeral. Many people sent flowers and condolence cards anonymously.

If Petri had resided in West Germany, where conviction rates of Nazi war criminals were low by comparison, she would probably not have been tried; and if she had been tried, she would probably not have received a life sentence. She would most likely have slipped back into society and gone unnoticed, an ordinary *Hausfrau*. A detailed confession of her crimes in Poland would not have been documented. There would be no trace of her misdeeds, or of her victims. In Erna's own pleas to the court, she blamed her husband for her wartime cruelties. It is true that Erna's marriage transformed her from an ordinary German farm girl into the Missus of the Grzenda plantation, but Horst was not the sole reason why Erna became a murderer.

Explaining the causes of women's genocidal behaviour is as difficult as trying to pin down the motivations of their male counterparts and, given the gender bias then and now, arguably more complicated. The images of Nazi propagandists continue to resonate and distort. Goebbels's films presented German women as hysterical supporters of the regime, driven by their irrational emotions, not their individual ambitions. Such portraits of wild fanaticism distort the political convictions and 'correct' composure of most German women. Goebbels famously remarked that 'men organise life: women are their support and implement their decisions'. Nazi Germany was a participatory dictatorship in which women fully contributed, and our standard for measuring this contribution should not be defined exclusively by power as we know it in a 'man's world' of political office and social standing. Rather, understanding the roles and behaviour of women who were agents of a criminal regime should begin by identifying who they were, what they did and whether they were held accountable for their actions.

Even though mass murderers created false narratives about their experiences, these narratives tell us something. Erna Petri's husband wrote in his last letter to his wife and family on the eve of his execution that he was a victim of the East German system, which had betrayed him, the honest, hard-working farmer-socialist. Erna Petri, on the other hand, claimed that she was a victim of Nazi propaganda and had acted under the pressure of men who surrounded her, including her husband. 'Euthanasia' nurses presented themselves as upstanding medical professionals who heeded the authority of the doctors, fulfilled their duties and ultimately suffered for doing their job. These explanations are similar to countless written pleas submitted to the courts by the wives of Nazi perpetrators, in which they stressed their own struggles as single mothers who were subjected to a victor's justice, or to the revenge of the Jews. The persistence of anti-Semitism is also not to be underestimated. According to the research of the historian Katrin Himmler, some female perpetrators and their descendants who fumed about the meddling prosecutors and the victors' justice saw 'the new enemy as the old enemy: world Jewry'. The German victimisation narratives of the First World War, which incited the Nazi movement and anti-Semitism of the Holocaust, continued in post-war defences of male and female perpetrators.

The female biographies studied here are based largely on post-war investigations and trials. But very few women were prosecuted after the war; even fewer were judged and convicted. Witness testimony of survivors, often the only available evidence, was not considered strong enough, and many of the female defendants, especially those who appeared matronly and meek, did not seem capable of committing such atrocities. The physical appearance of the women and gender stereotypes held by the mostly male investigators and judges usually worked in favour of the female perpetrators, whose acts were in some instances as criminal as those of their male counterparts. The fact that thousands of women worked in agencies such as the SS, which was declared a criminal organisation, was also not taken seriously. The enormous amount of material booty that German women in the East either took themselves while stationed there or received from husbands, like Gertrude Segel's gold necklace, was also not the subject of investigations against women – this in spite of the fact that many personal possessions of persecuted and murdered Jews, Poles and Ukrainians ended up in German households, the primary domain of women.

Furthermore, the relatively few women who were tried after the war were featured in sensationalistic press coverage, portrayed as beasts, sadists and seductresses. Much of this coverage perpetuated pornographic images of Nazi women that distorted their violent behaviour as a form of sexual deviance. As the historian Claudia Koonz has observed, we live in a culture that has 'sensationalised Nazism by locating evil in eroticised women'. The multitude of roles and professions and the range of German female perpetration were not grasped at the time. Generalisations about female innocence prevailed.

Criminal police and prosecutors had specific goals – to establish the occurrence of the crime, to identify and apprehend the suspect, to collect testimony and evidence, to indict and secure a conviction, to put a law-breaking threat to society behind bars. The entire postwar history of female perpetrators was as much political as it was judicial. The contexts in which the investigation occurred – immediate post-war Austria, 1960s East Germany or 1970s West Germany – mattered a great deal, and could determine who was investigated, what testimony and evidence could be collected and was deemed credible, what crimes could be prosecuted and whether judges would issue mild or stiff sentences. German women were caught up in this tangled web of international and national justice. What happened to them? The short answer is that most got away with murder.

# EPILOGUE

After reading thousands of pages of wartime documents, court records and testimonies, I decided to visit a wartime crime scene. The archival record of Erna Petri's trial contained sketches and photographs of the Grzenda plantation in western Ukraine. Names and addresses of Ukrainian and Polish peasants who gave testimony concerning Petri's crimes were listed. I copied the material, thinking it might be useful. This would not be my first trip to Ukraine. Years before, I had travelled through the part of Ukraine where Petri's wartime house was located, and spent some time in Lviv, but I had not seen the landscape with the history of the Holocaust in mind. At that time the city and its surrounding villages still looked like architectural conglomerations of bygone eras – drab Soviet socialist-realist edifices, crumbled Jewish synagogues and cemeteries, glimmers of Austro-Hungarian *fin-de-siècle* ornamentation, sturdy foundations of *ancien régime* Polish rule. But when I returned to research the Holocaust, there were new hoardings in yellow and blue proclaiming a vibrant Ukrainian nation. Scarved Ukrainian *babushkas* with tanned, deeply wrinkled faces sat at roadsides with plastic buckets of apples for sale – and now some of these peasant women could be seen talking on mobile phones.

I was not sure what I would find at Grzenda. I did not know if the place actually still existed, or what I would do once I got there. I persuaded two colleagues to join me; one spoke fluent Ukrainian, the other one Polish. We found the location on a local map, a short taxi trip from Lviv heading north. Our car's path paralleled the same railway lines that had taken hundreds of thousands of Polish and Ukrainian Jews to the gassing facilities of Belzec and Sobibor. We turned down the same road that Erna Petri took that fateful day when she spotted the Jewish boys who had fled from the freight wagon. We entered the long driveway leading to the manor, which had changed from a stately home to a decrepit structure overgrown with weeds. The porch was two pillars with a sagging middle, precariously standing on breeze blocks. Given what I knew, the place felt haunted, but to the poor, elderly Ukrainians who eked out an existence there, it was home. The gilded ironwork on the terrace where Petri had served cake and coffee was rusted and flaking like brittle bones crumbling at the joints. Clean laundry had been hung there to dry. The women living at Grzenda immediately appeared when they saw us, strangers in city clothes with cameras, stepping out of a taxi.

Stalin completed the demographic engineering that Hitler started in Ukraine, and these women were the result. The Polish minority had been moved out of the region, and Ukrainians from Poland relocated there. Chronic housing shortages in the Soviet Union transformed historic manors such as this one into public housing for multiple families. The peasants we spoke with knew nothing of the wartime events in the home. Ironically, Soviet post-war population exchanges accomplished what Hitler's henchmen had desired: a displacement of local memory.

We walked a few hundred yards in the direction of the place that was described in the court record as the site where Petri had murdered the six boys. It was a strip of forest along a gully that divided two fields. I was momentarily distracted by the scene around me, which was picturesque and peaceful. Farmers were harvesting in the fields with horse-drawn ploughs and by hand. A crisp, colourful September sunset illuminated the rolling hills and flashed off several of Ukraine's newly restored church steeples. Every acre was being cultivated, except for two weedy swathes: an overgrown graveyard – an impenetrable mass of thorny bushes – and the forested gully we had come to see.

One could descend into the gully, but the prospect was not inviting. Passers-by threw their rubbish there – plastic bags, rags, booze bottles. Or perhaps the rains had carried the waste into this crevice. I knew it was not the only site in Ukraine where mass graves from the Holocaust, the bones and often personal possessions of Jewish victims, lie a few yards below a surface covered with weeds, empty bottles and other refuse. I stood there; I meditated, prayed and thought about what had happened there, and what those frightened Jewish children who whimpered when Erna Petri drew her pistol might have achieved had they lived. Apparently I stood there too long. A Ukrainian peasant with his wool cap, flannel shirt, threadbare jacket and mended trousers accosted me. It was time to go.

In many ways this book is about how we fail to reckon with the past, not so much as a historical reconstruction or morality tale, but as evidence of a recurring problem in which we all share responsibility. What are the blind spots and taboos that persist in our retelling of events, in individual accounts, memoirs and national histories? Why does this history continue to haunt us, several generations and many miles removed, in places such as Grzenda?

The teacher Ingelene Ivens attempted her own reckoning with the past. In the early 1970s she returned to her school near Poznań, Poland. Curious, concerned and nostalgic, she wanted to know what had happened there after she had hastily departed in 1943. She had often thought about her students, and looked at their photos, one showing the children climbing an apple tree in the playground. They were ethnic Germans from Romania and Ukraine whom she was supposed to transform into civilised Aryans. During that return trip Ingelene learned that in January 1945 Red Army conquerors, perhaps with the help of local Poles, gathered the children and other Germans who were left behind and, in a brutal act of revenge, killed them all in the school-yard. Ingelene mourned the children and struggled with her own role leading up to that tragic event. She wrote and published her memoir about her time in the East, but she decided to omit parts of her story, such as her visit to a Jewish labour camp in Poland. What other stories have been left out?

The secretaries and wives who became killers, such as Johanna Altvater in Volodymyr-Volynsky and Josefine Block in Drohobych, could not possibly have been as rare as we would like to assume. Specifics about who perpetrated the violence in the ghettos and mass-shooting sites across the Nazi-occupied East are most often simply lacking. The Germans concealed or destroyed this information, and witnesses and survivors could seldom identify their persecutors by name. The Nazi-hunter Simon Wiesenthal pursued hundreds of leads for decades, an endeavour detailed in his private correspondence in the Simon Wiesenthal Archive. An informant in the 1960s beseeched him to investigate a couple in Poland, a German gendarme named Franz Bauer and his wife. This duo and their German shepherd terrorised inhabitants in Miedzyrzec-Podlaski, near Lublin. The witness stated that Bauer's wife personally took part in the mass shootings of Soviet prisoners of war. The behaviour of the wife was widely discussed among the local inhabitants. Wiesenthal was able to determine that Franz Bauer had died in 1958, but the wife could not be found. Perhaps she had remarried and changed her name. The wife of the commandant at the Jaktorow camp, near Lviv, was also known for her German shepherd. She ordered her dog to attack the Jewish children who worked in the camp garden. The dog tore them apart. I interviewed a sur-vivor who, as a young girl in the camp, had had the gruesome task of pick-ing up the limbs of the victims of the commandant's wife and her dog.

Even when there were eyewitnesses, often the suspects could not be tracked down after the war, and victim testimony alone was not strong enough evidence to mount a case, especially in the case of female sus-pects who did not hold an official position in the system. Given the fact that in places such as Ukraine less than 2 per cent of the local Jewish population survived the war, the existence of *any* testimony naming German perpetrators, male or female, is itself astounding.

Again, none of the women in this book had to kill. Refusing to kill Jews would not have resulted in punishment. If one chose to *help* victims, however, the regime showed no mercy. Women of all ages and professions were not spared the terror of Nazi special courts. The German wife of a forester near Lviv provided aid to Jewish refugees who had fled the final deportations to the killing centres and camp liquidations in the autumn of 1943. For her bravery she was sentenced to death. The judge ruled that this defendant had had the proper anti-Semitic education at home, and that after being a member of the German community in occupied Poland, where the policy regarding Jews was 'common talk in the streets', she should have known better than to sabotage it. In the final months of the war, German leaders in the Justice Ministry, the armed services and the SS and police ordered that anyone who sabotaged the war effort could be shot on the spot. In the Reich itself, as many as ten thousand Germans were executed. At least fifteen thousand German soldiers were branded deserters and shot. A German businessman thrown into the civil defence of Danzig in early 1945 observed the chilling aftermath of such a drumhead court-martial: 'The streets of Danzig look like a desert. Although the authorities repeatedly issued decrees that nobody is to abandon his workplace, anyone who could, fled. Where the boulevard opens at the Oliva Gate, German soldiers were hanged as deserters, 6 of them, among them also a young nurse.'

We do not know the name, let alone the biography, of this young nurse. The stories of German women who were morally courageous and defiant are difficult to uncover. The cases of these women, branded criminals by the Nazis and considered traitors by many Germans, were not reopened after the war.

When I returned to Munich from my research trip to the former Petri plantation in Ukraine, I realised that this journey was not the end of the story. I learned that one of my interview subjects in Germany, Maria Seidenberger, had just died. Ms Seidenberger was not an accomplice or perpetrator in the Nazi machinery of destruction. During the Nazi era, Ms Seidenberger and her family lived in a house that was along the perimeter of the Dachau concentration camp. When she and her mother stood at their kitchen window, they saw prisoners being marched into the camp, and heard gunfire. Some four and a half thousand Soviet prisoners of war were shot outside the camp's walls at a shooting range near the Seidenbergers' back yard. Maria helped the camp inmates by serving as their courier to the outside world, sending letters to their loved ones, hiding their personal belongings in her family's beehive and feeding them. In 2005, sixty years after the end of the war, the city of Dachau recognised Maria Seidenberger with a prize for her civil courage. This public event was a high point in her life, but could not make up for the many years of isolation she had experienced. Neighbours and even relatives who did not behave as admirably during the war viewed Seidenberger with suspicion.

Like the stories of female witnesses, accomplices and perpetrators featured in this book, Seidenberger's story *has* come to light, but only recently. We will never know all there is to know about Nazism, the Second World War and the Holocaust. No single story can relate it all, and the pieces that we uncover may not fit together to our satisfaction. But the collage of stories and memories, of cruelty and courage, while continuing to test our comprehension of history and humanity, helps us see what human beings – not only men, but women as well – are capable of believing and doing.

# ACKNOWLEDGEMENTS

I could not have completed this study without the generous support of several institutions, funders and colleagues. The German Research Foundation (DFG) awarded me a grant to write a book on biographies in the age of extremes. I am grateful to the Foundation and the evaluators who approved my application. During my time as a researcher in Germany, I was supported by the Modern History Department of Ludwig Maximilian University, especially by Petra Thoma and Professors Michael Brenner, Michael Geyer, Martin Schulze-Wessel, Margit Szollosi-Janze and Andreas Wirsching. My stay in Munich was sustained as well by the US Holocaust Memorial Museum and colleagues who agreed to my proposal to collect oral histories from German witnesses. As I completed this book, I joined the History Department at Claremont McKenna College, and during that transition my new colleagues granted me the time and support needed to complete my final edits and photo research.

Researching the Holocaust requires work in several archives across Europe, North America and Israel. While the digital age has made the material easier to access, we scholars still rely on archivists and colleagues in the field to help us find the material, obtain copies of it and analyse it.

I am grateful to staff at the Bundesarchiv in Ludwigsburg, Kirsten Goetze, Tobias Hermann and Abdullah Toptanci. At the US Holocaust Memorial Museum I received assistance from Vadim Altskan, Michlean Amir, Susan Bachrach, Judy Cohen, Bill Connolly, Michael Gelb, Neal Guthrie, Dieter Kuntz, Jan Lambertz, Steve Luckert, Jacek Nowakowski, Paul Shapiro, Caroline Waddell and Leah Wolfson. My discovery of the Petri case occurred in the summer of 2005, when I was a participant in the museum's Center for Advanced Holocaust Studies research workshop on punishing perpetrators in war-crimes trials. In the summer of 2010 I experienced another windfall, this one at Yad Vashem, where I was a participant in a summer research workshop on grass-roots violence. Colleagues in the workshop, including Rebecca Carter-Chand, David Cesarani, Wolf Gruner and Alexander Prusin, and scholars in the research institute and archives, including Hari Drefus, Bella Guterman, Dan Michman, Elliot Orvieto, Naama Shik, David Silberklang and Dan Uziel, shared material and provided invaluable feedback. Furthermore, Yad Vashem arranged my meeting with the *New York Times* correspondent Isabel Kershner, who published an article about my research. Nancy Toff at Oxford University Press was involved in the early development of my manuscript, and Lisbeth Cohen at Harvard University encouraged me to write a study that might reach a broader audience, and put me in touch with Geri Thoma. In Paris, I received support from Yahad in Unum; I thank Father Patrick Desbois and his team for sharing their findings. At the USC Shoah Foundation Visual History Archive, Crispin Brooks and Ita Gordon identified relevant material; at the LA Holocaust Museum, Vladimir Melamed helped me research the collection, a little-known treasure trove for scholars. Mike Constady at Westmoreland Research Group promptly responded to my numerous requests for material at the US National Archives. Dr Walter Rummel at the Speyer Archive helped me obtain rare photographs.

Several colleagues shared their research, taking the time to send me materials and to make suggestions about where to look. Among them were Andrej Angrick, Omer Bartov, Waitman Beorn, Ray Brandon, Martin Dean, Robert Ehrenreich, Christian Gerlach, Stephen Lehnstaedt, Jürgen Matthäus, Jared McBride, Marie Moutier, Dieter Pohl and Eric Steinhart. I benefited from discussions with Kimberly Allar, Betsy Anthony, Tracy Brown, Joyce Chernick, Marion Deshmukh, Deborah Dwork, Mary Fulbrook, Alexandra Garbarini, Ann Hajkova, Susannah Heschel, Marion Kaplan, Jeffrey Koerber, Deborah Lipstadt, Dalia Ofer, Katrin Paehler, John Roth, Corrine Unger and James Waller. Timothy Snyder introduced the term 'bloodlands' in his outstanding book on the Nazi East. Participants in the Soros ReSet seminar in Kiev and Odessa were also helpful: Anna Bazhenova, Olena Bettlie, Alexei Bratochkin, Oksana Dudko, Diana Dumitru, Anastias Felcher, John-Paul Himka, Georgiy Kasianov, Alexandr Marinchenko, Alexei Miller, Oleksandr Nadtoka, Irina Sklokina, Octavian Tacu and Oksana Vynnyk. I had the opportunity to present my findings in a workshop at the University of North Carolina, where Christopher Browning, Karen Hagemann, Claudia Koonz, Michael Meng, Karl Schleunes and Gerhard and Janet Weinberg graciously hosted me and offered valuable suggestions.

This book would not have happened without the support of my agent, Geri Thoma at Writers House. She advised me in preparing my proposal and made sure that my proposal fell into the right hands at Houghton Mifflin Harcourt. It was an honour and pleasure to collaborate with Deanne Urmy, an excellent executive editor and a wonderful person who moved the manuscript forward with diligence and care. Debbie Engel's enthusiasm and commitment to this research ensured that the book would reach international audiences. Katya Rice assiduously copy-edited the manuscript. The historians Richard Breitman and Atina Grossmann read through the final manuscript, catching errors and problems that only experts could detect. I am inspired by their erudition and appreciate their tireless mentoring and service.

Most of all I am grateful for the forbearance of my family and friends who have lived with this research too, and not by choice. This book is dedicated to my grandmothers, mother and sisters, but I also want to thank my father, James Lower; my brother, Joshua Lower;

my husband, Christof Mauch; my sons, Ian Maxwell Mauch and Alexander Morgan Mauch; and my other sisters, Millie Gonzalez, Sally George, Susan Hercher, Sylvia Szeker and Valerie Henry, for keeping me grounded in the present day and raising my spirits with their love and good humour.

It was possible to feature certain women in this study because they or their families responded to my enquiries and graciously opened their homes to me. The Petris, the Schücking-Homeyers, Ingelene Ivens Rodewald, Renate Summ Sarkar and the late Maria Seidenberger trusted me with their stories. I have tried my best to render their accounts with the understanding that they expect and with the integrity and compassion that the victims of the Holocaust deserve.

# NOTES

ARCHIVES

*Germany*

BAB    Bundesarchiv (Federal Archives), Berlin
BAK    Bundesarchiv (Federal Archives), Koblenz
BAL    Bundesarchiv (Federal Archives), Ludwigsburg
BSL    Bavarian State Library, Munich
ICH    Institute for Contemporary History, Munich
ITS    International Tracing Service, Bad Arolsen
LAS    Landesarchiv Speyer, Speyer
MCA    Munich City Archive, Munich

*Austria*

SWA    Simon Wiesenthal's Office Archive, Vienna Wiesenthal Institute for Holocaust
       Studies, Vienna
VCA    Vienna City and State Archive, Vienna

*Ukraine*

CSA    Central State Archives of Civic Organisations of Ukraine, Kiev
ZSA    State Archives, Zhytomyr

## United States

BDC   Berlin Document Center Collection, NARA, Washington, DC
IMT   International Military Tribunal at Nuremberg, NARA, Washington, DC
NARA   US National Archives Record Administration, Washington, DC
SFA   Shoah Foundation Visual History Archive, University of Southern California, Los Angeles
USHMMA   US Holocaust Memorial Museum Archives, Washington, DC

## France

Yahad   Yahad in Unum Collection, Paris

## Israel

YVA   Yad Vashem Archive, Jerusalem

### INTRODUCTION

*Page*

3   'just that a few Jews . . .': Elisabeth H., Neustadt, 11 Aug. 1977, BAL, 76-K 41676-Koe.

   studies by pioneering historians: Theresa Wobbe, ed., *Nach Osten: Verdeckte Spuren nationalsozialistischer Verbrechen* (Verlag Neue Kritik, 1992); Gudrun Schwarz, *Eine Frau an seiner Seite: Ehefrauen in der 'SS-Sippengemeinschaft'* (Hamburger Edition, 1997); Elizabeth Harvey, *Women and the Nazi East: Agents and Witnesses of Germanization* (Yale University Press, 2003); Susannah Heschel, 'Does Atrocity Have a Gender? Feminist Interpretations of Women in the SS', in Jeffrey Diefendorf, ed., *Lessons and Legacies*, vol. 6, *New Currents in Holocaust Research* (Northwestern University Press, 2004), pp. 300–321.

5   'Our people immigrating here . . .': Christa Schroeder, *He Was My Chief: The Memoirs of Adolf Hitler's Secretary* (Frontline Books, 2009), pp. 99, 114–15. The German edition appeared in 1985.

6   recognised their imperial role: Lora Wildenthal, *German Women for Empire, 1884–1945* (Duke University Press, 2001). For the related pre-Nazi history, also see Katharina Walgenbach, *Die weisse Frau als Trägerin deutscher Kultur: Koloniale Diskurse über Geschlecht, 'Rasse' und Klasse im Kaiserreich* (Campus Verlag, 2005). On the integration of female aristocrats into the imperial projects, see the biography of Hildegard von Rheden, department leader for ideological work in the Reich Main Office of the Reich Nährstandes, and active in the German Red Cross; and von Rheden's appointment with Himmler, 17 June 1941, as the Landesbauerführerin, in Peter Witte et al., eds, *Der Dienstkalender Heinrich Himmlers 1941/42* (Christians Verlag, 1999).

   Hitler's Furies: Rosemarie Killius, ed., *Frauen für die Front: Gespräche mit Wehrmachtshelferinnen* (Militzke Verlag, 2003), pp. 69–70; and Franka Maubach, 'Expansionen weiblicher Hilfe: Zur Erfahrungsgeschichte von Frauen im Kriegdienst,' in Sybille Steinbacher, ed., *Volksgenossinnen: Frauen in der NS-Volksgemein-schaft* (Wallstein Verlag, 2007), pp. 93–94. Women were sent to the police training school in Erfurt, and graduates from this school were allowed to enter the SS train-ing school in Alsace in early 1945. See Gudrun Schwarz, 'Verdrängte Täterinnen: Frauen im Apparat der SS, 1939–1945', in Theresa Wobbe, ed., *Nach Osten: Verdeckte Spuren nationalsozialistischer Verbrechen* (Verlag Neue Kritik, 1992), p. 210.

8   women set up refreshment tables: In one especially revealing piece of testimony, an ethnic German cook from Lida told of having been put in charge of feeding the lo-cal policemen. One day the German gendarme captain asked her to quickly prepare meals for one hundred people who would be arriving in town the next day for a spe-cial action. In the early morning hours she fed them, and they departed into the darkness; a few hours later, the gunfire started. Working in shifts, the executioners, whom she described as German SS officers and greenish-grey-uniformed Lithuanian auxiliaries, came back to eat periodically. This went on past midnight and into the next day. Local auxiliaries told her the horrific details of the execution site, includ-ing the throwing of babies into the air and the burying of those who were still alive. She recalled the beating of a Jewish woman on the street outside the gendarme of-fice and other Jews who had worked in their office and were hunted down by the SS executioners and their auxiliaries. Maria Koschinska Sprenger, 20 Apr. 1966, BAL, 162/3446.

Gertrud Scholtz-Klink: Scholtz-Klink led the Nazi Women's League and a host of other organisations. As the 'Frau of the Volk', she called for a new age of woman-hood that was anti-feminist. To this end, she produced eleven children and married three times. She preached a life of purity, thrift and discipline, but she lived a life of debauchery and infidelity. According to Claudia Koonz, who researched and inter-viewed her, Scholtz-Klink was ambitious but weak. See Koonz, *Mothers in the Fa-therland: Women, the Family, and Nazi Politics* (St Martin's Press, 1988), p. 6. Also see Scholtz-Klink's self-serving account, *Die Frau im Dritten Reich* (Grabert, 1978).

9   in the killing fields: My choice of the term *killing fields* is deliberate. Though the Khmer Rouge terror came much later – three decades after the Second World War – this case of genocide drew popular attention to the historically more common non-industrialised methods of mass murder and to the role of Khmer women as revolu-tionaries and killers. See Ben Kiernan, *The Pol Pot Regime: Race, Power, and Genocide in Cambodia under the Khmer Rouge, 1975–1979*, 3rd edn (Yale University Press, 2008). As an example of the view that the two were quite different, the German case be-ing thought to involve just a few thousand camp guards as compared with the wide-spread participation of women in the Khmer Rouge, see Roger W. Smith, 'Perpetra-tors', in *Encyclopedia of Genocide and Crimes against Humanity* (Macmillan, 2004).

did not speak openly: Ursula Mahlendorf, *The Shame of Survival: Working through a Nazi Childhood* (Penn State University Press, 2009).

There were ample rations: On excessive female plundering, see the report (*Schenk Bericht*) of the Commander of the Security Police and Security Service for District Galicia, Verhalten der Reichsdeutschen in den besetzten Gebieten, 14 May 1943. The full report is at ITS; several pages are missing from the copy in BAK, R58/1002. See also Martin Dean, *Robbing the Jews: The Confiscation of Jewish Property in the Holocaust, 1933–1945* (Cambridge University Press, 2008).

10 This sympathetic image: Margarete Dörr, *'Wer die Zeit nicht miterlebt hat . . .': Frauenerfahrungen im Zweiten Weltkrieg und in den Jahren danach*, vol. 2, *Kriegsalltag* (Campus Verlag, 1998), p. 109. Women's accounts of the rubble have contributed to this narrative of victimisation; see Antonia Meiners, ed., *Wir haben wieder aufgebaut: Frauen der Stunde null erzählen* (Sandmann, 2011).

11 'endowed with innocence . . .': Ann Taylor Allen, 'The Holocaust and the Modernization of Gender: A Historiographical Essay', *Central European History* 30 (1997): 349–64 (see p. 351). Only in passing are women analysed in Gerhard Paul, ed., *Die Täter der Shoah: Fanatische Nationalsozialisten oder ganz normale Deutsche?* (Wallstein Verlag, 2002).

agency of women in the crimes: In Karen Hagemann and Jean H. Quataert, eds, *Gendering Modern German History: Rewriting Historiography* (Berghahn, 2007), see Karen Hagemann, 'Military, War, and the Mainstreams: Gendering Modern German Military History', especially pp. 70–75, and the excellent review of the literature by Claudia Koonz, 'A Tributary and a Mainstream: Gender, Public Memory, and Historiography of Nazi Germany', pp. 147–68.

regime's genocidal machinery: Raul Hilberg, *Perpetrators, Victims, Bystanders: The Jewish Catastrophe, 1933–1945* (HarperCollins, 1992), p. 53.

12 a female chief detective: She was the only section head in the Reich Security Main Office (Reichssicherheitshauptamt, or RSHA). There were seventy-one female senior officers in the Criminal Police (Kriminalpolizei, or Kripo), working in sixty-one offices in May 1943. See Michael Wildt, *An Uncompromising Generation: The Nazi Leadership of the Reich Security Main Office* (University of Wisconsin Press, 2009), pp. 177–78, 482 n. 35.

13 There are significant differences: See Henry Greenspan, *On Listening to Holocaust Survivors: Recounting and Life History* (Praeger, 1998); Christopher Browning, *Collected Memories: Holocaust History and Post-war Testimony* (University of Wisconsin Press, 2003); Harald Welzer, *'Opa war kein Nazi': Nationalsozialismus und Holocaust im Familiengedächtnis* (Fischer Verlag, 2002); and Dörr, *'Wer die Zeit nicht miterlebt hat . . .'*

## 1. THE LOST GENERATION OF GERMAN WOMEN

15 The men and women who established: See Ernest M. Doblin and Claire Pohly, 'The Social Composition of the Nazi Leadership', *American Journal of Sociology* 51, no. 1 (1945): 42–49; Michael Mann, 'Were the Perpetrators of Genocide "Ordinary Men" or "Real Nazis"? Results from Fifteen Hundred Biographies', *Holocaust and Genocide Studies* 14 (Winter 2000): 331–66; and Daniel Brown, *The Camp Women: The Female Auxiliaries Who Assisted the SS in Running the Nazi Concentration Camp System* (Schiffer, 2002), especially John Roth's foreword, pp. 6–7.

16 One historian: Michael Wildt, *An Uncompromising Generation: The Nazi Leadership of the Reich Security Main Office* (University of Wisconsin Press, 2009).

baby boomers of the First World War: Between 1914 and 1964, the greatest number of births occurred in the years 1920–1922. The birthrate plummeted during the First World War to 14.3 per 1,000 people in 1918, then spiked in 1920 to 25.8, only to decline again with the depression in 1930 to 17.5. This demographic trend, though common in Europe, was extreme in Germany, and was one of the main causes of the anti-feminist backlash that tried to drive women back into the home and controlled contraception and abortions while elevating the social status of mothers. See Michelle Mouton, *From Nurturing the Nation to Purifying the Volk: Weimar and Nazi Family Policy, 1918–1945* (Cambridge University Press, 2007), pp. 108, 272–82. The largest number of marriages in Germany between 1908 and 1964 occurred in 1919–1920. See Elizabeth D. Heineman, *What Difference Does a Husband Make? Women and Marital Status in Nazi and Post-war Germany* (University of California Press, 1999), Appendix A.

17 The Weimar Republic saw an explosion: For example, the German National People's Party, the Christian Socialist People's Party, the German People's Party, the Christian National Farmer's and Rural Folk's Party, and the Bavarian People's Party. See Larry Eugene Jones and James Retallack, eds, *Elections, Mass Politics and Social Change in Modern Germany* (Cambridge University Press, 1992); George L. Mosse, *The Crisis of German Ideology: Intellectual Origins of the Third Reich* (Grosset & Dunlap, 1964); and Mosse, *Toward the Final Solution: A History of European Racism* (Howard Fertig, 1997).

Feminism lacked: Ute Frevert, *Women in German History: From Bourgeois Emancipation to Sexual Liberation* (Berg, 1989).

18 housewife wearing a spotless apron: See Nancy R. Reagin, *Sweeping the German Nation: Domesticity and National Identity in Germany, 1870–1945* (Cambridge University Press, 2006), pp. 61–69, 97–101; and Renate Bridenthal, Atina Grossmann and Marion Kaplan, eds, *When Biology Became Destiny: Women in Weimar and Nazi Germany* (Monthly Review Press, 1984), p. xiii.

19 extreme turn to the right: Eva Schöck-Quinteros and Christiane Streubel, eds, *'Ihrem Volk verantwortlich': Frauen der politischen Rechten (1890–1933); Organisationen – Agitationen – Ideologien* (Trafo Verlag, 2007).

20 'Women could not remain . . .': Erna Günther, 'Wir Frauen im Kampf um Deutschlands Erneuerung', *NS-Frauen-Warte* 2, no. 17 (25 Feb. 1934): 507. German Propaganda Archive, http://www.calvin.edu/academic/cas/gpa/fw2-17.htm.

women cannot be blamed: Women were not a majority of those who voted for Hitler, even at the peak of the Party's popularity in 1932. In the presidential election of March 1932, 51.6 per cent of female voters voted for Hindenburg while 26.5 per cent went for Hitler. In the 1931 September elections, 3 million women voted for NSDAP candidates, almost half of the total of 6.5 million votes cast for the NSDAP. Most women cast their ballots for the conservative nationalist parties. See Richard Evans, 'German Women and the Triumph of Hitler', *Journal of Modern History* 48 (March 1976): 156–57. Regional variations were significant, however, and religion mattered – for example, those in the Catholic Centre Party (Amalie Lauer) and leftists in the SPD and the Communist Party (Clara Zetkin) opposed Hitler's fascism. Among the more liberal conservative female leaders who warned women against the Nazi Party was the jurist Elisabeth Schwarzhaupt, in 'Was hat die deutsche Frau vom Nationalsozialismus zu erwarten?', originally published in 1932 in Berlin, excerpted in Annette Kuhn and Valentine Rothe, *Frauen im deutschen Faschismus*, vol. 1 (Schwann, 1982), pp. 80–83. See also Michael Kater, *The Nazi Party: A Social Profile of Members and Leaders* (Harvard University Press, 1983); and Raffael Scheck, 'Women on the Weimar Right: The Role of Female Politicians in the Deutschnationale Volkspartei', *Journal of Contemporary History* 36, no. 4 (2001): 547–60.

As soon as Hitler was in office: This history began in 1933 with the dissolution of the largest women's organisation, the Association of German Women (BdF). As traditional women's groups and professions were taken over by Nazi fanatics, Jewish women were forced out. See Bridenthal, Grossmann and Kaplan, *When Biology Became Destiny*, pp. 21–22.

were among the persecuted: Sybil Milton, 'Women and the Holocaust: The Case of German and German-Jewish Women', in Bridenthal, Grossmann and Kaplan, *When Biology Became Destiny*, pp. 298, 300, 305. There were about 150,000 communists in Nazi concentration camps between 1933 and 1939, and 30,000 were executed. Female prisoners were later transferred to Lichtenburg and then Ravensbrück. Among those in the earliest camps at Gotteszell and then Lichtenburg was the communist Lina Haag.

21  'very quietly and carefully': Lina Haag's 1947 memoir, *Eine Hand voll Staub – Widerstand einer Frau 1933 bis 1945* (Fischer Verlag), 1995, pp. 10, 53.

'When you leave . . .': Barbara Distel, 'In the Shadow of Heroes: Struggle and Survival of Centa Beimler-Herka and Lina Haag', in Wolfgang Benz and Barbara Distel, eds, *Dachau Review: History of Nazi Concentration Camps; Studies, Reports, Documents*, vol. 1 (Berg, 1988), p. 201; see also author interview with Lina Haag and Dr Boris Neusius, 9 Feb. 2012, Munich (interview is available in USHMMA).

The increase in female prisoners: Reports on camp personnel from January 1945, listing 3,508 female guards, cited by Karin Orth, 'The Concentration Camp Personnel', in Jane Caplan and Nikolaus Wachsmann, eds, *Concentration Camps in Nazi Germany: The New Histories* (Routledge, 2010), p. 45. The total number of women who served in the prison system (not camps) is not known. For portraits of female guards, see Luise Rinser, *Gefängnistagebuch (1944–1945)*, excerpted in Kerrin Gräfin Schwerin, ed., *Frauen im Krieg: Briefe, Dokumente, Aufzeichnungen* (Nicolai Verlag, 1999), pp. 117–24. On Stutthof, where there were 30,000 prisoners, see Rita Malcher, 'Das Konzentrationslager Stutthof', in Theresa Wobbe, ed., *Nach Osten: Verdeckte Spuren nationalsozialistischer Verbrechen* (Verlag Neue Kritik, 1992), pp. 161–74. See also Elissa Mailänder Koslov, *Gewalt im Dienstalltag: Die SS-Aufseherinnen des Konzentrations- und Vernichtungslagers Majdanek, 1942–1944* (Hamburg Institute for Social Research, 2009); Brown, *The Camp Women*; and Jürgen Matthäus, ed., *Approaching an Auschwitz Survivor: Holocaust Testimony and Its Transformations* (Oxford University Press, 2009).

Female guards at Camp Neuengamme: See Marc Buggeln, *Arbeit und Gewalt: Das*

*Aussenlagersystem des KZ Neuengamme* (Wallstein Verlag, 2009). In January 1945 there were 322 female guards at Neuengamme.

22  when one's neighbours: On the self-policing in German society, see Robert Gellately, *The Gestapo and German Society: Enforcing Racial Policy, 1933–1945* (Oxford University Press, 1991).

'What man offers in heroism . . .': Speech excerpted in Benjamin Sax and Dieter Kunz, eds, *Inside Hitler's Germany: A Documentary History of Life in the Third Reich* (D. C. Heath, 1992), pp. 262–63.

'since it draws the woman . . .': Hitler quoted in George L. Mosse, ed., *Nazi Culture: Intellectual, Cultural, and Social Life in the Third Reich* (Grosset & Dunlap, 1966), p. 39.

'Hence all possibilities . . .': Rosenberg quoted in Mosse, *Nazi Culture,* p. 40.

23  In the Reich's battle for births: See Gisela Bock, 'Ordinary Women in Nazi Germany: Perpetrators, Victims, Followers, and Bystanders', in Dalia Ofer and Lenore Weitzman, eds, *Women in the Holocaust* (Yale University Press, 1999). See also the racial guidelines for conception, pregnancy, birthing and midwifery in a standard manual of the day (republished in the immediate post-war period) by Frau Dr Johanna Haarer, *Die deutsche Mutter und ihr erstes Kind* (J. F. Lehmanns Verlag, 1938). All female marriage candidates had to undergo invasive medical examinations and were evaluated for so-called hereditary diseases that included prostitution, gambling and vagrancy. See 'Richtlinien für die ärztliche Untersuchung der Ehestandsbewerber vom 3.1.1939', excerpted in Kuhn and Rothe, *Frauen im deutschen Faschismus,* vol. 1, p. 95; and 'Die geschichtliche Entwicklung der deutschen Schwesternschaften', in *Lehrbuch für Säuglings- und Kinderschwestern* (Stuttgart, 1944), p. 11.

historian Gisela Bock: Bock, 'Ordinary Women in Nazi Germany', p. 87.

24  'incredibly authoritarian': Dagmar Reese, *Growing Up Female in Nazi Germany,* trans. William Templer (University of Michigan Press, 2006), p. 148. See also Michael Kater, *Hitler Youth* (Harvard University Press, 2004), pp. 100–103.

'emancipate women . . .': Alfred Rosenberg, quoted in Frevert, *Women in German History,* p. 207. See also Matthew S. Seligmann, John Davison and John McDonald, *Daily Life in Hitler's Germany* (St Martin's Press, 2003), p. 75; Kirsten Heinsohn, Barbara Vogel and Ulrike Weckel, eds, *Zwischen Karriere und Verfolgung: Handlungsräume von Frauen im nationalsozialistischen Deutschland* (Campus Verlag, 1997), p. 7; and Bock, 'Ordinary Women in Nazi Germany', p. 93.

25  its own female aesthetic: Mosse, *Nazi Culture,* p. 21; and Irene Guenther, *Nazi Chic? Fashioning Women in the Third Reich* (Berg, 2004), pp. 83–85, 92, 106–8.

26  act on the ambitious notion: On the appeal of 'becoming someone', Ulrike Gaida, *Zwischen Pflegen und Töten: Krankenschwestern im Nationalsozialismus* (Mabuse Verlag, 2006), pp. 7–8.

27  In secondary schools: Lisa Pine, *Education in Nazi Germany* (Berg, 2011), pp. 57–58. A Mardi Gras parade: Jürgen Matthäus, 'Antisemitic Symbolism in Early Nazi Germany, 1933–1935', *Leo Baeck Institute Yearbook* 45 (2000): 183–203.

in the streets and at school: Jews were barred from German public schools in November 1938. Henny Adler, interview 10481; Susi Podgurski, interview 5368; both in SFA. Thanks to Danielle Knott for the interview sources.

28 'you can't fight back': Marion A. Kaplan, *Between Dignity and Despair: Jewish Life in Nazi Germany* (Oxford University Press, 1999), p. 108.

historian Richard Evans: Richard Evans, *The Third Reich in Power* (Penguin, 2006), pp. 584–86; the estimate of the death toll is on p. 590.

'the night of broken glass': Alan E. Steinweis, *Kristallnacht 1938* (Harvard University Press, 2009); Beate Meyer, Hermann Simon and Chana Schütz, eds, *Jews in Nazi Berlin: From Kristallnacht to Liberation* (University of Chicago Press, 2009); and Thomas Kühne, *Belonging and Genocide: Hitler's Community, 1918–1945* (Yale University Press, 2010), pp. 38–40.

'The Jews are the enemy . . .': Evans, *The Third Reich in Power*, p. 587.

29 removed from management boards: Evans, *The Third Reich in Power*, pp. 378–88.

integrated women into a martial society: Kaplan, *Between Dignity and Despair*. On the training of girls in military-style exercises, see Reese, *Growing Up Female in Nazi Germany*, p. 4. On German militarism and 'final solutions', see Isabel V. Hull, *Absolute Destruction: Military Culture and Practices of War in Imperial Germany* (Cornell University Press, 2005); and on the militarism of women in the Red Army, see Anna Krylova, *Soviet Women in Combat: A History of Violence on the Eastern Front* (Cambridge University Press, 2011). German women were brought into combat roles out of necessity in the latter stages of the war, but they had already become part of the martial culture and underwent physical training.

not necessary for future mothers: On the racial state and women's role, see Michael Burleigh and Wolfgang Wippermann, *The Racial State: Germany, 1933–1945* (Cambridge University Press, 1991); and Evans, *The Third Reich in Power*, pp. 331, 523.

'In my state the mother . . .': Quoted in Frevert, *Women in German History*, p. 207. See also Christina Thürmer-Rohr, 'Frauen als Täterinnen und Mittäterinnen im NS-Deutschland', in Viola Schubert-Lehnhardt and Sylvia Korch, eds, *Frauen als Täterinnen und Mittäterinnen im Nationalsozialismus: Gestaltungsspielräume und Handlungsmöglichkeiten* (Universität Halle-Wittenberg, 2006), p. 22.

30 did not yield the results: 1939 was an exception when the marriage rate jumped, but between 1933 and 1945 the overall birthrate was not much higher than in the 1920s, and in the war years (1940–1945) it was significantly lower. See Jill Stephenson, *Women in Nazi Germany* (Longman, 2001), pp. 24, 31–35; and Frevert, *Women in German History*, pp. 218–19.

'everyone had to have a profession . . .': Reese, quoting an interview subject born in Minden in 1921, *Growing Up Female in Nazi Germany*, p. 126.

it would be inaccurate: Besides working on a farm, one could still choose a particular assignment to fulfil one's labour duty, and for women this usually meant in 'clerical work, auxiliary nursing, social welfare, public transport, [and] munitions work' (Stephenson, *Women in Nazi Germany*, p. 81). Obligatory labour service of single women was expanded under the Four Year Plan, but because these women preferred to work in offices and retail, Goering required them to spend at least one year as household help and in agriculture, where there were labour shortages. See Goering's decree of 15 Feb. 1938 and Elisabeth Sedlmayr's *Frauenberufe der Gegenwart und ihre Verflechtung in den Volkskörper* (Munich, 1939), excerpted in Kuhn and Rothe, *Frauen im deutschen Faschismus,* vol. 1, pp. 125–26.

## 2. THE EAST NEEDS YOU

32 'Just as our ancestors…': Adolf Hitler, *Mein Kampf,* trans. Ralph Manheim (Houghton Mifflin, 2001; orig. pub. 1943), pp. 653–54. According to Albert Speer's account, Hitler also stated that the loss of a few hundred thousand Germans on the battlefield did not play a role, since these losses could easily be made up in two or three years. Albert Speer, *Spandau: The Secret Diaries* (Macmillan, 1976).

33 'The German colonist…': Monologues of 8–10 Sept. 1941, Adolf Hitler, *Table Talk, 1941–1944* (Enigma Books, 2008), p. 24.

'essence of blood purity': Lisa Pine, *Education in Nazi Germany* (Berg, 2011), p. 56.

a best-selling novel: Woodruff Smith, 'The Colonial Novel as Political Propaganda: Hans Grimm's *Volk ohne Raum*', *German Studies Review* 6, no. 2 (May 1983): 215–35.

34 'Into the east wind…': Verses in *Wir Mädel singen,* 1938 edition of the BdM songbook, cited in Michael Kater, *Hitler Youth* (Harvard University Press, 2004), pp. 102–3.

a major exhibit in Berlin: *Das Sowjet-Paradies: Ausstellung der Reichspropagandaleitung der NSDAP; Ein Bericht in Wort und Bild* (Berlin: Zentralverlag der NSDAP, 1942; excerpted at www.calvin.edu). On 18 May, 1942, a group of leftist resisters, including Herbert Baum and four other Jews, bombed the exhibit. Goebbels and the SS and police retaliated with the arrest of 500 Jews and their families; 250 of the men were shot immediately, the others sent to camps. The event figures in the diaries of Goebbels and Victor Klemperer. See Regina Scheer, *Im Schatten der Sterne: Eine jüdische Widerstandsgruppe* (Aufbau Verlag, 2004).

'the expanses in the East': Elizabeth Harvey, *Women and the Nazi East: Agents and Witnesses of Germanisation* (Yale University Press, 2003), p. 92. See also Nicholas Stargardt, *Witnesses of War: Children's Lives under the Nazis* (Random House, 2005), p. 120; and the memoir by Hildegard Fritsch, *Land, mein Land: Bauerntum und Landdienst, BDM-Osteinsatz, Siedlungsgeschichte im Osten* (Schütz, 1986).

35 In the Nazi imagination: Wendy Lower, 'Living Space', in Peter Hayes and John K. Roth, eds, *The Oxford Handbook of Holocaust Studies* (Oxford University Press, 2011), pp. 310–25; Carroll P. Kakel III, *The American West and the Nazi East: A Comparative and Interpretive Perspective* (Palgrave Macmillan, 2011), p. 1; Hitler, *Table Talk*; Götz Aly, *Hitlers Volkstaat: Raub, Rassenkrieg und Nationalsozialismus* (Fischer Verlag, 2005), pp. 230–44; Johnpeter Horst Grill and Robert L. Jenkins, 'The Nazis and the American South in the 1930s: A Mirror Image?', *Journal of Southern History* 58, no. 4 (1992): 667–94; and Gert Gröning and Joachim Wolschke-Bulmahn, *Der Drang nach Osten: Zur Entwicklung der Landespflege im Nationalsozialismus und während des 2. Weltkrieges in den eingegliederten Ostgebieten* (Minerva, 1987), p. 132.

in wagon trains: For photos of migrating Volhynian *Volksdeutsche* in covered wagons, see Maximilian du Prel, ed., *Das deutsche Generalgouvernement Polen: Ein Überblick über Gebiet, Gestaltung und Geschichte* (Buchverlag Ost Krakau, 1940).

36  'those deep layers . . .': Siegfried Kracauer, *From Caligari to Hitler: A Psychological History of the German Film* (Princeton University Press, 1947; reprinted 2004), p. 6. See also Eric Rentschler, *Ministry of Illusion: Nazi Cinema and Its Afterlife* (Harvard University Press, 1996).

campaigns of kidnapping: Himmler's Hegewald speech, 16 Sept. 1942, NARA, Record Group 242, T175, R 90. The International Tracing Service is still reuniting families: http://www.its-arolsen.org/en/archives/collection/organisation/child-tracing-service/index.html. During the war children were exploited as labourers and subjected to medical experiments. Karoline Diehl and her husband, the SS doctor Sigmund Rascher (a Himmler confidant known for his cruel medical experiments at Dachau), kidnapped their children; arrested in late 1944, Diehl and Rascher were killed in concentration camps in April 1945 for their deceit and financial wrongdoings. See Stanislav Zamečnik, *Das war Dachau* (Comité International de Dachau, 2002).

37  roles as resettlement administrators: Isabel Heinemann, *Rasse, Siedlung, deutsches Blut* (Wallstein Verlag, 2003), p. 520.

38  'euphoria of victory': Christopher R. Browning, with Jürgen Matthäus, *The Origins of the Final Solution: The Evolution of Nazi Jewish Policy, September 1939–March 1942* (Yad Vashem, 2004), p. 427.

how many Germans: The figures for German personnel in the East are scattered in the documentation, and the reports that do exist are from specific agencies at different points in time. The figures presented here are mainly from the Reich Commissariat Ukraine, the Reich Commissariat Ostland, and the General Government. Women were among the staff of more than 15,000 German personnel in SS offices in the Reich Commissariat Ukraine and Ostland in 1942, the 14,000 agricultural inspectors and the 6,600 Germans in the Central Trade Corporation East (ZHO); in Ukraine there were more than 440 rural outposts that made up the commissariat, and each had at least one secretary. See the statistics in Timothy Patrick Mulligan, *The Politics of Illusion and Empire: German Occupation Policy in the Soviet Union, 1942–1943* (Praeger, 1988), pp. 22–23, 26, 28–29, 64 (n. 18) and 72. Mulligan's source is NARA, Record Group 242, 'Übersicht über die Verwaltungseinteilung des Reichskommissariats Ukraine nach dem Stand vom 1. Januar 1943', T454, reel 92, frame 000933. The figures for occupied Poland are from Bogdan Musial's *Deutsche Zivilverwaltung und Judenverfolgung im Generalgouvernement* (Harrossowitz Verlag, 1999), pp. 82–90. Within the figures cited by Musial were local ethnic Germans (*Volksdeutschen*). Additional personnel records that show female typists and administrators in the Ostland are in Record Group 242, A3345-DS-A156, Ostministerium, frame 316, selections for Riga, 'Einsatz in den besetzten Ostgebieten', 28 Nov. 1941, Zentral- und Personalabteilung RKO-RmfdbO, NARA, Record Group 242, T454, roll 15.

nineteen thousand young German women: Kater, *Hitler Youth*, p. 89.

39 'burn the racial sense...': Richard Evans, *The Third Reich in Power* (Penguin, 2006), p. 273; see also pp. 265, 268.

'observe the Jew...': George L. Mosse, ed., *Nazi Culture: Intellectual, Cultural, and Social Life in the Third Reich* (Grosset & Dunlap, 1966), p. 80, excerpted from Jakob Graf, *Familienkunde und Rassenbiologie für Schüler* (Munich, 1935).

'Go to the back...': Susi Podgurski, interview 5368, segment 32; Henry Adler, interview 10481; both in SFA. See Pine, *Education in Nazi Germany*, pp. 15–16. Thanks to Danielle Knott for her research help.

40 The child never returned: Author interview with one of Ottnad's students, friend of the epileptic child, Friedrich and Freya K., 11 Apr. 2011. Letter from witnesses to author, Reichersbeuern, 6 May 2011. Local history corroborated in the personnel and party records of Ottnad, who was an active Party member, a district leader of the NS Women's League after July 1933, in the Nazi Teachers' League and local manager of youth programmes beginning in 1934. See NARA, Record Group 242, BDC records, NSDAP Parteikorrespondenz: A3340-PK-I450, frames 1336–1340; NS Lehrerbund: A3340-MF-B095 frames 96–98, NSDAP, MFOK: A3340-MFOK-Q036, frame 1496. Author interview with Ottnad's student has been deposited in USHMMA. For teachers' reliance on the Party for basic materials, see Kalender 1938-NS Lehrerbund, private collection of former teacher, Weil im Schönbuch, Germany.

Claudia Koonz has observed: Claudia Koonz, *The Nazi Conscience* (Harvard University Press, 2005), p. 154.

41 'You are hereby assigned...': Ingelene Rodewald, ... *und auf dem Schulhof stand ein Apfelbaum: Meine Zeit in Polen, 1942–1944* (Cimbrian, 2007), pp. 8–11.

42 one of several hundred: Harvey, *Women and the Nazi East*, pp. 97, 98–101.

43 'Sisyphean task': Rosemarie Killius, ed., *Frauen für die Front: Gespräche mit Wehrmachtshelferinnen* (Militzke Verlag, 2003). See correspondence from Eugenie S., pp. 59–60.

Of all the professions: See Jean H. Quataert, 'Mobilizing Philanthropy in the Service of War: The Female Rituals of Care in the New Germany, 1871–1914', in Manfred F. Boemeke, Roger Chickering and Stig Förster, eds, *Anticipating Total War: The German and American Experiences, 1871–1914* (Cambridge University Press, 1999). Within the 1930s network of organisations were the Evangelical-Lutheran and Catholic associations of nurse-nuns (for example, the Diakonissen des Kaiserswerther Verbandes, the Caritasschwestern des dritten Ordens) and the National Association for Nurses (Reichsbund für Schwestern); the Blue Sisterhood merged with the Nazi Schwesterschaft.

44 'angels of the front': See Birgit Panke-Kochinke and Monika Schaidhammer-Placke, *Frontschwestern und Friedensengel: Kriegskrankenpflege im Ersten und Zweiten Weltkrieg; Ein Quellen- und Fotoband* (Mabuse Verlag, 2002), p. 18; and Ulrike Gaida, *Zwischen Pflegen und Töten: Krankenschwestern im Nationalsozialismus* (Mabuse Verlag, 2006).

During the Nazi era: For the interconnections between the DRK, NSV and

NSDAP, see record of the German Red Cross at NARA, Record Group 242, Deutsches Rotes Kreuz, Göttingen Stab, BDC, A 3345-DS-N001, frame 298. Gaida, *Zwischen Pflegen und Töten.*

The Nazi Party regulated: Vorschlagsliste DRK to NSDAP, Ortsgruppenleiter Aschaffenburg, 7 Dec. 1938. NARA, Record Group 242, Misc. Collection, Personnel Records, Göttingen, A 3345-DS-N001. Decree of the Reich Ministry of the Interior, 28 Sept. 1938, on the segregation of Jewish nurses' training and patient care. Joseph Walk, ed., *Das Sonderrecht für die Juden im NS-Staat* (C. F. Mueller Verlag, 1996), p. 243.

'hatred is noble': Lotte Guse, *Kriegserlebnisse einer Krankenschwester: Vom Kreuz beschützt, Der Spiegel,* August 11, 2008, http://einestages.spiegel.de/static/authoralbumbackground/2413/vom_kreuz_beschuetzt.html. The quote is taken from the recollections of a former wartime nurse, Lotte Guse.

45 'evil people in Russia': *Frauen an der Front: Krankenschwestern im Zweiten,* documentary film, Henrike Sandner and Dirk Otto (MDR, 2010). Thanks to Renate Sarkar for sharing this film with me.

46 Ohr found them inspiring: Erika Summ, *Schäfers Tochter: Die Geschichte der Frontschwester* (Zeitgut Verlag, 2006), p. 76.

'I wanted more': Erika Summ, 'Ich will mehr', quoted in Jürgen Kleindienst, ed., *Als wir Frauen stark sein mussten: Erinnerungen 1939–1945* (Zeitgut Verlag, 2007), p. 60; and in Summ, *Schäfers Tochter,* p. 89, the same phrase is used as a heading, with an exclamation mark.

nurses and female health aides: See Panke-Kochinke and Schaidhammer-Placke, *Frontschwestern und Friedensengel*; and Birgitt Morgenbrod and Stephanie Merkenich, *Das Deutsche Rote Kreuz unter der NS-Diktatur, 1933–1945* (Ferdinand Schöningh), 2008.

47 two years of intensive training: Summ, *Schäfers Tochter,* pp. 95–115.

48 A patriot and an idealist: Author interview with Annette Schücking-Homeyer, 30 March 2010, Lünen, Germany.

49 barred women from the judiciary: Diemut Majer, *'Non-Germans' under the Third Reich: The Nazi Judicial and Administrative System in Germany and Occupied Eastern Europe, with Special Regard to Occupied Poland, 1939–1945* (Johns Hopkins University Press, 2003), p. 638.

her wartime labour duty: On the obligatory labour of German women during the war, see Ute Frevert, *Women in German History: From Bourgeois Emancipation to Sexual Liberation* (Berg, 1989), p. 227.

50 Of all the female professions: Michael Burleigh, *Death and Deliverance: 'Euthanasia' in Germany, 1900–1945* (Cambridge University Press, 1994), p. 159; and Henry Friedlander, *The Origins of Nazi Genocide: From Euthanasia to the Final Solution* (University of North Carolina Press, 1997).

51 'The Führer developed...': NARA, RG 238, NMT, NO-470; Pauline Kneissler, Nazi Party #3892898. She was born in Kurdjunowka, Ukraine. Nazi Party Card, BDC, NARA II, A3340-MFOK-L005, frame 0972.

'not all particularly serious cases': All quotations in this paragraph and the next two are from Kneissler and testimonies cited in Gaida, *Zwischen Pflegen und Töten,* p. 176.

53 rise of the modern workplace: The metropolitan scene was bewildering for young women from the countryside. They experienced new forms of stress as well as liberation. See Katharina von Ankum, ed., *Women in the Metropolis: Gender and Modernity in Weimar Culture* (University of California Press, 1997), pp. 2–4; and Frevert, *Women in German History*, pp. 156–57, 218.

54 'Thank God . . .': Ilse Schmidt, *Die Mitläuferin: Erinnerungen einer Wehrmachtsangehörigen* (Aufbau Verlag, 2002), p. 16.

55 some five hundred thousand: The largest employer of German female clerical aides during the war was the German military. The most numerous female military aides, the *Blitzmädchen* or 'lightning girls', were a wartime version of the Weimar New Woman, not the virtuous, milk-maiden types who embodied the home front. For one secretary's story, see Killius, *Frauen für die Front,* testimony entitled 'Ich hatte es nicht schlecht', pp. 69–70. Women who were assigned to military support positions 'to free up men for the front' were placed in a hierarchy with the power to issue orders, from the senior staff leader down to a regular military aide. See Franka Maubach, 'Expansionen weiblicher Hilfe: Zur Erfahrungsgeschichte von Frauen im Kriegdienst', in Sybille Steinbacher, ed., *Volksgenossinnen: Frauen in der NS-Volksgemeinschaft* (Wallstein Verlag, 2007), p. 105. See also Ingeburg Hölzer's memoir, *'Im Sommer 1944 . . .'* (Wim Snayder Verlag, 1994); and Franz Wilhelm Seidler, *Blitzmädchen* (Wehr und Wissen, 1979).

She grew up in the Saxon town: Liselotte Meier Lerm, statement of 19 Sept. 1963, BAL, 162/3425.

higher status as a civil servant: Dagmar Reese, *Growing Up Female in Nazi Germany*, trans. William Templer (University of Michigan Press, 2006), p. 128.

'strong, brave women': Reese, *Growing Up Female in Nazi Germany*, p. 41, quoting Hitler and von Schirach at a BdM rally in 1936. See also pp. 72, 101, 133, 237.

56 'very punctual, hard-working . . .': Biographical material in the indictment of Altvater and verdict, BAL, B162/4524, pp. 20, 22.

57 Sabine Dick: Dick testimony, 27 and 29 Apr. 1960, Berlin, Oberstaatsanwalt Koblenz files, Koblenz 9 Js 716/59, Sonderkommission P. Thanks to Jürgen Matthäus for these files from the Heuser and RSHA investigations.

secretaries who worked in this: Gerhard Paul, '"Kämpfende Verwaltung" Das Amt IV des Reichssicherheitshauptamtes als Führungsinstanz der Gestapo', in Gerhard Paul and Klaus-Michael Mallman, eds, *Die Gestapo im Zweiten Weltkrieg: 'Heimatfront' und besetztes Europa* (Primus Verlag, 2000), pp. 45, 47. There were 31,374 in the Secret State Police (Gestapo), 12,792 in the Criminal Investigation Police (Kripo) and 6,482 in the Security Service (SD); see Klaus Hesse, Kay Kufeke and Andreas Sander, eds, *Topographie des Terrors* (Stiftung Topographie des Terrors, 2010), p. 127. Thanks to Rachel Century for sharing her sources on secretaries.

58 'open, honest character': NARA, RG 242, BDC, RuSHA marriage application, and A3343-RS-D-490, frames 1584, 1640 and 1656.

scholar Michael Mann: Michael Mann determined that Germans who lived in territories lost or occupied under terms of the Treaty of Versailles (such as Silesia and

Rhineland), and who were active in the Nazi era, were ultra-nationalist, and constituted a higher percentage of perpetrators. See his 'Were the Perpetrators of Genocide "Ordinary Men" or "Real Nazis"?' *Holocaust and Genocide Studies* 14 (Winter 2000): 331–66, especially pp. 343–46.

Josefine Krepp: Biographical information on Josefine Krepp Block, Vernehmung, VCA, Strafbezirksgericht Wien, 15 Oct. 1946, Wiener Stadt- und Landesarchiv, Vg 8514/46.

60 Austrians cemented their future: On the Vienna Model, see Hans Safrian, *Eichmann's Men* (Cambridge University Press, 2010).

passed the SS examiners' test: Katrin Himmler, '"Herrenmenschenpaare": Zwischen nationalsozialistischem Elitebewusstsein und rassenideologischer (Selbst-) Verpflichtung', in Marita Krauss, ed., *Sie waren dabei: Mitläuferinnen, Nutzniesserinnen, Täterinnen im Nationalsozialismus* (Wallstein Verlag, 2008), pp. 65–66.

The route to success: Additional cases of female stenographers sent from Gestapo offices in the Reich to the occupied territories are in Michael Wildt, *An Uncompromising Generation: The Nazi Leadership of the Reich Security Main Office* (University of Wisconsin Press, 2009), pp. 116–19.

61 The tremendous growth: According to Richard Evans in *The Coming of the Third Reich* (Penguin, 2004): 'The rapid emergence of a service sector in the economy, with its new employment possibilities for women, from sales positions in the great department stores to secretarial work in the booming office world (driven by the powerful feminising influence of the typewriter), created new forms of exploitation but also gave increasing numbers of young, unmarried women a financial and social independence they had not enjoyed before' (p. 127). According to Elizabeth D. Heineman in *What Difference Does a Husband Make? Women and Marital Status in Nazi and Post-war Germany* (University of California Press, 1999): 'Whether they enthusiastically or reluctantly joined the war effort, women born roughly from 1918 to 1928 who remained single during the war contributed to it more directly than any other working group of German women' (p. 64).

'failing to meet their obligations . . .': Frevert, *Women in German History*, p. 186.

62 two understandings of marriage: Michael Burleigh and Wolfgang Wippermann, *The Racial State: Germany, 1933–1945* (Cambridge University Press, 1991), pp. 49–50; and Wildt, *An Uncompromising Generation*, p. 111.

some 240,000 German women: See Gudrun Schwarz, *Eine Frau an seiner Seite: Ehefrauen in der 'SS-Sippengemeinschaft'* (Hamburger Edition, 1997), p. 11; and Kathrin Kompisch, *Täterinnen: Frauen im Nationalsozialismus* (Böhlau, 2008), p. 204. Documentation on SS marriage applications survived the war and is archived in the United States and Germany, as part of the collection of the Berlin Document Center. See also Isabel Heinemann, *Rasse, Siedlung, deutsches Blut* (Wallstein Verlag, 2003), pp. 54, 62 n. 47.

63 Vera Stähli: She was born in 1912, in Hamburg, so she does not fit into the category of post-First World War baby boomers, but her professional pre-Second World War experience was largely shaped by First World War backlashes of late Weimar and Nazi era and by earlier trends of women in the emerging metropolitan working culture.

When asked in her marriage application about the history of her family, she stated that she did not know much about her parents. Either she was concealing something considered by SS examiners to be 'harmful' in her genetic past, or she was not close to her parents. 'Fragebogen' Wohlauf, NARA, BDC, A3343-RS-G5348, frames 2214–2326.

65 'most private wishes': Urteil Landegericht Zivilkammer Hamburg, 10 June 1942, NARA, BDC, RuSHA file Wohlauf, A3343-RS-G5348, frames 2214–2326.
Vera and Julius were in a rush: Christopher R. Browning, *Ordinary Men: Reserve Police Battalion 101 and the Final Solution in Poland* (HarperCollins, 1993), p. 92.

67 Liesel Riedel and her SS fiancé: Willhaus marriage application, NARA, BDC, Ru-SHA files, A3343-RS-G5242, frames 2524–2710. See Ernst Klee, *Das Personenlexikon zum Dritten Reich: Wer war was vor und nach 1945* (Fischer Verlag, 2003).

68 'In the end, blood . . .': Evans, *The Third Reich in Power*, p. 626.

69 'political organisation that was . . .': 2 July 1935 letter of Stabsführer to RuSHA Leader of the 85th Standarte, Cottbus. RuSHA file Willhaus. In 1943 the SS was still investigating the issue of his unapproved marriage. NARA, BDC, A3343-RS-G5242. See Michael Burleigh, *The Third Reich: A New History* (Hill & Wang, 2000), pp. 102, 116.

70 developed a split personality: In and around Erna's home town, racial anti-Semites and 'blood and soil' agitators infiltrated state institutions, with immediate effect. Boycotting of Jewish business started in December 1932 along with the reissuing of school textbooks to re-educate youth. Among the regional Nazi leaders in Thuringia who would later rise and fall with the regime were Fritz Sauckel (later Hitler's wartime 'czar' of forced-labour deportations from the East to the Reich, hanged at Nuremberg in 1946), Richard Walter Darré (Himmler's farming specialist and first chief of the SS racial office) and Professor Dr Hans F. K. Günther (the intellectual populariser of Nordicism, a paganist known as the 'Race Pope'). But it was Himmler's trusted expert in matters of colonisation, Walter Darré, who would have a direct role in shaping Erna's future. See Lower, 'Living Space', pp. 310–25; and Evans, *The Third Reich in Power*, p. 9.

71 'blood and soil' expert: Darré proposed the creation of a new agrarian nobility founded on pure German blood of men and women in monogamous relationships cultivating large families and large estates, in *Neuadel aus Blut und Boden* (Munich, 1930), pp. 131, 152, 153. Darré was the son of a merchant in a German trade firm in Argentina; having returned to Germany, he was schooled at the German Colonial School at Witzenhausen and completed a degree in agricultural science at the University of Halle. He was a staunch advocate of *völkisch* theories. See Klee, *Das Personenlexikon zum Dritten Reich*.

72 After a year-long courtship: NARA, BDC, RuSHA file Petri, SSOK, roll 373A, frames 2908, 2910–2936. See Heineman, *What Difference Does a Husband Make?* Appendix A.
no longer the farmer's daughter: Many farmers' daughters and wives were not formally registered as labourers, but as 'assisting family members'. The centuries of the traditional household economy persisted. See Jill Stephenson, *Women in Nazi Germany* (Longman, 2001), p. 68.

73 Motor Vehicle Corps: Shelley Baranowski, *Nazi Empire: German Colonialism and Imperialism from Bismarck to Hitler* (Cambridge University Press, 2011), p. 154.

New Woman of the Weimar era: Frevert, *Women in German History*, p. 203.

'superior' methods of housekeeping: Nancy Reagin, *Sweeping the German Nation: Domesticity and National Identity in Germany, 1870–1945* (Cambridge University Press, 2006).

### 3. WITNESSES

75 'everything looked totally different…': Erika Summ, *Schäfers Tochter: Die Geschichte der Frontschwester* (Zeitgut Verlag, 2006), p. 117. Ohr's description here fits into the typical colonialist discourse about foreign landscapes that lack life and culture, and the dark depths of the Russian steppe.

77 emaciated Soviet prisoners: See Dieter Pohl, *Die Herrschaft der Wehrmacht: Deutsche Militärbesatzung und einheimische Bevölkerung in der Sowjetunion, 1941–1944* (Oldenbourg, 2008). See also Christian Streit, 'The Fate of the Soviet Prisoners of War', in Michael Berenbaum, ed., *A Mosaic of Victims: Non-Jews Persecuted and Murdered by the Nazis* (New York University Press, 1990).

'like animals hanging . . .': Nurse quoted in Birgit Panke-Kochinke and Monika Schaidhammer-Placke, *Frontschwestern und Friedensengel: Kriegskrankenpflege im Ersten und Zweiten Weltkrieg; Ein Quellen- und Fotoband* (Mabuse Verlag, 2002), pp. 193–96. See also Magdalena Wortmann, *Was haben wir nicht alles mitgemacht: Kriegserinnerungen einer Rotkreuzskrankenchwester* (Wim Snayder Verlag, 1995); Lora Wildenthal, *German Women for Empire, 1884–1945* (Duke University Press, 2001); and Elfriede Schade-Bartkowiak, *Sag mir, wo die Blumen sind . . . Unter der Schwesternhaube: Kriegserinnerungen einer DRK-Schwester im II. Weltkrieg an der Ostfront* (Hamburg, 1989), excerpted in Panke-Kochinke and Schaidhammer-Placke, *Frontschwestern und Friedensengel*, pp. 191–92.

78 'eyes wide open': Brigitte Erdmann letter to mother, 24 Jan. 1943, reprinted in Walter Kempowski, *Das Echolot* (btb Verlag, 2001), p. 339.

letters she sent home: Jens Ebert and Sybille Penkert, eds, *Brigitte Penkert: Briefe einer Rotkreuzschwester von der Ostfront* (Wallstein Verlag, 2006).

Nurses, teachers and secretaries: Franka Maubach, 'Expansionen weiblicher Hilfe: Zur Erfahrungsgeschichte von Frauen im Kriegdienst', in Sybille Steinbacher, ed., *Volksgenossinnen: Frauen in der NS-Volksgemeinschaft* (Wallstein Verlag, 2007); and Marita Krauss, ed., *Sie waren dabei: Mitläuferinnen, Nutzniesserinnen, Täterinnen im Nationalsozialismus* (Wallstein Verlag, 2008), p. 13.

Stories about the mass shootings: Karel Berkhoff, 'Babi Yar: Site of Mass Murder, Ravine of Oblivion', J. B. and Maurice C. Shapiro Annual Lecture, 9 Feb. 2011 (United States Holocaust Memorial Museum, Occasional Paper Series, May 2012); Peter Longerich, *'Davon haben wir nichts gewusst!' Die Deutschen und die Judenverfolgung, 1933–1945* (Siedler, 2006); and Jeffrey Herf, *The Jewish Enemy: Nazi Propaganda during World War II and the Holocaust* (Belknap Press, 2008).

79 operations such as those at Belzec: For an example of an exchange about mass murder in Belzec as a train passed by the camp, see 'Aufzeichnungen eines deutschen Unteroffiziers vom 31 August 1942, Rawa Ruska, Anlage 36', in Raul Hilberg, *Sonderzüge nach Auschwitz: The Role of the German Railroads in the Destruction of the Jews* (Dumjahn Verlag, 1981), pp. 188–91. Similar recollections about train conversations are in Alison Owings, *Frauen: German Women Recall the Reich* (Rutgers University Press, 1995).

an inadequately heated train: Paul Salitter, captain of the *Schutzpolizei* in Düsseldorf, was assigned by the Gestapo to guard this transport. At Konitz the local German train official tried to prevent the train from passing through; Salitter denounced him as a friend of the Jews, and not a member of the German racial community. Salitter went to the German Red Cross station to deal with a medical issue and the train departed without him. His wartime report is reprinted in Hilberg, *Sonderzüge nach Auschwitz*, p. 134. See also Andrej Angrick and Peter Klein, *Die 'Endlösung' in Riga: Ausbeutung und Vernichtung 1941–1944* (Wissenschaftliche Buchgesellschaft, 2006).

80 'killing all the Jews there': Quotations in this paragraph and the next are from Annette Schücking-Homeyer interview with author and Dr Christof Mauch, 30 Mar. 2010, Lünen, Germany. Some of the material used here appeared first in an interview conducted by Martin Doerry and Klaus Wiegrefe and published in *Der Spiegel* online, 25 Jan. 2010, 'They Really Do Smell Like Blood: Among Hitler's Executioners on the Eastern Front'. Thanks to Mr Wiegrefe for his assistance.

81 'shoot a Jewish woman in Brest': On massacres and ghettoisation in and around Brest, see the German military commander's report of 11 Oct. and 10 Nov. 1941, cited in Christian Gerlach, *Kalkulierte Morde. Die deutsche Wirtschafts- und Vernichtungspolitik in Weissrussland 1941 bis 1944* (Hamburger Edition, 1999), p. 610. See also Jürgen Matthäus, Konrad Kwiet and Jürgen Förster, eds, *Ausbildungsziel Judenmord? 'Weltanschauliche Erziehung' von SS, Polizei und Waffen-SS im Rahmen der 'Endlösun'* (Fischer Verlag, 2003).

Their responses ranged: Frau Leonhard, for instance, who went to the ghetto out of curiosity, also secretly gave food to the Jewish labourer. She was reprimanded but not punished (BAL, B162/1682; testimony of Erna Leonhard, 14 Dec. 1960). Helmy Spethmann, too, cared for Jews in the ghetto. An older nurse with experience in the First World War, Spethmann entered the Warsaw ghetto in August 1941, despite the ban (the ghetto was under quarantine). She brought her camera and photographed the extreme poverty and suffering of the Jews. After the war, she hid the photos; shortly before her death, she asked her niece to care for them and publicise them after she died. See 'Zeugin des Grauens: Lazarettschwester im Warschauer Ghetto', 24 Sept. 2010, *Der Spiegel* online http://einestages.spiegel.de/static/authoralbumbackground/15081/zeugin_des_grauens. html. Thanks to Susan Bachrach for bringing this article to my attention.

82 sites of German tourism: Erdmann letter to her mother, 30 Jan. 1943, in Kempowski, *Das Echolot* (2001), pp. 613–14. See also Alexander B. Rossino, 'Eastern Europe through German Eyes: Soldiers' Photographs, 1939–42', *History of Photography* 23, no. 4 (Winter 1999): 313–21.

'Today we are going in the ghetto': Quoted in Susi Gerloff, 'Kriegsschwestern: Erlebnisberichte, 1995', in Panke-Kochinke and Schaidhammer-Placke, *Frontschwestern und Friedensengel*, p. 196.

83 'death crates', in Goebbels's term: See Philip Friedman, *Roads to Extinction: Essays on the Holocaust* (Jewish Publication Society, 1980), p. 69. See also Eric Sterling, ed., *Life in the Ghettos during the Holocaust* (Syracuse University Press, 2005); and Daniel Michman, *The Emergence of Jewish Ghettos during the Holocaust* (Cambridge University Press, 2011).

showgirl Brigitte Erdmann: Erdmann letter to her mother, 30 Jan. 1943, in Kempowski, *Das Echolot* (2001), pp. 613–14. Approximately 55,000 Jews were living in Minsk at the time of the Germans' arrival there on 28 June 1941. Most were shot or shoved into gas vans along with the thousands who, starting in November 1941, were deported to Minsk from Hamburg, Frankfurt, Berlin, Vienna and other cities in the Reich. See deportation lists of Jews from Hamburg to Minsk ghetto, 18 Nov. 1941, Bundesarchiv, Dahlwitz Hoppegarten Records on microfilm at USHMMA, RG 14.050, reel 1, frames 827–841. On the Organisation Todt, the Minsk ghetto and ghetto tourism in Minsk, see Christian Gerlach, *Kalkulierte Morde*, pp. 57–63.

84 'filth, laziness, primitiveness . . .': Letter of Marianne Peyinghaus, 17 July 1942, on Plöhnen in the Warthegau, reprinted and analysed in Margarete Dörr, '*Wer die Zeit nicht miterlebt hat . . .': Frauenerfahrungen im Zweiten Weltkrieg und in den Jahren danach*, vol. 2, *Kriegsalltag* (Campus Verlag, 1998), p. 132.

'unreal city' and 'greasy kaftans': Elizabeth Harvey, *Women and the Nazi East: Agents and Witnesses of Germanisation* (Yale University Press, 2003), pp. 130–31, 122.

85 'It's really fantastic . . .': Letter quoted in Catherine Epstein, *Model Nazi: Arthur Greiser and the Occupation of Western Poland* (Oxford University Press, 2010), p. 169. The letter continues with the young woman's statement that if she were a Jew in the ghetto, she would be outraged by the confinement.

For the young women: In the summer of 1944 a German secretary in a construction office near Danzig watched each morning as 100–150 Polish Jewish female labourers were herded to work. They had come from the Stutthof concentration camp. They were guarded by SS women dressed in black with whips and boots. See Walter Kempowski, *Das Echolot* (btb Verlag, 1979), pp. 107–8.

'nice lads in the office': Erna Leonhard, statement of 14 Dec. 1960, BAL, 162/1682; and Rosemarie Killius, ed., *Frauen für die Front: Gespräche mit Wehrmachtshelferinnen* (Militzke Verlag, 2003), pp. 71–74.

86 'it stuck on me . . .': Anna Luise von Baumbach, *Frauen an der Front: Krankenschwestern im Zweiten Weltkrieg*, 2010 (DVD).

the water tasted strange: Testimony of Henriette Bau, former wife of Richard Lissberg, 23 Apr. 1969, BAL, 162/1673. Thanks to Omer Bartov for sharing this source.

Mass murder transforms: The wife of a railway official in Lida recalled the mass shooting of 5,200 Jews in a mass grave that was covered with chlorine, which in the heat of the day exploded 'like a fountain'. Testimony of Liselotte Wagentrotz, 11 Oct. 1965, Staatsanwaltschaft Mainz, 3 Js 155/64, BAL, 162/3446. See also Father Patrick Desbois, *The Holocaust by Bullets* (Macmillan, 2008).

87 'as big as our house . . .': Testimony of Florentina Bedner, 29 Nov. 1976, BAL, Bayer, Landeskriminalamt 76-K 41676, Koe. See NSV 'tasks' under the district commissars, 'IV. Vorläufige Aufgaben', regarding 'Judennachlass'. CSA, Kiev, 3206–6–254, microfilm held at USHMMA, RG31.002M, reel 6, p. 5.

away from the street in Zhytomyr: Erika Ohr's daily routine included a walk through the city to the canteen where they had lunch. Summ, *Schäfers Tochter*, pp. 132, 141.

'fenced, miserable ghetto . . .': The reference to Rivne/Rovno's Jewish community as a 'nest' also appeared in the testimony of the Commander of the Order Police for Ukraine, Otto von Oelhafen, 7 May 1947, NARA, RG 238, roll 50, M1019. See Ilse Schmidt, *Die Mitläuferin: Erinnerungen einer Wehrmachtsangehörigen* (Aufbau Verlag, 2002), pp. 73–75.

88 'One night I was awakened . . .': Schmidt, *Die Mitläuferin*, pp. 74–76. See also Shmuel Spector, *The Holocaust of Volhynian Jews, 1941–1944* (Yad Vashem, 1990), pp. 113–15, 184–85. On the massacres of Jews in Rivne, see testimony of Herman Graebe, NARA, RG 238, Document 2992-PS, International Military Tribunal Nuremberg. See also Dieter Pohl, 'The Murder of Ukraine's Jews under German Military Administration and in the Reich Commissariat Ukraine', in Ray Brandon and Wendy Lower, eds, *The Shoah in Ukraine: History, Testimony, Memorialisation* (Indiana University Press, 2008), p. 49. According to Pohl's research, local collaborators and the first company of Order Police Battalion 33 supported the SD units. The ghetto liquidation probably witnessed by Struwe occurred on 13 July 1942.

90 She could close her eyes: Another, more famous witness, Melita Maschmann, stated that when she saw the violence she went blind. See Maschmann's *Fazit: Mein Weg in der Hitler-Jugend* (dtv, 1983).

orders of Heinrich Himmler: On Himmler's verbal order in Zhytomyr, see Lower, *Nazi Empire Building and the Holocaust in Ukraine* (University of North Carolina Press, 2005), p. 8; testimony of Paul Albert Scheer, 29 Dec. 1945, USHMMA RG 06.025 Kiev; and Peter Witte et al., eds, *Der Dienstkalender Heinrich Himmlers 1941/42* (Christians Verlag, 1999), pp. 498–99.

91 'What am I doing here . . .': Schmidt, *Die Mitläuferin*, p. 81.

'crumpled down . . .' and 'a part of me . . .': Schmidt, *Die Mitläuferin*, pp. 38, 76–77.

'I have unlearned my *Todesangst* . . .': Brigitte Erdmann, letter of 21 Jan. 1943, in Kempowski, *Das Echolot* (2001), p. 237.

92 On her first day in Novgorod Volynsk: The destruction of the Jews of Zwiahel (Novgorod Volynsk) began in July 1941, when the command staff of Einsatzgruppe C established headquarters there. A sub-unit, Sk4a, with the help of local Ukrainian and ethnic German collaborators and Waffen-SS units under HSSPF Jeckeln, identified and arrested Jewish men and women. Wehrmacht units assisted the effort by organising and carrying out 'reprisal' measures: local Jews and Jewish POWs were killed as retaliation for any attacks against Germans and German installations. A mass grave unearthed in May 1945 revealed the 'half rotten women's and children's clothes, shoes, cemented by blood'. According to Soviet Extraordinary Commission investigators, the corpses lay in chaos; heads and skulls were damaged; some women were hugging children and toys. According to an eyewitness, a Ukrainian peasant,

the shooting took place at the end of August 1941. On the POWs, see Fernspruch 16 Pz.-Div. 14 July 1941, NARA, RG 242, T314, roll 1146, frame 000467. On the massacres of Jews, see Ereignismeldung 38, Einsatzgruppe C, 30 July 1941, NARA, RG 242, T175, reel 233; Soviet Extraordinary Commission reports, 24 May 1945, copy in ZSA, file 413, and copy at Jewish Culture Society in Novgorod Volynsk. I am grateful to Daniel Redman for sharing these Soviet reports. See also Jeckeln's *Einsatzbefehl* of 25 July 1941 for Novgorod Volynsk, NARA, RG 242, T501, roll 5, frames 000559–560, and *Unsere Ehre Heisst Treue: Kriegstagebuch des Kommandostabes Reichsführer SS, Tätigketisberichte der 1. Und 2. SS-Inf., Brigade der 1. SS-Kav.Brigade und von Sonderkommandos der SS* (Europa Verlag, 1965), pp. 95–96.

93 'Oftentimes conversations . . .': See letter of Annette Schücking-Homeyer to author, 17 May 2010, excerpted from her wartime correspondence. I am grateful to Ms Schücking-Homeyer for sharing copies of her letters. (Originals are deposited in the Warendorf district archive.)

94 'their eyes burning . . .': Brigitte Erdmann, letter of 15 Feb. 1943, quoted in Kempowski, *Das Echolot* (2001), p. 780.

'it would give him nightmares': Annette Schücking-Homeyer, letter to author, 17 May 2010. Massacres at Khmilnyk were corroborated in wartime documents and testimonies gathered by investigators at BAL – see Abschlussbericht, BAL II, 204 AR-Z, 135/67, 23–24.

'went on a rampage . . . *Jude kaput!*': Testimony of Blyuma Bronfin, 1944, in the form of a letter to Ilya Ehrenburg, reprinted in Joshua Rubenstein and Ilya Altman, eds, *The Unknown Black Book: The Holocaust in the German-Occupied Soviet Territories* (Indiana University Press, 2010), pp. 151–54.

clothing piled in a warehouse: Schücking-Homeyer interview with author and Christof Mauch, 30 Mar. 2010; also in *Der Spiegel* article, 28 Jan. 2010.

95 Every week she drove: On 5 November 1941, the district commissar of Rivne, Werner Beer, organised the massacre of about 17,000 Jews, which occurred on 6–7 November, 1941, and was carried out by Orpo 320, 315, 69 and EK 5. See Brandon and Lower, eds, *The Shoah in Ukraine*, p. 43.

'what an enormous slaughterhouse . . .': Letter of 5 Nov. 1941, Zwiahel, Annette Schücking to parents. Schücking-Homeyer, interview with author and Christof Mauch, 30 Mar. 2010, deposited in the USHMMA.

96 A secretary in Slonim: Frau Emilie Horst, statement of 10 May 1961, BAL, 162/5088.

## 4. ACCOMPLICES

97 few published or publicly spoke: Joanne Sayner, *Women without a Past? German Autobiographical Writings and Fascism* (Rodopi, 2007), p. 2. Thanks to Marion Deshmukh for this source.

encourages women to tell war stories: See Rosemarie Killius, ed., *Frauen für die Front: Gespräche mit Wehrmachtshelferinnen* (Militzke Verlag, 2003); and Margarete Dörr, '*Wer die Zeit nicht miterlebt hat . . .': Frauenerfahrungen im Zweiten Weltkrieg und in den Jahren danach*, vol. 2, *Kriegsalltag* (Campus Verlag, 1998).

98 hardships . . . on the home front: These accounts focus on the everyday household challenges of securing food, fuel, soap and clothing, on cooking, on bombing raids and on homelessness. See Kathrin Kompisch, *Täterinnen: Frauen im Nationalsozial-ismus* (Böhlau, 2008), p. 85; Nicole Ann Dombrowski, 'Soldiers, Saints, or Sacrificial Lambs? Women's Relationship to Combat and the Fortification of the Home Front in the Twentieth Century', in Nicole Ann Dombrowski, ed., *Women and War in the Twentieth Century* (Routledge, 2004), pp. 2–3; and Joanna Bourke, *An Intimate History of Killing: Face-to-Face Killing in Twentieth-Century Warfare* (Basic, 2000), especially chap. 10, 'Women Go to War.'

99 As Hitler's empire expanded: Women filled positions left vacant by men in 1944–45. In Vienna the Gestapo office had 180 female administrators, and in Berlin there were 600 women out of 1,500 associates. See Kompisch, *Täterinnen*, p. 85.

access to higher education: Many secondary schools were converted into military quarters and hospitals, but with young men on the front, women returned to the universities in greater numbers. Female enrolment sky-rocketed, reaching more than 50 per cent of the student body at the University of Frankfurt in 1943. A wartime hit comedy film, *Unser Fräulein Doktor* (1940), featured a wily, intelligent, university-educated woman who supplanted her lover, a medical doctor, in a twist of roles that emboldened women, not mocked them. See Christoph Dorner et al., *Die Braune Machtergreifung: Universität Frankfurt, 1930–1945* (Nexus/Druckladen, 1989), p. 96; and Dörr, '*Wer die Zeit nicht miterlebt hat . . .* ', p. 125.

Women secretaries, file clerks: The number of Reich Germans employed in the commissariat offices varied, but in the office in Lida, for example, there were eighty-six. In Baranowitsche's district office in September 1941 there were six German men on staff; by 20 January 1943, there were nineteen men and seven women (and from the local population ninety-five men and sixty-six women); on 24 June 1944, there were twenty-six men and ten women, plus four men in the German court with two female assistants, and three women (including two nurses) in the National Socialist Welfare Association. The *Gebietskommissar* for this district, Werner, brought his wife and four children to live with him in November 1942. See NARA, RG 242, T454, roll 102, Report by Gebietskommissar Hennig, Lida, 15 Aug. 1944; and Situation and Activity Report of Gebietskommissar Werner, Baranowitsche, 11 Aug. 1944.

100 'yellowhammers': *Goldammern* are described in Erika Summ's memoir, *Schäfers Tochter: Die Geschichte der Frontschwester* (Zeitgut Verlag, 2006), p. 130.

office work in the East: The commissar who would succeed Hermann Hanweg in Lida complained in the summer of 1944 that many women went east not to serve the Reich but to serve themselves. He contrasted the women there with those at home who had to clean and do their own laundry. Those in the East behaved like prima donnas with domestic servants and private dressing rooms. (He was referring here to the officials' female secretaries and wives.) Gebietskommissar Kennig, report of 15 Aug. 1944, NARA, RG 242, T454, roll 102, frame 000162.

a sinecure in the empire: Hanweg wanted to retain labourers for his building projects, to fulfil his imperial fantasies and personal demands. He was not as brutish as his deputy Windisch, but he also did not object to or impede the mass-murder operations. Hanweg interacted closely with 'his' Jewish labourers with some decency and appreciation for their work. For his relative leniency, Hanweg had to answer to complaints against him lodged by Windisch and the SS and police. NARA, RG 242, roll 21, frames 000580 and 000587, report of 29 Dec. 1942, Wilhelm Kube to Personnel Advisor to Rosenberg, and response to Kube, 15 Jan. 1943.

Hanweg's duty to make the region: In their testimony to the Central Committee of Liberated Jews in Munich in 1947, most survivors named Hanweg's deputy, Windisch, as the worst perpetrator in the Lida administration. Hanweg was identified as having been present at selections as well, but it was Windisch who took every opportunity to beat, shoot and humiliate Jews. Record Group M.21, War Criminals' Section, Legal Department at the Central Committee of Liberated Jews, File 184, 28 pp., YVA. I am grateful to Waitman Beorn for sharing archival references to Lida and Slonim testimonies.

101 'Vice-Mama': Statement of Eberhard Hanweg, 15 Oct. 1964, BAL, 162/3433. Hanweg testified in 1964 that he arrived in Lida with Meier in the spring of 1942, and shortly thereafter the massacre occurred. On the Nazi occupation of Lida, see Christian Gerlach, *Kalkulierte Morde: Die deutsche Wirtschafts- und Vernichtungskriegpolitik in Weissrussland 1941 bis 1944* (Hamburger Edition, 1999); Bernhard Chiari, *Alltag hinter der Front: Besatzung, Kollabouration und Widerstand in Weissrussland, 1941–1944* (Droste Verlag, 1998); and statement of Joachim L. (former 727th Infantry Regiment, in Lida), 7 May 1965, BAL, B162/3440.

Today the commissar's ring: Hanweg interview with author, 20 Sept. 2010, Langgoens, Germany; and see *Sefer Lida*, Lida Memorial Book, ed. Alexander Manor, Itzchak Ganusovitch and Aba Lando (Tel Aviv, 1970), p. 294. A similar case is documented in Buczacz, Ukraine. The *Landkommissar* brought his wife and three children. One son received a carved toy horse from a Jewish labourer, to the disapproval of the SS commander Otto Waechter, who asked him where he got the nice toy. B 162/1673, testimony of Henriette Bau, former wife of Richard Lissberg, 23 Apr. 1969. Thanks to Omer Bartov for sharing this source.

102 critical reports and investigations: See the *Schenk Bericht* on the behaviour of Reich Germans in the occupied territories (Galicia) of May 1943, located in ITS. This particular report was an attempt by the SS police to expose and weaken rivals in the civil administration, such as mayors, district officials and local developers. Such a power struggle may have led to exaggerated accounts of misconduct, but at the very least the report documents trends of corruption related to the Holocaust and the collusion of German women in the East. On the availability of foodstuffs in the East being shipped back to the Reich, see letters intercepted by the Abwehr about shipments in March and April 1943, and the Wehrmacht's critique of the black market and plundering, in ZSA, P1151-1-1, P1151-1-21. See also Götz Aly, *Hitler's Beneficiaries: Plunder, Racial War, and the Nazi Welfare State* (Picador, 2008); and Catherine Epstein, *Model Nazi: Arthur Greiser and the Occupation of Western Poland* (Oxford University Press, 2012), especially p. 269 (on Greiser's castle at Mariensee) and p. 276 (on his wine collection, valued at $300,000).

Operation (*Aktion*) Reinhardt: See Peter Black, 'Foot Soldiers of the Final Solution: The Trawniki Training Camp and Operation Reinhard', *Holocaust and Genocide Studies* 25, no. 1 (2011): 1–99; also by Peter Black, 'Odilo Globocnik – Himmler's Vorposten im Osten', in Ronald Smelser et al., eds, *Die Braune Elite* (Wissenschaftliche Buchgemeinschaft, 1993); and Dieter Pohl, 'Die Stellung des Distrikts Lublin in der "Endlösung der Judenfrage"', in Bogdan Musial, ed., *'Aktion Reinhardt': Der Völkermord an den Juden im Generalgouvernement 1941–1944* (Fibre Verlag, 2004).

secretaries 'cheerfully' prepared lists: Runhof statement to Wiesbaden court, 15 Sept. 1961, presented in Berndt Rieger, *Creator of Nazi Death Camps: The Life of Odilo Globocnik* (Vallentine Mitchell, 2007), pp. 72, 82. Hillmann was 'relieved' of her duties in Lublin, owing to a health issue and rumours of having Jewish ancestry. See Joseph Poprzeczny, *Odilo Globocnik, Hitler's Man in the East* (McFarland, 2004).

top managers, such as Globocnik: By the end of the summer of 1943, however, Globocnik fell out of favour with the Reichsführer because of his excessive behaviour. See Bogdan Musial, *Deutsche Zivilverwaltung und Judenverfolgung im Generalgouvernement* (Harrossowitz Verlag, 1999), pp. 201–8. See also David Silberklang, 'Only the Gates of Tears Were Not Locked: The Holocaust in the Lublin District of Poland' (forthcoming); and Peter R. Black, 'Rehearsal for "Reinhard"? Odilo Globocnik and the Lublin Selbstschutz', *Central European History* 25, no. 2 (1992): 204–26.

One day when Hanweg's son: The ghetto workshops were liquidated on 18 September 1943. Remaining Jewish labourers were deported to the gassing facility of Sobibor and the Majdanek camp. Hanweg's son, who was gone from Lida before September 1943, must have recollected an earlier massacre. See statement of Eberhard Hanweg, 15 Oct. 1964, BAL, 162/3433, and in interview with author, 31 July 2010.

first and largest massacre: During the first two weeks of May 1942, especially 5–12 May several massacres occurred in the Lida region (Radun, Woronowo, Szczuczyn) in which more than twenty thousand Jews were shot. See survivor testimony (Churban Wilno), German report of the General Commissar Weissruthenian (month illegible, but not earlier than 29 July 1942) on 'Partisan Warfare and Jewish Actions', excerpts of the Soviet investigation, and grave exhumations of September 1947 in ITS, Doc No. 82176805 #1 (1.2.7.6/0007/1383/0233, Archivnummer 3090). In 1962 testimony, the survivor Sioma Pupko refers to Hanweg and Meier as 'Hanenberg along with his girlfriend Merkel, a sadistic person'. Quoted in *Sefer Lida*, Lida Memorial Book, translated at http://www.jewishgen.org/Yizkor/lida/lid307.html#Page311. The massacre on 8 May was carried out by former members of Einsatzkommando 9 (based in the SD office in Baranowitsche) and native auxiliaries. Also see *The Yad Vashem Encyclopedia of the Ghettos during the Holocaust* (Yad Vashem, 2009), vol. 1, *Lida*, pp. 396–97. The local auxiliaries might have been Lithuanian, Polish, Belarusian or Latvian; the testimony on nationality is inconsistent. See Wolfgang Curilla, *Die deutsche Ordnungspolizei und der Holocaust im Baltikum und in Weissrussland* (Ferdinand Schöningh, 2006), pp. 885–86. Three hundred Jews survived the war in

Lida. Many who escaped to the forests joined the Bielski partisans, a resistance force recently featured in the film *Defiance,* which is based on the work of Nechama Tec, *Defiance: The Bielski Partisans* (Oxford, 1994).

103 'better informed . . .': Statement of Johanna Luise Zietlow, 9 Oct. 1964, BAL, 162/3433.

A certified bookkeeper: Liselotte Meier Lerm, statement of 19 Sept. 1963, BAL, 162/3425, and statement of 5 Sept. 1966, BAL, 162/3450. Lerm explained in the statement of 19 Sept. 1963 that the last time she saw Altmann was in the autumn of 1943, when the ghetto was liquidated. Hanweg's son remembered Tenenbaum, who is also mentioned in Lerm's testimony.

'Commissariat officials . . .': *Sefer Lida,* Lida Memorial Book, p. 294. The female exploitation of Jewish labourers for personal items was investigated by the Sipo SD Lettland, in a case concerning a local leather factory where several women were connected with the Gebietskommissariat Schaulen. KdS Lettland, Ermittlungsverfarhen betr Lederwerk in Schaulen, 10 Jan. 1943, NARA, RG 242, T454, roll 15.

constructing a swimming pool: Liselotte Meier Lerm, statements of 19 Sept. 1963, 6 Oct. 1964 and 6 Sept. 1966, BAL, 162/3425. Thanks to Waitman Beorn for bringing Lerm to my attention.

104 'eastern rush': *Ostrausch,* 'intoxication with the East', as a spatial-colonial high rather than a sexual one, is treated in Elizabeth Harvey, *Women and the Nazi East: Agents and Witnesses of Germanisation* (Yale University Press, 2003), p. 125.

sex and violence: Non-German women who were raped were often killed by German men who wished to conceal the crime of racial mixing. Testimony of Erna Leonhard, 14 Dec. 1960, BAL, 162/1682. Testimony of Frau Ingeborg Gruber (b. 1922), Mannheim, 11 Oct. 1960, BAK, 9 Js 716/59. Grihory Denisenko, ZSA, interview by author, 11 Aug. 1993, Zhytomyr, Ukraine. Also see Abschlussbericht, Becker Case, BAL, 204 AR-Z 129/67, 1023; and Dagmar Herzog, ed., *Brutality and Desire: War and Sexuality in Europe's Twentieth Century* (Palgrave Macmillan, 2011). On the intertwining of male brain circuits that control sexual and violent behaviour, see *Scientific American,* 'Sex and Violence Linked in the Brain', February 2011. The co-occurrence of raping and killing of Jewish women by German men has been documented, but how widespread this phenomenon was is unclear because the Nazi authorities prosecuted Germans for racial mixing, and Jewish victims and witnesses were mostly killed. To protect privacy and honour, Jewish female survivors were reluctant to speak about this type of assault. A Jewish survivor who lived in Vienna, Julie Sebek, was questioned in several cases about crimes in Minsk. She had been sent in May 1942 to Minsk and Trostenets. She mentioned incidents of Jewish women who were raped and then killed (20 Mar. 1962, BAK, Sta, 9 Js 716/59). See Sonja M. Hedgepeth and Rochelle G. Saidel, eds, *Sexual Violence against Jewish Women during the Holocaust* (Brandeis University Press, 2010); and John Roth and Carole Rittner, eds, *Rape: Weapon of War and Genocide* (Paragon, 2012).

He gave Meier special access: Liselotte Meier Lerm, statement of 6 Sept. 1966, BAL, 162/3450. The personal secretary of Arthur Greiser, Elsa Claassen, was the only one besides Greiser who had special access to the safe where top-secret Reich orders and correspondence were kept. See Epstein, *Model Nazi*, p. 142.

commissar and his staff had the authority: 'Die Zivilverwaltung in den besetzten Ostgebieten, Teil II: Reichskommissariat Ukraine' (Brown File), Osobyi Moscow 7021-148-183.

105 'had not finished knitting . . .': Frau Emilie Horst, another secretary at the local sawmill, statement of 10 May 1961, BAL, 162/5088.

'On one Sunday . . .': Quoted in the chapter 'Life in the Lida Ghetto', p. 289, by D. S. Amarant, translated by Don Goldman, in *Sefer Lida*, Lida Memorial Book, http://www.jewishgen.org/yizkor/lida/lida.html. The incident is also described by Elise Barzach (b. 1913), Interview 1995, Sydney, Australia (interviewer Anna Friedlander), SFA. Likewise, the district captain in Tarnopol and Rawa Ruska, Gerhard Hager, was described as a corrupt philanderer in a critical SS report (in large part a smear campaign against rivals in the civilian government), who took his ladies on boar hunts and showered them with gifts that were stolen Jewish belongings. See *Schenk Bericht* on corruption in Galicia, Verhalten der Reichsdeutschen in den besetzten Gebieten, 14 May 1943. The full report is at ITS; several pages are missing from the copy in BAK, R58/1002. See also the photo album and testimonies on Lida massacres, LAS, Bestand J76, Nr. 569.

107 'Trees saved us': Elise Barzach, Interview 1995, Sydney, Australia (interviewer Anna Friedlander), Title 4, SFA. Barzach also described the mistress of one of Hanweg's deputies, who was present when the deputy, named Werner, killed Jews. Thanks to staff of the USHMM for providing a copy of this interview.

Lida's Jews would reappear: Liselotte Meier Lerm, statement of 6 Sept. 1966, BAL, 162/3450. The Germans in town (Meier, Hanweg, Windisch, Werner) were with other German visitors when they came upon the shovelling Jews. See interrogation of Meier, 19 Sept. 1963, BAL, 162/3425.

Historians of the Holocaust: Hilary Earl, *The Nuremberg SS-Einsatzgruppen Trial, 1945–1958: Atrocity, Law, and History* (Cambridge University Press, 2010). Interview with former prosecutor of the Einsatzgruppen Trial, Benjamin Ferencz and his wife, Gertrude Ferencz, conducted with author, Nicole Dombrowski, and Linda Bishai. New Rochelle, NY, 15 Oct. 2005.

at least thirteen: Gudrun Schwarz, 'Verdrängte Täterinnen: Frauen im Apparat der SS, 1939–1945', in Theresa Wobbe, ed., *Nach Osten: Verdeckte Spuren national-sozialistischer Verbrechen* (Verlag Neue Kritik, 1992), p. 207. For years after the war, Gestapo chief Heinrich Mueller's secretary Barbara Hellmuth was questioned by West German and American authorities hunting for Mueller. Hellmuth appears in the recently declassified CIA name files: http://www.archives.gov/iwg/declassified-records/rg-263-cia-records/rg-263-mueller.html. Mueller's mistress Anna Schmid was also questioned. See Richard Breitman, Norman Goda, Tim Naftali and Robert Wolfe, *U.S. Intelligence and the Nazis* (Cambridge University Press, 2005, p. 150). The wife of Wily Suchanek, SS adjutant of Himmler, who herself served as Himmler's secretary, was pursued after the war as a witness. See Simon Wiesenthal correspondence regarding investigation of SS Officer Horst Bender, 2 Jan. 1975, SWA.

thousands of pages of such reports: On the reports, see Ronald Headland, *Messages of Murder: A Study of the Reports of the Einsatzgruppen of the Security Police and the Security Service, 1941–1943* (Fairleigh Dickinson University Press, 1992).

108 Himmler realised: Himmler speech at Poznań, 4 Oct. 1943, full text with appeal for SS female auxiliaries, http://www.nizkor.org/hweb/people/h/himmler-heinrich/posen/oct-04-43/. The SS school for women was intended for those who experienced 'an awakening of their sense of honour'. By the end of the war, about three thousand women, one-quarter of the applicants, were accepted into auxiliary and command positions. See SS Obersturmbannführer, Commander of the SS Helferinnenschule, Dr Mutschler, on applicant Dorothea Seebeck (b. 1925), Prüfung, Dienstleistungzeugnis and Verhandlung, 19 Feb. 1945, NARA, RG 242, BDC, Misc. recs., DRK personnel files, A 3345-SF B021, 130, 156. For more on the training and assignments of the graduates, see Jutta Mühlenberg, *Das SS Helferinnenkorps: Ausbildung Einsatz und Entnazifizierung der weiblichen Angehörigen der Waffen-SS 1942–1949* (Hamburger Edition, 2011), p. 264.

109 'women's camp must be . . .': Langefeld complained about the encroachments of SS men Aumeier and Mulka. Himmler sided with her. See Peter Witte et al., eds, *Der Dienstkalender Heinrich Himmlers 1941/42* (Christians Verlag, 1999), entry of 18 July 1942, p. 483; and the biography of Langefeld by Irmtraud Heike, 'Johannes Langefeld: Die Biographie einer KZ-Oberaufseherin', in *Werkstatt Geschichte* 12 (1995): 7–19.

'In the hallway . . .': Quoted in Thomas Kühne, *Belonging and Genocide: Hitler's Community, 1918–1945* (Yale University Press, 2010), p. 149.

110 'hold down the fort' and 'Look, here is a drop . . .': Helene Dowlad, Euskirchen, 21 Apr. 1966, BAL, B162/2110, fol. 1, copy provided by Marie Moutier, Yahad in Unum. Also see testimony of Maria Koschinska Sprenger, 20 Apr. 1966, BAL, 162/3446. On the Holocaust in Tarnopol, from the perspective of a Jewish woman who was murdered there in 1943, see 'Briefe einer unbekannten Jüdin an ihre Familie (geschrieben kurz vor ihrer Hinrichtung, 1943)', Tarnopol, 7 Apr. and 26 Apr. 1943, ed. Kerrin Gräfin von Schwerin, *Frauen im Krieg: Briefe, Dokumente, Aufzeichnungen* (Nicolai Verlag, 1999), pp. 127–30. There was a similar piece of testimony from a German secretary in Minsk confronted by a shooter after an action with a finger in a splint, explaining a mass shooting in Maly Trostenets in 1943. The SS first lieutenant also invited the secretary to the execution site, since he thought that she might like to pick through the clothing. Testimony of Frau Ingeborg Gruber (b. 1922), Mannheim, 11 Oct. 1960, BAK, Js 716/59.

She was looking to advance: In addition to the women featured here, Birgit Classen (b. 1921) was working in the Nazi Party's Association of Lawyers, and heard through a relative of Wilhelm Kube that there were good opportunities in the East. She arrived in August 1941 in Belarus, with a group of six to seven other women, assigned to General Commissar Kube's office in Minsk, and was questioned in Heuser case, 20 Nov. 1959, BAK, Staatsanwalt, file 9, Js 716/59.

'Sabine, quickly write this up!': Sabine Dick testimony, 27–29 Apr. 1960, BAL, 162/5183; 14 Dec. 1960, BAL, 162/1682. Thanks to Stephan Lehnstädt, Jürgen Matthäus and Andrej Angrick for bringing this testimony to my attention. Erna Leonhard testified against Heuser, explaining that people in the office spoke about Heuser going into the ghetto with his pistol at night, running around shooting, terrifying the Jews, who walled themselves up in fear. Statement of 14 Dec. 1960, BAL, 162/1682.

111 'sought our company': Erna Leonhard testimony (14 Dec. 1960) also referred to ten other German women working in the Sipo-SD office in Minsk. Leonhard typed interrogation reports into the night, and she attended the interrogations of Jews.

decisions on the spot: Witte et al., *Der Dienstkalender Heinrich Himmlers*, 15 Aug. 1941. On Himmler decision-making, see Wendy Lower, '"Anticipatory Obedience" and the Nazi Implementation of the Holocaust in the Ukraine: A Case Study of Central and Peripheral Forces in the Generalbezirk Zhytomyr, 1941–1944', *Holocaust and Genocide Studies* 16, no. 1 (Spring 2002): 1–22.

112 who slept in the basement: Testimony of Ingeborg Gruber, Mannheim, 11 Oct. 1960, BAK, Sta, 9 Js 716/59, B162/1682.

*Judenwurst:* Testimony of Erna Leonhard, 14 Dec. 1960, BAL, 162/1682.

wanted more than Jewish food: The episode described in this paragraph relies on Sabine Dick testimony, 27–29 Apr. 1960, BAL, 162/1583. Leonhard also described the property depot at Gut Trostenets, statement of 14 Dec. 1960, BAL, 162/1682.

113 high concentrations of ethnic Germans: A series of articles appeared in July 1942 about the ethnic German celebrations in Zhytomyr surrounding the building of the kindergarten. *Deutsche Ukraine-Zeitung* (Luzk), 1 July, 2 July, 5 July, and 9 July 1942, all on p. 3, Library of Congress Newspaper Collection. See 'Vermerk', 9 June 1942; 'Einweisung von 14 Kindergärtnerinnen zur Betreuung Volksdeutscher in der Ukraine', 21 July 1942; and 'Lagebericht', NSV, 29 Sept. 1942, Zhytomyr – all CSA, 3206-6-255, microfilm held at USHMMA, RG 31.002M, reel 6. On 16 December 1942, commissars announced that schooling was mandatory for ethnic German children. *Deutsche Ukraine Zeitung* (Luzk), 16 Dec. 1942, p. 3.

They taught ethnic Germans: This file on educational materials for German youth in the East is undated; it is probably from late 1942 or early 1943. ZSA P1151-1-139. See Koch memo to general commissars about educating *Volksdeutsche* about racial crimes and punishment vis-à-vis the Jews. 13 May 1942, ZSA, P1151-1-120. Hoffmeyer report, 12 Oct. 1941, NARA, RG 242, T454, roll 100, frames 000661–670. See the NSV report of 11–12 June 1942 and RmfdbO report of 15 June 1942, CSA, 3206-6-255, microfilm held at USHMMA, RG 31.002M, reel 6. Irma Wildhagen and her staff of nurses set up infant-mother stations in Cherniakhiv, Novgorod Volynsk, Andreyiv, Horoshkyn and Sadki. See the overview of NSV staff dated 11 Aug. 1942. CSA, 3206-6-255, microfilm held at USHMMA, RG 31.002M, reel 6.

114 wives of SS men: On Greiser's wife, see Epstein, *Model Nazi*, pp. 64–66, 70.

Vera Wohlauf: Schwarz, *Eine Frau an seiner Seite*, pp. 191–94; and Christopher R. Browning, *Ordinary Men: Reserve Police Battalion 101 and the Final Solution in*

*Poland* (HarperCollins, 1993), pp. 91–94. The German perpetrators were from platoons of the first, second and third companies of the Order Police Battalion 101, a unit of Hiwis, and the Radzyń Security Police.

116 Two months before the massacre: Wohlauf's marriage application, NARA, BDC, A3343-RS-G5348, frames 2214–2326. One child is listed in Julius Wohlauf's personnel file, born 6.2.43, NARA, BDC, A3343 SSO 006C, frame 1182. See Daniel Jonah Goldhagen, *Hitler's Willing Executioners: Ordinary Germans and the Holocaust* (Knopf, 1996), pp. 241–42.

'before a rather large gathering . . .': Goldhagen, *Hitler's Willing Executioners,* pp. 244, 558 nn. 9, 12, 16.

'outrageous that women . . .': Statement of the wife of Lieutenant Brand; quoted in Goldhagen, *Hitler's Willing Executioners,* p. 243.

Embodying the home front: The research of Claudia Koonz and Gitta Sereny, among others, established that male perpetrators returned from killing centres and concentration camps to nurturing wives and lovers who eased their conscience and in some cases incited their husbands to commit more crimes. When the commandant of Treblinka and Sobibor was asked how he endured the daily strain of running a mass-murder factory, he replied, 'I don't know. My wife. Perhaps my love for my wife'. Gitta Sereny, *Into That Darkness: An Examination of Conscience* (Vintage, 1983), p. 348; on Frau Stangl, pp. 210–11, 361–62.

117 so reasoned a Nazi perpetrator: Steven K. Baum, *The Psychology of Genocide: Perpetrators, Bystanders, and Rescuers* (Cambridge University Press, 2008), pp. 131–32.

liquidation at Hrubieszow: Schwarz, *Eine Frau an seiner Seite,* p. 189.

## 5. PERPETRATORS

120 All of this was done: Henry Friedlander, *The Origins of Nazi Genocide: From Euthanasia to the Final Solution* (University of North Carolina Press, 1997), pp. 4, 54, 231–32; and Michael Burleigh, *Death and Deliverance: 'Euthanasia' in Germany, 1900–1945* (Cambridge University Press, 1994). See also the USHMM *Deadly Medicine* online exhibition: http://www.ushmm.org/wlc/article 'euthanasia' Programme.

121 physicians and midwives: On midwives, see Wiebke Lisner, '"Mutter der Mütter – Mütter des Volkes"? Hebammen im Nationalsozialismus', in Marita Krauss, ed., *Sie waren dabei: Mitläuferinnen, Nutzniesserinnen, Täterinnen im Nationalsozialismus* (Wallstein Verlag, 2008).

shootings of Polish psychiatric patients: Richard Evans, *The Third Reich at War* (Penguin, 2010), pp. 75–76.

122 asylums at Grafeneck and Hadamar: Interrogation summaries of nurses and office personnel at Hadamar (Irmgard Huber, Margarete Borkowski, Lydia Thomas, Agnes Schrankel, Isabella Weimer, Judith Thomas, Paula Siegert, Johanna Schrettinger, Hildegard Ruetzel, Elfriede Haefner, Elisabeth Utry, Ingeborg Seidel, Margot Schmidt, Christel Zielke, Lina Gerst), in trials against Wahlmann, Gorgass et al., OLG Frankfurt am Main, SS 10.48, 188/48. B162/28348 fol. 1, Urteil, 68–98. Experienced euthanasia nurse and early Nazi Party member Maria Appinger was also

sent to Minsk for five months in the first part of 1942; see Friedlander, *The Origins of Nazi Genocide*, p. 235.

'relieved the suffering' of German soldiers: Burleigh, *Death and Deliverance*. Bishop von Galen had suspected this would happen; on 3 August 1941, in his famous speech in Münster denouncing euthanasia, he warned that 'it will require only a secret order to be issued that the procedure which has been tried and tested with the mentally ill should be extended to other "unproductive" persons, that it should also be applied to those suffering from incurable tuberculosis, the aged and infirm, persons disabled in industry, soldiers with disabling injuries!'

123 Those killed were 'our own': Pauline Kneissler's public statement about deployment to Minsk, reprinted in Ulrike Gaida, *Zwischen Pflegen und Töten: Krankenschwestern im Nationalsozialismus* (Mabuse Verlag, 2006), p. 176. Kneissler had been transferred to several facilities to introduce lethal procedures and expand the killing. Promoted to deputy senior nurse, Kneissler could order others to kill and administer deadly doses of sedatives, such as Vernal and Luminal. According to Kneissler, each day about seventy-five patients died in her ward. When her boss asked her if she was ready to murder without his guidance and supervision, she responded that she could, and had done so already. See Burleigh, *Death and Deliverance*, p. 254. Georg Lilienthal's research on biographies of Hadamar perpetrators focuses in part on a medical aide Lydia Thomas, whose story follows the same outlines as that of Pauline Kneissler, with deployment to the East in early 1942, and provides confirmation of gassings of German civilians injured in bombing raids and wounded Wehrmacht and SS soldiers. See Georg Lilienthal, 'Personal einer Tötungsanstalt. Acht biographische Skizzen', in Uta George et al., *Hadamar: Heilstätte, Tötungsanstalt, Therapienzentrum* (Jonas Verlag, 2006), p. 286. See also Ernst Klee, *Euthanasie (NS-Staat): Die 'Vernichtung lebensunwerten Lebens'* (Fischer Taschenbuch 1983), pp. 372–73; Burleigh, *Death and Deliverance*, pp. 231–32; and Friedlander, *The Origins of Nazi Genocide*, pp. 153, 160, 296–97.

124 an asylum in Meseritz-Obrawalde: Susan Benedict and Tessa Chelouche, 'Meseritz-Obrawalde: A "Wild Euthanasia" Hospital of Nazi Germany', *History of Psychiatry* 19 (1): 68–76; Bronwyn Rebekah McFarland-Icke, *Nurses in Nazi Germany: Moral Choice in History* (Princeton University Press, 1999), p. 214. One of the chief doctors at Meseritz-Obrawalde was a woman, Dr Hilde Wernicke. Additional sites in Poland were the former Bernardine Monastery at Koscian, about thirty miles from Poznań, and Tiegenhof or Dziekanka in the Warthegau.

'a place of immense misery': Quoted in Benedict and Chelouche, p. 71. See also Claudia Koonz, *The Nazi Conscience* (Harvard University Press, 2005) and Friedlander, *The Origins of Nazi Genocide*, p. 153.

'caused extra work . . .'. and 'who had fled . . .': Indictment text quoted in Friedlander, *The Origins of Nazi Genocide*, p. 160.

it took at least two nurses: Testimony of nurse Anna Gastler, reprinted in Gaida, *Zwischen Pflegen und Töten*, p. 170.

125 A county seat: Material in this section relies on *Der Generalbezirk Wolhynien, Der Reichsminister für die besetzten Ostgebiete, Hauptabteilung I, Raumplanung*, 5 Dec.

1941, 9, 30; and Yitzhak Arad, Shmuel Krakowski and Shmuel Spector, eds, *The Einsatzgruppen Reports: Selections from the Dispatches of the Nazi Death Squads' Campaign Against the Jews in the Occupied Territories of the Soviet Union, July 1941– Jan 1943* (Holocaust Library, 1989), Report #24, 16 July 1941.

'gimlet-eyed runt': Statement of Karl Wetzle, Oberhausen, 21 June 1963, BAL, 162/4522 fol. 1, II, 204 AR-Z 40/1961.

126  the 'dead' one: Statement of Moses Messer, date unclear, corroborated by Arie Go-mulka, 3 May 1964, Haifa. The testimonies were mostly given to the Untersuchun-gsstelle für NS-Gewaltverbrechen beim Landesstab der Polizei, Israel. Originals are deposited at BAL, B162/4522, fol. 1, II, 204 AR-Z 40/1961. Many of the testimonies were published earlier in the memorial book *Pinkas Ludmir: Sefer-zikaron li-kehilat Ludmir* (Tel Aviv, 1962).

'Such sadism ...': Statement of Moses Messer, date unclear, corroborated by Arie Go-mulka, 3 May 1964, Haifa.

127  'like a cattle herder': Testimony of Kurt Bettins, who from September 1941 to April 1943 was the chief of the POW camp in Volodymyr-Volynsky, reprinted in *Die Tat*, 27 Oct. 1978. Press clippings file, trial records, BAL, II, 204 AR-Z 40/61, Band II.

'nasty habit': Arie Gomulka, 3 May 1964, Haifa, BAL, B162/4522, fol. 1.

'did not think highly ...': Statement of Erna Schirbel Michels, 12 June 1968, p. 434, BAL, B162/4523, fol. 1. See Judith Halberstam, *Female Masculinity* (Duke University Press, 1998).

128  farmers who were working: Banquet scene in Piatydny, testimony of Josef Opa-towski, p. 7, Jewish Historical Institute, Warsaw, ZIH 301/2014. I am grateful to Ray Brandon for providing this document. Other witnesses in Ukraine have described the banquet-table scene at other mass shootings. See *The Holocaust by Bullets: The Mass Shooting of Jews in Ukraine, 1941–1944,* Exhibition Catalogue, Fondation pour la Mémoire de la Shoah and Yahad in Unum, p. 44.

'Polish woman ...': Ginsburg was born in 1932, in the nearby town of Maciejow. Thanks to his daughter Suzanne Ginsburg for providing the memoir *Noike: A Mem-oir of Leon Ginsburg,* 2011 (see pp. 120–21). See also Martin Dean, ed., *Encyclopedia of Ghettos and Camps,* vol. 2, *Ghettos in German-Occupied Eastern Europe* (Indiana University Press, 2011); and Shmuel Spector, *The Holocaust of Volhynian Jews, 1941– 1944* (Yad Vashem, 1990), pp. 127, 145, 186. There was a smaller ghetto in the nearby town of Ustilug. Spector's account of the ghetto is derived from testimonies pub-lished in the Volodymyr-Volynsky Memorial Book.

129  'wooded area ...': Dieter Pohl, 'The Murder of Ukraine's Jews under German Mili-tary Administration and in the Reich Commissariat Ukraine', in Ray Brandon and Wendy Lower, eds, *The Shoah in Ukraine: History, Testimony, Memorialisation* (In-diana University Press, 2008), pp. 50, 52, 58.

132  Petris led their visitors: Horst Petri recalled the date of the visit as the autumn of 1943; Erna dated it to the summer of 1943. However, the SS official, Fritz Katzmann, had been assigned to Danzig–West Prussia by the end of April of that year. In the Grzenda guest book, Hilde Katzmann expressed gratitude for an afternoon visit

on 3 November 1942, and a similar signature appears for a visit of 29 March 1943. Horst interrogation of 8 Sept. 1961; Erna interrogation of 15 Sept. 1961. File archive no. 403/63, BStU Aussenstelle Erfurt, fol. 2 Untersuchungsvorgang, 000131, Stasi Archive, BAB. On Katzmann's role in the Holocaust in Galicia, see Dieter Pohl, *Nationalsozialistische Judenverfolgung in Ostgalizien, 1941–1944: Organisation und Durchführung eines staatlichen Massenverbrechens* (Oldenbourg, 1996). In the famous 'Katzmann report' of 30 June 1943 presented at the Nuremberg trials (Nuremberg material, USA Exhibit 277, Document L-18), Katzmann detailed the ghettoisation, murder, forced labour, and property theft carried out against the 434,329 Jews in the region. Katzmann was not captured after the war and is believed to have died in 1957.

As the women walked away: Erna Petri, first interrogation, 25 Aug. 1961, File archive no. 403/63, BSTu aussenstelle Erfurt, fol 2 Untersuchungsvorgang, 000131. Stasi Archive, BAB.

'these were the children . . .': Interrogation of Erna Petri, 19 Sept. 1961, pp. 1–7. Horst and Erna P. Trial, BAB, BStU 000050–57; USHMMA, RG 14.068, fiche 566. Also see Wendy Lower, 'Male and Female Holocaust Perpetrators and the East German Approach to Justice, 1949–1963', *Holocaust and Genocide Studies* 24, no. 1 (Spring 2010): 56–84, where some of this material on Erna Petri was published. I thank Oxford University Press and the US Holocaust Memorial Museum for permission to use passages (in altered form) from that article.

134 'bloodthirsty camp commandant': Recollection of Stepan Yakimovich Shenfeld, 1943, quoted in Joshua Rubenstein and Ilya Altman, *The Unknown Black Book: The Holocaust in the German-Occupied Soviet Territories* (Indiana University Press, 2010), p. 91.

'natural-born killer' and 'chaff cutter': Excerpted testimony, BAL, Indictment Lemberg Trial, p. 273; USHMMA, RG 17.003m, reel 98, included in the preliminary Austrian investigation of Karl Kempka. Indictment of Hansberg, formerly Willhaus, BAL, 162/4688, 208 AR-Z 294/59. The Lemberg Prozess, April 1968, BAL, 162/2096, 274.

'the sport of it . . .': Philip Friedman, *Roads to Extinction: Essays on the Holocaust* (Jewish Publication Society, 1980), p. 311. One account has Heike also shooting at 'Jewish targets' with a pistol supplied by her parents as a birthday gift. Eliyahu Yones, *Smoke in the Sand: The Jews of Lvov in the War Years, 1939–1944* Gefen House, 2004.

135 labourers in the garden: Similar balcony shootings occurred not far away at the Jaktorow camp and in the Plaszow camp near Cracow. Author interview with Gisela Gross, 3 Nov. 2005, Baltimore.

136 'marriage markets': There are numerous examples of SS men who married or had office relationships with their secretaries, including the Reichsführer Heinrich Himmler himself, whose 'second wife' was his assistant Hedwig Potthast; Gestapo chief Heinrich Mueller and his secretary Barbara Hellmuth; general of the Waffen-SS Jochen Peiper and his secretary Sigrid Hinrichsen; Alois Brunner and his aide Anni Roeder. In these cases and many more, the separation of private and public spheres

was not so clear-cut. See Gudrun Schwarz, *Eine Frau an seiner Seite: Ehefrauen in der 'SS-Sippengemeinschaft'* (Hamburger Edition, 1997), pp. 201–2.

The children of the new elite: As the Hanweg case shows, children became embroiled in the Holocaust. In a number of cases they were brought to the workshops and inter-acted with Jewish labourers, who were then killed. See Nicholas Stargardt, *Witnesses of War: Children's Lives under the Nazis* (Random House, 2005). See also Schwarz, *Eine Frau an seiner Seite*, pp. 219–21, for the case of an SS father, Hermann Blache, who brought his son to the Tarnów ghetto for target shooting.

child-rearing, femininity and pleasure: On the sexual revolution, see Dagmar Herzog, *Sex after Fascism: Memory and Morality in Twentieth-Century Germany* (Princeton University Press, 2005).

137 'his lovely bunny': Landau, in Walter Kempowski, *Das Echolot: Ein kollektives Tage-buch, Barbarossa 1941* (btb Verlag, 2002), pp. 215, 243, 261, 282, 297, 714. Landau's entries are corroborated by official reports of Einsatzgrupppe C. Ereignismeldung UdSSR Nr. 21, 13 July 1941. Excerpts of original diary are held in the Staatsarchiv Ludwigsburg, reference E1 317 III Bue 1103–1113. Excerpted copies of the diary are in investigation files BAL 162/22380. Passages of the 13 July entry are excerpted and translated in Ernst Klee, Willi Dressen and Volker Riess, eds, *'The Good Old Days': The Holocaust as Seen by Its Perpetrators and Bystanders* (Konecky & Konecky, 1991), pp. 97–98.

Drohobych: Omer Bartov, *Erased: Vanishing Traces of Jewish Galicia in Present-Day Ukraine* (Princeton University Press, 2007), pp. 50–60.

138 beautiful, fanciful paintings: In recent years the murals were at the centre of an inter-national scandal and diplomatic crisis when the Ukrainian government objected to the murals' removal to Israel, where they are displayed at Yad Vashem, Israel's official Holocaust memorial and museum.

had a balcony on their villa: Schwarz, *Eine Frau an seiner Seite,* pp. 201–9.

testimony of a Jewish witness: Chaim Patrich, 3 July 1947 and 6 Sept. 1947, VCA, Po-lizeidirektion Vienna, People's Court investigation, Vg 3b Vr 7658/47.

reclined on upholstered chairs: Austrians referred to this chair as a 'Canadian', a modish design in the 1930s. Gertrude Landau, statement of 27 Feb. 1948, VCA, Po-lizeidirektion Vienna, People's Court investigation, Vg 3b Vr 7658/47.

working in the garden below: Gertrude Landau, statement of 29 May 1947, VCA, Po-lizeidirektion Vienna, People's Court investigation, Vg 3b Vr 7658/47.

started to shoot pigeons: Gertrude Landau, 2 June and 17 June 1947 additions to statement of 29 May 1947, VCA, Polizeidirektion Vienna, People's Court investiga-tion, Vg 3b Vr 7658/47.

largest was in November 1942: 'Jew General' Indictment of Landau, 20 Apr. 1961, 14 Js 3808/58, BAL 162/3380. It was not long after this massacre that Landau's colleague shot Bruno Schulz on the streets of Drohobych.

139 'Don't be such an idiot . . .': Quoted in Schwarz, *Eine Frau an seiner Seite,* p. 204.'

trampled a Jewish child: See the Judgement of the Stuttgart Court from 16 Mar. 1962, published in *Justiz und NS-Verbrechen*, vol. 18, pp. 364–65.

140 'I will help you!': Statement of Josefine Block, 18 May 1948, VCA, Vg 8514/46.

Indictment, 3 March 1949, 15 St 1617/49. In 1946 she had a five-year-old and a three-year-old. Thus in 1942–43, at the time of her killing sprees, she had a toddler and an infant, or was pregnant with the second.

Desperate Jewish labourers: One victim was able to flee. The three who were killed were identified as Vera Zuckermann, Dora Sternbach and Paula Winkler (witness statements of Katz, Fischer and Weidemann). On the pleasure Block and her husband both derived from abusing Jews in random encounters, see courtroom testimony of Regina Fritz, 12 Dec. 1946, and statement of Weiss, 19 Feb. 1947, Vg 8514/46, Investigation and Trial of Josefine Block (b. 1910), 19 Nov. 1946, VCA, Polizeidirektion Wien an Staatsanwaltschaft Wien; Stadtarchiv Wien.

witnesses would later state: Statements of Fischer, 3 Oct. 1946, and Katz, VCA, Polizeidirektion Vienna, 21 Sept. 1946, and Katz, 12 Dec. 1946, Vg 8514/46.

could not make any decisions: Statements of Fischer, 16 Dec. 1946, and Dengg, 17 Jan. 1947, VCA, Vg 8514/46.

141 approached fellow Germans: Heinrich Barth testimony of 2 Mar. 1977, BAL, 76-K 41676-Koe. Wetzle testimony on Westerheide 'invitation' to shoot Jews: Karl Wetzle, Statement, Oberhausen 21 June 1963, BAL, LKA-NW, B162/4522 fol. 1, II, 204 AR-Z 40/1961.

As 'packers' . . . as 'hemp collectors': Father Patrick Desbois, *The Holocaust by Bullets* (Macmillan, 2008).

Crime scenes included: In Riga, an ethnic German female translator attended one of these 'funeral banquets' and recalled people raising their schnapps glasses, toasting to the death of the Jews. A Latvian police chief summoned everyone – 'Ladies and gentlemen, now it is time' – and all were led about 150 yards from the banquet hall to a fresh grave that had been dug, about fifteen yards long and two yards wide. Ten Jews stood by the grave, stripped to their underwear; another ten were in the pit moaning. The Latvian ordered his unit to shoot; he also placed a pistol in the hands of one woman and told her to try, aiming for the Jews. Regular German soldiers who were also there did not shoot, and complained that this scene was a mess. They returned to the banquet, which lasted until dawn. Violetta Liber, BAL, B162/8978, interrogation of 16 Feb. 1972, Riga. Thanks to Martin Dean for sharing this source.

### 6. WHY DID THEY KILL?

145 One young schoolteacher: Eugenie S. on Chernihiv school, in Rosemarie Killius, ed., *Frauen für die Front: Gespräche mit Wehrmachtshelferinnen* (Militzke Verlag, 2003), pp. 59–60.

146 The entire staff: Erika Summ, *Schäfers Tochter: Die Geschichte der Frontschwester* (Zeitgut Verlag, 2006), p. 144.

'transported away': Summ, *Schäfers Tochter*, p. 153.

147 dead children on the hooks: Summ, *Schäfers Tochter*, pp. 165–66. Erika Ohr married one of her patients, a German soldier who had lost his legs in the war. After the war, Summ (as she was now called) worked as a nurse in Sindelfingen and Marbach and then had children. Five or six times she met up with other nurses from the war at re-

unions in southern Germany. Summ relied on her faith to cope with what she had witnessed and done during the war. She tended to look forward; until her ninetieth birthday, one of her mottos was 'Es muss weitergehen' (Life must go on). She focused on small pleasures and trained herself to suppress bigger fantasies and ambitions. Author telephone interview with Summ's daughter, 4 Aug. 2011.

'For the last time . . .': Proclamation of Adolf Hitler, 15 Apr. 1945, published in German newspapers. Quoted in Ian Kershaw, *Hitler: Nemesis, 1936–1945* (W. W. Norton, 2000), p. 793.

148 women who were raped: Estimates of rapes vary in part because victims were raped repeatedly and because many were killed or committed suicide afterwards (ten thousand died in Berlin alone). French troops committed mass rapes in south-western Germany. There were also cases among American soldiers, and to a lesser degree within the British Army. See Richard Evans, *The Third Reich at War* (Penguin, 2010); Michael Kater, *Hitler Youth* (Harvard University Press, 2004), p. 241; and Norman M. Naimark, *The Russians in Germany: A History of the Soviet Zone of Occupation, 1945–1949* (Harvard University Press, 1995). On the mass rapes and discourses of German victimisation, see Atina Grossmann, 'A Question of Silence: The Rape of German Women by Soviet Occupation Soldiers', in Nicole Ann Dombrowski, ed., *Women and War in the Twentieth Century* (Routledge, 2004), pp. 162–83; *Die deutschen Trümmerfrauen* (documentary film), Hans Dieter Grabe (1968); Elizabeth D. Heineman, 'The Hour of the Woman: Memories of Germany's "Crisis Years" and West German National Identity', *American Historical Review* 101, no. 2 (April 1996): 354–95; and [Anon.,] *A Woman in Berlin: Eight Weeks in the Conquered City* (Metropolitan Books, 2005).

life without Hitler: The schoolteacher Frau Ottnad in Reichersbeuern, for instance, committed suicide on 9 May 1945, when the Allies arrived. Author interview with Ottnad's former student and his wife, Friedrich and Freya K., 11 Apr. 2011, deposited in USHMMA. See also Evans, *The Third Reich at War*; and Margaret Bourke-White, *Dear Fatherland, Rest Quietly: A Report on the Collapse of Hitler's Thousand Years* (Literary Licensing, 2012).

would be punished: On early trials and vigilante justice, see Ilya Bourtman, '"Blood for Blood, Death for Death": The Soviet Military Tribunal in Krasnodar, 1943', *Holocaust and Genocide Studies* 22 (Autumn 2008): 246–65; Gary Bass, *Stay the Hand of Vengeance: The Politics of War Crimes Tribunals* (Princeton University Press, 2000); and Donald Bloxham, *Genocide on Trial: War Crimes Trials and the Formation of Holocaust History and Memory* (Oxford University Press, 2001).

149 escaped Soviet custody: Christiane Berger, 'Die Reichsfrauenführerin Gertrud Scholtz-Klink', in Marita Krauss, ed., *Sie waren dabei: Mitläuferinnen, Nutzniesserinnen, Täterinnen im Nationalsozialismus* (Wallstein Verlag, 2008); and Claudia Koonz's interview with Klink in *Mothers in the Fatherland: Women, the Family, and Nazi Politics* (St Martin's Press, 1988).

150 twenty thousand were arrested: Gudrun Schwarz, 'Verdrängte Täterinnen: Frauen im Apparat der SS, 1939–1945', in Theresa Wobbe, ed., *Nach Osten: Verdeckte Spuren nationalsozialistischer Verbrechen* (Verlag Neue Kritik, 1992), p. 212.

'I might as well hang myself . . .': Ilse Schmidt, *Die Mitläuferin: Erinnerungen einer Wehrmachtsangehörigen* (Aufbau Verlag, 2002), pp. 38, 61, 76–77.

Erika Ohr was also swept up: Summ, *Schäfers Tochter*, p. 176.

151 cruel medical experiments: Dr Oberheuser had worked her way up through the Nazi Party. She volunteered to serve as a camp doctor at Ravensbrück and received a German War Merit Medal for assisting with gruesome medical experiments (lethal injections, bone transplants, inserting glass and wood splinters into wounds) that killed Polish labourers, among other victims. She told the Nuremberg court that she was always interested in surgical procedures and that it was hardly possible for a woman in Germany to be a surgeon. In the women's concentration camp of Ravensbrück she had the opportunity to be a surgeon and to perform experiments on healthy 'living objects'. See Paul Weidling, *Nazi Medicine and the Nuremberg Trials* (Palgrave Macmillan, 2004); and Robert Jay Lifton, *The Nazi Doctors: Medical Killing and the Psychology of Genocide* (Basic Books, 2000). Original documents from the Doctors' Trial, including Oberheuser's testimony (Document NO-487, NO-862), have been digitised and are online in Harvard University's Law Library, http://nuremberg.law. harvard.edu. NO-470. NARA, RG 238.

Inge Viermetz: On the US case against members of the SS organisation that carried out kidnapping campaigns (among other crimes of 'Germanisation'), and Viermetz, see Kathrin Kompisch, *Täterinnen: Frauen im Nationalsozialismus* (Böhlau, 2008), pp. 33–36; and Andrea Böltken: *Führerinnen im Führerstaat: Gertrud Scholtz-Klink, Trude Mohr, Jutta Rüdiger und Inge Viermetz* (Centaurus Verlag, 1995), pp. 105–29.

Emmy Hoechtl: From 1925 to 1933, Emmy Hoechtl was secretary in the Prussian Ministry of the Interior (with Robert W. Kempner); from 1933 to 1936, secretary at Polizeipräsidium Berlin; from 1936 to 1942, secretary of Arthur Nebe at Reichskriminalpolizeiamt; from October 1945 to 30 November 1948, secretary of Kempner at Nuremberg; from 1948 to 1949, secretary of the representative of the Landesregierung, Nordrhein-Westfalen, with the Zweizonenregierung Frankfurt; and from 1950 to 1959, located in Bonn as secretary of the representative of the government of Berlin (West). When she was interrogated in 1961 as part of the investigations of Albert Widman and Dr Werner concerning the gas vans in the East, Hoechtl claimed that she could not remember anything about the crimes or any criminal activity of Nebe or other people she knew in the Kripo. During the war she was not stationed in the East. But her knowledge of the documentation on the Final Solution and offices of the Reich may have been one of the reasons that the prosecutor Kempner turned up so much evidence, including the Wannsee Protocol, when she was his secretary at Nuremberg. See BAL, B162/1604, fol. 1, 556–568. I am grateful to Christian Gerlach for bringing Hoechtl to my attention.

152 'without illusions . . .': Ruth Kempner and Robert M. W. Kempner, *Women in Nazi Germany* (1944), p. 46.

153 'It could not be established who he was . . .': Summ, *Schäfers Tochter*, p. 152.

'as a civil servant . . .': Quoted from Susan Benedict, 'Caring While Killing', in Elizabeth R. Baer and Myrna Goldenberg, eds, *Experience and Expression: Women, the Nazis and the Holocaust* (Wayne State University Press, 2003), p. 105.

'I would never have committed . . .': Testimony quoted in Harald Welzer, *Täter: Wie aus ganz normalen Menschen Massenmörder werden* (Fischer Verlag, 2007), p. 67. Dr Wernicke at Meseritz-Obrawalde also used her authority to order nurses to give lethal injections. See Bronwyn Rebekah McFarland-Icke, *Nurses in Nazi Germany* (Princeton University Press, 1999) pp. 233, 248.

154  Besides sharing tools of violence: Men's and women's methods overlapped in most ways, but women seem to have had some preferences that men did not have. In the literature on the concentration camps, one often reads of the distinctive manner of female guards who regularly relied on attack dogs, and who screamed, slapped and kicked. See Elissa Mailänder Koslov, *Gewalt im Dienstalltag: Die SS-Aufseherinnen des Konzentrations- und Vernichtungslagers Mayjdanek, 1942–1944* (Hamburg Institute for Social Research, 2009); and author interview with Helen Tichauer, commenting on Irma Grese at Birkenau and female guards at Malchow, 23 June 2010, Ludwig Maximilians University, Munich; corroborated in Donald McKale, *Nazis after Hitler: How Perpetrators of the Holocaust Cheated Justice and Truth* (Rowman & Littlefield, 2012), p. 42.

denial and repression: Typical responses include 'Mir ist nichts daruber bekannt' (I know nothing about that), 'Ich kann nicht sagen' (I cannot say), 'Ich weiss nicht mehr' (I don't know any more) and 'Ich habe nichts davon gehört' (I heard nothing about it). Elisabeth Hoeven (b. Bork 1922), Kassel, 10 Oct. 1978, BAL, 634-K41676-Koe.

Germans and Austrians investigated: The latest estimate on German and Austrian perpetrators who had a direct hand in the killing process – those in the SS and police, and those in the camp system – is about 200,000 to 250,000 people. Across Europe, as many as 330,000 Germans and Austrians were investigated and accused, and of this about 100,000 were actually judged and received some sentence by a court. Between 1945 and 1989, in East Germany, 12,890 people stood trial for Nazi-related war crimes and crimes against humanity, about twice as many as in West Germany. Ninety per cent occurred prior to 1955, under Soviet pressure. Conviction rates were high, and the death sentence was imposed until the mid-1980s. See Norbert Frei, ed., *Transnationale Vergangenheitspolitik. Der Umgang mit deutschen Kriegsverbrechern in Europa nach dem Zweiten Weltkrieg* (Wallstein, 2006); and Jürgen Matthäus and Patricia Heberer, eds, *Atrocities on Trial: Historical Perspectives on the Politics of Prosecuting War Crimes* (University of Nebraska Press, 2008).

'I never understood . . .': Pauline Kneissler quoted in Michael Burleigh and Wolfgang Wippermann, *The Racial State: Germany, 1933–1945* (Cambridge University Press, 1991); and in Ulrike Gaida, *Zwischen Pflegen und Töten: Krankenschwestern im Nationalsozialismus* (Mabuse Verlag, 2006), p. 160. Kneissler killed as long as she could. In her last placement, at Kaufbeuren-Irsee, a four-year-old boy was killed on 29, May 1945, thirty-three days after US troops had marched into Kaufbeuren. See Ernst T. Mader, *Das erzwungene Sterben von Patienten der Heil- und Pflegeanstalt Kaufbeuren-Irsee zwischen 1940 und 1945 nach Dokumenten und Berichten von Augenzeugen* (Blöcktach, 1992). The historian Peter Witte has pieced together the documentation of these last days at Kaufbeuren, based on a US intelligence report of

2 July 1945, Nuremberg Doc. PS-1696 (unpublished). See excerpts in Henry Fried-lander's *The Origins of Nazi Genocide: From Euthanasia to the Final Solution* (University of North Carolina Press, 1997), pp. 218–19; 'Massenmord in der Heilanstalt' in the *Münchner Zeitung* on 7 July 1945; and Ernst Klee, *'Euthanasie' im NS-Staat: Die 'Vernichtung lebensunwerten Lebens'* (Fischer Verlag, 1983), pp. 452–53.

'may see something wrong . . .': Roy Baumeister, *Evil: Inside Human Violence and Cruelty* (W. H. Freeman, 1997), p. 47.

Erna Petri did not deny her killing: According to Insa Eschenbach, the judge-ment of women on trial in the GDR for Nazi crimes was influenced by three fac-tors: consideration of their behaviour as an anomalous lapse, their youth or naiveté and their status as workers in the emerging socialist state. Erna's self-presentation played into all of these considerations – but apparently the court was not sympa-thetic: she still received a life sentence. See Insa Eschenbach, 'Gespaltene Frauen-bilder: Geschechterdramaturgien im juristischen Diskurs ostdeutscher Gerichte', in Ulrike Weckel and Edgar Wolfrum, eds, *'Bestien' und 'Befehlsempfänger': Frauen und Männer in NS-Prozessen nach 1945* (Vandenhoeck & Ruprecht, 2003), p. 99.

155 'In those times . . .': Interrogation of Erna Petri, 18 Sept. 1961. Horst and Erna Petri Trial, BStU 000050–57, USHMMA, RG 14.068, fiche 566.

156 'I am unable to grasp . . .': Interrogation of Erna Petri, 18 Sept. 1961.

157 'the treatment we Germans . . .': Norman Goda, *Tales from Spandau: Nazi Crimi-nals and the Cold War* (Cambridge University Press, 2008), p. 147.

female killers stood out: Roger Brown and James Kulik, 'Flashbulb Memories', *Cog-nition 5* (1977): 73–99.

158 not a feminine characteristic: Susannah Heschel, 'Does Atrocity Have a Gender? Feminist Interpretations of Women in the SS', in Jeffrey Diefendorf, ed., *Lessons and Legacies*, vol. 6, *New Currents in Holocaust Research* (Northwestern University Press, 2004), pp. 300–321.

creates a false shield: Of course, as the social psychologist James Waller points out, 'to offer a psychological explanation for the atrocities committed by perpetrators is not to forgive, justify, or condone their behaviors. Instead, the explanation simply al-lows us to understand the conditions under which many of us could be transformed into killing machines'. James Waller, *Becoming Evil: How Ordinary People Commit Genocide and Mass Killing* (Oxford University Press, 2002), p. xiv.

criminologist Cesare Lombroso: Cesare Lombroso and Guglielmo Ferrero, *Crimi-nal Woman, the Prostitute, and the Normal Woman,* trans. Nicole Hahn Rafter and Mary Gibson (Duke University Press, 2004).

likening them to underdeveloped primates: Eileen MacDonald, *Shoot the Women First* (Random House, 1991), pp. xi–xii. Thanks to Robert Ehrenreich for bringing this source to my attention.

'naturally deceitful': Cited in Steven Barkan and Lynne Snowden, *Collective Violence* (Allyn & Bacon, 2000), p. 85.

studies of animal behaviour: Richard Wrangham and Dale Peterson, *Demonic Males: Apes and the Origins of Human Violence* (Houghton Mifflin, 1996); and Frans B. M.

de Waal, 'Evolutionary Ethics, Aggression, and Violence: Lessons from Primate Research', *Journal of Law, Medicine, and Ethics* 32 (Spring 2004): 18–23. Adam Jones provides a good summary of similar literature, such as Michael Ghiglieri's *The Dark Side of Man*, in *Genocide: A Comprehensive Introduction*, 2nd edn (Routledge, 2011), pp. 477–82.

'an insult to the animal kingdom . . .': Yehuda Bauer, *Rethinking the Holocaust* (Yale University Press, 2000), p. 21.

159   Perpetration of genocide requires: See Roger W. Smith's entry, 'Perpetrators', in *Encyclopedia of Genocide and Crimes against Humanity* (Macmillan, 2004); Baumeister, *Evil*, p. 137; Beatrice Hanssen, *Critique of Violence: Between Poststructuralism and Critical Theory* (Routledge, 2000); and Steven K. Baum, *The Psychology of Genocide: Perpetrators, Bystanders, and Victims* (Cambridge University Press, 2008), p. 123.

preponderance of male violence: James Blair, Derek Mitchell and Karina Blair, *The Psychopath: Emotion and the Brain* (Blackwell, 2005), p. 20. Community samples in the present-day United States show that cruel conduct (bullying, torturing pets) and delinquent behaviour (shoplifting, truancy) are exhibited in 6–16 per cent of men and 2–9 per cent of women. More extreme forms of psychopathic tendencies appear in 1–3 per cent of men and 1 per cent of women. According to psychologists, extreme forms of criminal behaviour can be measured along a spectrum of emotional and interpersonal factors. Typically, such a diagnosis relies on a point system of factors, or a checklist such as Robert Hare's list of certain traits, behaviours and emotional responses (lack of empathy, self-centredness, lack of remorse, aggression and impulsivity). These lists of traits are more descriptive than explanatory. The childhoods of the killers could be important indicators, since psychopathy and antisocial behaviour are manifested at an early age and become pronounced in the teen years.

A recent study of female criminals: There are gender differences as well; see Dana Britton, *The Gender of Crime* (Rowman & Littlefield, 2011). Waller, *Becoming Evil*, also stresses the importance of socialisation, and a similar conclusion was reached in an important study by Adam Jones, 'Gender and Genocide in Rwanda', in Adam Jones, ed., *Gendercide and Genocide* (Vanderbilt University Press, 2004), pp. 127–28. The Wiggershaus study of guards and wardens – cited in Jill Stephenson, *Women in Nazi Germany* (Longman, 2001), p. 113 – stressed their deprived backgrounds and dysfunctional family. From a biological standpoint, recent psychological research has linked hormones (such as serotonin) and brain damage caused by birth complications to psychological abnormalities and violent behaviour. See Blair, Mitchell and Blair, *The Psychopath*, pp. 32, 42; Peter Loewenberg, 'Psychohistorical Perspectives on Modern German History', *Journal of Modern History* 47 (1975): 229–79; Richard Bessel and Dirk Schumann, eds, *Life after Death: Approaches to a Cultural and Social History of Europe during the 1940s and 1950s* (Cambridge University Press, 2003); and Dirk Schumann, ed., *Raising Citizens in the Century of the Child* (Berghahn, 2010), pp. 111–13.

160   Other studies, including Theodor Adorno's: Theodor Adorno et al., *The Authoritarian Personality* (W. W. Norton, 1950); Aurel Ende, 'Battering and Neglect: Children

in Germany, 1860–1978', *Journal of Psychohistory* 7 (1979): 249–79; Raffael Scheck, 'Childhood in German Autobiographical Writings, 1740–1820', *Journal of Psychohistory* 15 (1987); and Sigrid Chamberlain, 'The Nurture and Care of the Future Master Race', *Journal of Psychohistory* 31 (2004): 374–76.

Rorschach inkblot test: See Molly Harrower, 'Rorschach Records of the Nazi War Criminals: An Experimental Study after Thirty Years', *Journal of Personality Assessment* 40, no. 4 (1976): 341–51; and George Kren and Leon Rappoport, *The Holocaust and the Crisis of Human Behavior* (Holmes & Meier, 1994).

'sadist, a pervert or a lunatic': Quoted in the introduction to Joshua Rubenstein and Ilya Altman, eds, *The Unknown Black Book: The Holocaust in the German-Occupied Soviet Territories* (Indiana University Press, 2010), p. 35. On Ohlendorf, also see Hilary Earl, *The Nuremberg SS-Einsatzgruppen Trial, 1945–1958: Atrocity, Law, and History* (Cambridge University Press, 2010).

161 'neither sick nor unusual...': Douglas Kelley report, quoted in Welzer, *Täter,* p. 9.

Such psychological experiments: Most of the post-war psychological research on Nazi perpetrators, done by Milgram, Adorno, Ritzler and others, concluded that Nazi leaders and functionaries were normal. According to clinical criteria applied to perpetrator testimony, about 10 per cent of those studied would be diagnosed as pathological. In fact, most were highly intelligent, creative and energetic. Dr Ritzler found in his analysis of the Rorschach inkblot tests that five out of the sixteen people examined in Nuremberg drew chameleon-like images. That image, he argued, was the most revealing. Cited in Welzer, *Täter,* pp. 9, 11. On the chameleon effect, see also Eric Steinhart, 'The Chameleon of Trawniki: Jack Reimer, Soviet *Volksdeutsche*, and the Holocaust', *Holocaust and Genocide Studies* 23 (Spring 2009): 239–62.

not been published: Eleanor Baur, otherwise known as Bloody Sister Pia, is one of the few known cases in which a woman was given a psychiatric evaluation. A hardcore Nazi, she was seen in Dachau observing medical experiments. On more than one Christmas Eve, she abused prisoners while singing carols and handing out packages. Baur was arrested in 1945. A German doctor from a nerve clinic in Munich examined her during her incarceration and determined that she was a 'primitive, incapable character ... dominated by a strong ego and sexual drives'. A Munich court sentenced her in 1949 to ten years of forced labour, the maximum sentence allowable in that denazification court. She was released in 1950 for health reasons, and died in 1981 at the age of ninety-five. See Ulrike Leutheusser, ed., *Hitler und die Frauen* (DVA, 2001), pp. 178–86. See also Hans Holzhaider, '"Schwester Pia": Nutzniesserin zwischen Opfern und Tätern', in *Dachauer Hefte* 10 (1994).

'The individuals were not insane...': Author interview with Hermann Weissing, 10 Mar. 2010, Münster, Germany.

162 There is no contradiction: Baum, *The Psychology of Genocide,* pp. 122–25.

163 'masculine' and 'ice cold': Author interview with Hermann Weissing, 10 Mar. 2010.

164 women in the elite ranks: Dora Maria Kahlich, a Viennese anthropologist, visited the Tarnów ghetto to conduct racial research on Jews. See Evan Bukey, *Jews and Intermarriage in Nazi Austria* (Cambridge University Press, 2011), p. 51.

dynamic of male-female relationships: The importance of marital relationships should be stressed not only as a causative factor in persecution, but also as a decisive part of the rescue activity. A spouse in the Third Reich could be an extreme liability or an asset. Besides the well-known story of German wives in Berlin married to Jewish men (Rosenstrasse protest), consider the following case: In Riga, the resident adviser in a special dormitory for army secretaries, a German woman, befriended a Jewish woman who had arrived in Latvia from their home town of Nuremberg. The German woman sneaked food from the residence-hall kitchen to the Jewish labourers who worked in the military motor pool. The SS found out and arrested the German woman and indicted her husband, a senior lieutenant also stationed in the East. When he learned of his wife's crimes and that he would be held responsible for her actions, he committed suicide. His wife survived the war. See Yad Vashem Righteous File, no. 49, file 2828. Also see Killius, *Frauen für die Front*, p. 183.

perform for each other: Franz Bauer, a German gendarme in Miedzyrzec-Podlaski, kept score with his wife, according to an eyewitness, a former Jewish POW who was in the ghetto there. Sworn testimony of Daniel Dworzynski, Linz, 28 Feb. 1962. Correspondence between Wiesenthal and Staatsanwalt Zeug, Zentrale Stelle der Landesjustizverwaltungen, 8 AR-Z 236/60, 5 Feb. 1962. An investigation was opened in Dortmund, file no. 45 Js 28/61. Correspondence from Wiesenthal to the Investigative Office for Nazi War Crimes, Tel Aviv, 28 Mar. 1963, SWA.

166  Moral codes of conduct: Gisela Bock, 'Ordinary Women in Nazi Germany: Perpetrators, Victims, Followers and Bystanders', in Lenore Weitzman and Dalia Ofer, eds, *Women in the Holocaust* (Yale University Press, 1999), p. 96.


## 7. WHAT HAPPENED TO THEM?

167  35 per cent of the SS staff: See Kathrin Kompisch, *Täterinnen: Frauen im Nationalsozialismus* (Böhlau, 2008), pp. 77, 84. In 1944 there were some 31,000 staff members in the Gestapo and 13,000 in the Kripo.

168  not threats to post-war German society: Gudrun Schwarz, 'Verdrängte Täterinnen: Frauen im Apparat der SS, 1939–1945', in Theresa Wobbe, ed., *Nach Osten: Verdeckte Spuren nationalsozialistischer Verbrechen* (Verlag Neue Kritik, 1992), p. 209. See also Hilary Earl, *The Nuremberg SS-Einsatzgruppen Trial, 1945–1958: Atrocity, Law, and History* (Cambridge University Press, 2010), pp. 40–44.

the 'rubble women': Elizabeth D. Heineman, 'The Hour of the Woman: Survival in Defeat and Occupation' and 'Marriage Rubble', in *What Difference Does a Husband Make? Women and Marital Status in Nazi and Post-war Germany* (University of California Press, 1999).

German women as martyrs: On the gendered metaphors of modern German history, and Nazism, see Elizabeth D. Heineman, 'Gender, Sexuality, and Coming to Terms with the Nazi Past', *Central European History* 38 (2005): 41–74.

Such a display of emotion: The interrogator of the Lida secretary Liselotte Meier Lerm explained that she broke out in tears, was distraught and confused while she got caught up in her own lies, denied her love affair with her boss and tried to conceal her knowledge. Her actual culpability was not determined. 6 Oct. 1964, BAL, 162/3433.

After the war, Annette Schücking: Schücking was one of the first female judges in a criminal court in Duisburg. Between 1954 and 1957 she was a judge in the civil court in Düsseldorf, and from there she moved to the courts in Detmold. She married the journalist Helmut Homeyer in 1948, and they had two children. Schücking-Homeyer was considered a potentially valuable witness. In May 1974, Dr Rückerl, the head of the West German Central Office of the State Justice Administration for the Investigation of National Socialist Crimes in Ludwigsburg, wrote a memo to a prosecutor stating that Schücking-Homeyer should be contacted as a witness if their investigation of the *Gebietskommissar* and German policemen in Zwiahel/ Novgorod Volynsk went to trial. No trial occurred. The memo from Dr Rückerl regarding Schücking-Homeyer as a witness, attached to her reports, is in the Investigation of Gebietskommissar Schmidt, BAL, II, 204a ARZ 132/67, p. 574.

169 'It was impossible . . .': Schücking-Homeyer interview with author and Christof Mauch, 30 Mar. 2010, Lünen, Germany.

in the minority: Women made up between 5 and 18 per cent of the murderers and accomplices to murder who were indicted in Austria, West Germany and East Germany. Twenty-two per cent of defendants in euthanasia cases were women, and 9 per cent in cases against camp guards. See Claudia Kuretsidis-Haider and Winfried R. Garscha, eds, *Keine 'Abrechnung': NS-Verbrechen, Justiz und Gesellschaft in Europa nach 1945* (Akademische Verlagsanstalt, 1998), pp. 200–205. See also Alexandra Przyrembel, 'Ilse Koch', in Klaus-Michael Mallmann and Gerhard Paul, eds, *Karrieren der Gewalt: Nationalsozialistische Täterbiographien* (Wissenschaftliche Buchgesellschaft, 2004), pp. 126–27, 130–31.

their role as administrators: When Hannah Arendt fashioned her thesis of the banality of evil based on her study of Adolf Eichmann and the Nazi bureaucracy, she neglected the role of female administrators. The sociologist Zygmunt Bauman, whose work was heavily influenced by Arendt's, also crafted a theory that failed to account for the role of women. About six years after the Eichmann trial, one female desk murderer was put on trial: Gertud Slottke, a thirty-nine-year-old specialist in Department 'J' (Jewish Matters) in the Nazi secret police office in the Netherlands. Historians scrutinising German documents from the summer and autumn of 1941 to reconstruct the origins of the Final Solution have found clues in regional initiatives such as a document prepared by Slottke on 31 Aug. 1941, 'Combating Jewry in its totality', which proposed 'the final solution of the Jewish question by way of the removal of all Jews'. Slottke had her own support staff of typists and clerks, and she actively participated in meetings with her boss, the commander of the Security Police and Security Service, Wilhelm Harster. She drafted lists of Jews to be deported to Mauthausen, Auschwitz and Sobibor, and observed at least one round-up of 'hysterical' Jewish women, as she described them in her report of 27 May 1943. Jews in the Westerbork transit camp named her the Angel of Death, because she circulated around the camp making her selections. Anne Frank's family was on her list of deportees. At the trial against Slottke and her male bosses, Anne's father, Otto, questioned the defendants and showed them the photograph of Anne on the cover of her published diary. Slottke received a five-year jail sentence for her role as an accomplice in the murder of nearly 55,000 deported Jews. The 1967 trial of this female desk murderer and the convictions were unusual; the international attention, media coverage and involvement of Otto Frank as well as the prominent Nazi-hunter Simon Wiesenthal and former Nuremberg lawyer Robert Kempner may have strengthened the prosecution's case. For Gertrude Slottke's testimony and other trial material, see BAL, 107 AR 518/59, Band II. See also Yaacov Lozowick, *Hitler's Bureaucrats: The Nazi Security Police and the Banality of Evil* (Continuum, 2000), pp. 165–66, 171, 269; and Elisabeth Kohlhaas, 'Weibliche Angestellte der Gestapo, 1933–1945', in Marita Krauss, ed., *Sie waren dabei: Mitläuferinnen, Nutzniesserinnen, Täterinnen im Nationalsozialismus* (Wallstein Verlag, 2008), pp. 154–61.

outside institutional settings: On the complicity of women managers of Jewish apartment houses and property in Berlin, see Brigitte Scheiger, '"Ich bitte um baldige Arisierung der Wohnung": Zur Funktion von Frauen im buerokratischen System der Verfolgung', in Theresa Wobbe, ed., *Nach Osten: Verdeckte Spuren nationalsozialistischer Verbrechen* (Verlag Neue Kritik, 1992), pp. 175–96; Krauss, *Sie waren dabei*, p. 11; and Jill Stephenson, *Women in Nazi Germany* (Longman, 2001), pp. 112–13. Female denouncers were pursued, though women were not disproportionately represented among those who denounced and those who were prosecuted for denouncing. See Robert Gellately, *The Gestapo and German Society: Enforcing Racial Policy, 1933–1945* (Oxford University Press, 1991); and Ulrike Weckel and Edgar Wolfrum, eds, *'Bestien' und 'Befehlsempfänger': Frauen und Männer in NS-Prozessen nach 1945* (Vandenhoeck & Ruprecht, 2003).

171 'act of fate . . .': Quoted in Katharina Kellenbach, 'God's Love and Women's Love: Prison Chaplains Counsel the Wives of Nazi Perpetrators', *Journal of Feminist Studies in Religion* (Autumn 2004): 11–13, 23. I thank Susan Bachrach for this source.

When I telephoned: Author telephone interview with Edith N., 22 Apr. 2010. Edith stressed that she had met her husband after the war and that as an elderly invalid he needed her continued care. She cried about the early death of her troubled son, who investigated his father's past and was devastated by what he discovered. Her husband was in an SS Death's Head division and served as a mass shooter with Sonderkommando 10a in Taganrog in 1942. Prior to that he was a guard in the Warsaw prison.

Pacts of loyalty: See Jürgen Matthäus, '"No Ordinary Criminal" Georg Heuser, Other Mass Murderers and West German Justice', in Patricia Heberer and Jürgen Matthäus, eds, *Atrocities on Trial: Historical Perspectives on the Politics of Prosecuting War Crimes* (University of Nebraska Press, 2008).

secretary for the district commissar in Slonim: Gerda Rogowsky, statement of 14 Mar. 1960, BAL, 162/5102.

Of course, not everyone abided: Vorermittlungsverfahren der Zentralen Stelle der Landesjustizverwaltungen wegen NS-Verbrechen im Bereich des ehemaligen Generalbezirks Shitomir/Ukraine, II, 204a AR-Z 131/67, Abschlussbericht, Das Gebietskommissariat Tschudnow. Beweismittel, Witness Statements, Erna Barthelt, Elisabeth Tharun, Elfriede Büschken, Friedrich Paul, Otto Bräse, Elfriede Bräse, Staatsanwaltschaft, Handakten, I 13 Js 60/51, Landgericht I 13 ERKs 35/51. BAB, BStU 000199–202. Herr Richter, Volkspolizei Oberwachtmeister, VPKA-Wittenberg, 'Bericht', 3 Feb. 1950, BStU 00035, Archiv Staatsanwalt des Bezirkes Halle, Fach Nr. 2052. MfS BV Halle, Ast 5544, BStU 00133–138, Urteilurschrift, Strafsache gegen den Arbeiter Bruno Sämisch aus Mühlanger Landesgreicht Dessau, and 'Gründe', pp. 1–5. BAB, BStU 00133–138, Archiv Staatsanwalt des Bezirkes Halle, Fach Nr. 2052.

172 covered for their bosses: When questioned after the war, Mimi Trsek, Globocnik's secretary, remained steadfastly loyal to her boss and maintained her ignorance about the Final Solution. She claimed that she knew nothing of the gassing centres. Yes, she had heard terms such as 'resettlement' and 'evacuations', but she did not realise that these were code words for death. Mimi stuck with this defence when she was interviewed by a German film-maker in 2001. See Berndt Rieger, *Creator of Nazi Death Camps: The Life of Odilo Globocnik* (Vallentine Mitchell, 2007), p. 201.

motive was anti-Semitic hate: Cited in Kerstin Freudiger, *Die juristische Aufarbeitung von NS-Verbrechen* (Mohr Siebeck, 2002), p. 214.

rubber-stamping a document: '*Erledigt!*' telephone conversations with Ruth P., 7 June and 2 Aug. 2011. Thanks to Andrej Angrick for this source. The West German investigation of the RSHA was the most extensive, involving the identification of about 730 members of the RSHA and the indictment of about 50 men. Landgericht Berlin, 13 Oct. 1969, KS 1/69 (ZStL: VI 415 AR 1310/63, Sammelakte Nr. 341).

174 'dragged into this shit': Vermerk, 9 Oct. 1960, prosecutor's notes, BAL, 9 Js 716/59.

incriminating details: As special prosecutors moved outside the closed circle of Heuser's staff and friends, they found other German women who had worked in wartime Minsk who provided more objective testimony. One secretary who was in Minsk from September 1941 to December 1943 described the killing operations in credible detail. She remembered Heuser very well and could place him in the centre of the operations. Whenever Jewish transports arrived at Maly Trostenets, she said, Heuser stood on a barrel and made a speech. Greetings, he declared, in the name of the Great German Reich. He told the Jews they were being resettled, and during these tough times of war they must give up their valuables for the effort. All their items would be registered on a list, he told them, implying that they would eventually be compensated. They would be transferred to farms for agriculture work; he apologised for the poor accommodation and transportation. Then this secretary related what she heard from other women in Heuser's office and SS male colleagues about the events at the mass-murder sites and specific German methods of killing. She saw Jews being shot in the courtyard of her building and named the persons who shot the Jews. Eva Maria Schmidt testimony, 9 Nov. 1961. Landgericht Köln. Koblenz Sta, 9 Js/716/59. Such testimony, combined with wartime documentation, was sufficient to convict Heuser. He was sentenced to fifteen years for the murder of more than 11,103 persons, but released after ten, since the court determined that he 'was not a criminal in the usual sense'. Files of the Staatsanwalt Koblenz, Heuser case, Sonderkommission P. 9 Js 716/59. Interrogation notes on Sabine Dick, April–Oct. 1960.

Gender bias: Kuretsidis-Haider and Garscha, *Keine 'Abrechnung'*, pp. 204–6. See Heineman on West German widows and family law, *What Difference Does a Husband Make?*

175  loathsome reminders: Dagmar Herzog, *Sex after Fascism: Memory and Morality in Twentieth-Century Germany* (Princeton University Press, 2005), especially chap. 3, 'Desperately Seeking Normality'; and Krauss, *Sie waren dabei*, p. 13.

Hanweg's deputy was still in Mainz: Windisch, who was Austrian, had fled to West Germany and had hidden out in neo-Nazi circles in the Saarland. He died in jail after serving fifteen years.

He personally arrested: Author interviews with Herbert Hinzmann, former *Oberstaatsanwalt*, Mainz, 2 Aug. 2010, and with Hinzmann and Boris Neusius, Mainz, 14 Feb. 2012.

'I cannot remember', 'I cannot recall . . .': Liselotte Meier Lerm, statement of 19 Sept. 1963, BAL, 162/3425; statements of 5 and 6 Sept. 1966, BAL, 162/3449 and 3450.

176  the West German pursuit: A West German delegation, including the prosecutor, Hermann Weissing, and the defence lawyers for the accused, travelled to Lutsk, where Soviet Ukrainian and Polish witnesses presented their accounts. Author interview with Weissing, Münster, 9 Mar. 2010.

177  'She can be usefully employed': Biographical material in the indictment of Altvater and verdict, BAL, B162/4524, pp. 20, 22.

Nazi Youth in Minden: Dagmar Reese, *Growing Up Female in Nazi Germany*, trans. William Templer (University of Michigan Press, 2006), quoting the recollections of one of Altvater's contemporaries in Minden, p. 154.

During the public trial proceedings: A key witness in the trial against Johanna Altvater Zelle and Wilhelm Westerheide was a former German colleague, a driver with the Wehrmacht (Technical Battalion 6, First Company) stationed near Westerheide's office. This driver often met Westerheide on the streets of Volodymyr-Volynsky. They would walk and chat. In 1943, when they encountered Jewish labourers, the Jews would stop and kneel down to Westerheide. The driver asked Westerheide: Why do the Jews do that? Because I ordered them to do so, Westerheide replied, and then boasted that he used to have about 30,000 Jews in his district, crammed into the ghettos, but already 18,000 had been 'knocked off', with the remainder yet to be killed. Westerheide added that he was looking for shooters and asked the driver if he would be interested in killing Jews, but he declined. Others in his military unit were approached by Westerheide and served as shooters in a massacre at the old cemetery in 1943. Among the shooters Westerheide recruited, the driver recalled, was a band of musicians. Statement of Karl Wetzle, 21 June 1963, Oberhausen, BAL, 162/4522, fol. 1. These musicians were probably the ones who played at the banquet table and then put down their instruments to do some shooting, described by Polish witnesses. Testimony of Josef Opatowski, 7. Jewish Historical Institute Warsaw, ZIH 301/2014.

'his city', 'his Jews' and 'Herr Westerheide . . .': Quoted in *Die Tat*, 6 Oct. 1978.

'Das Todes-Getto war "unsagbar freundlich"', newspaper coverage of the trial. Band IV, bl 773–1004. Westerheide, II, 204 AR-Z 40/61, B162/4523, fol 1. Strafsenat of the Bundesgerichtshof.

179  'insufficient evidence' and 'Despite strong suspicion . . .': Urteil, Bundesgerichtshof, in der Strafsache gegen Westerheide und Zelle, wegen Moerder, 4 StR 303/80. BAL, Band IV, II, 204 AR-Z 40/61.

The chief prosecutor in this office: During Weissing's tenure at the Central Office (1965–2000), he and his colleagues investigated more than 25,000 suspects and indicted 159. Among the other controversial cases that the office unsuccessfully prosecuted or rejected were the Erich Priebke and Heinrich Boere cases. Boere, a former Waffen-SS man (with Division Viking in Ukraine), was tried in Aachen for his crimes in the Netherlands and received a life sentence on 23 March 2010.

180  reflections on the proceedings: Author interview with Weissing, 9 Mar. 2010.

Another protest took place: 'Germans Protest Acquittal of Two in War Criminal Case', *New York Times,* 21 Dec. 1982.

'rule of Nobody': Hannah Arendt, *Eichmann in Jerusalem* (Viking, 1963). Defence lawyers could not turn up evidence that those who did not follow orders to rob, deport and kill Jews were punished by superiors. Putative duress as well as following orders did not hold up in court as a defence. The lack of an actual Führer Order also weakened the argument.

181  'it was not right . . .': Gertrude Segel Landau statement, 29 May 1947, VCA, Polizeidirektion Wien, People's Court investigation, Vg 3b Vr 7658/47. Felix Landau denied having responded in the way Gertrude claimed, and also insisted that his wife was lying when she told him not to shoot at people. Felix admitted that he confiscated a Jewish apartment in Vienna in 1938. In the course of this seizure of Jewish property he also bullied a family member (the Altmans, factory owners in Vienna) to give him gold jewellery. Felix Landau statement, 7 Aug. 1947. Camp Marcus, Abschrift in Wien Stadtarchiv, Vg 8514/46.

182  escaped from an Austrian jail: Apparently the Austrian jails were rather open – Franz Stangl also walked out of prison in 1947. See Gitta Sereny, *Into That Darkness: An Examination of Conscience* (Vintage, 1983), p. 353. To hide from investigators in Austria and Germany, Landau took on another identity, that of Rudolf Jaschke, claiming that he was a Sudeten ethnic German refugee; in fact, Landau was born in Vienna in 1910. (Preliminary investigation of Landau, and records of the Staatsanwaltschaft Stuttgart, 11 208 AR-Z 60a/1959, BAL/3380.) In 1958 Landau sought to obtain a marriage licence in Stuttgart. When he applied for his marriage certificate, he revealed his real name to the authorities and presented his Austrian birth certificate. It was the investigation over his false identity that led to his arrest, followed by a 1961 indictment for his Nazi-era crimes and a March 1962 murder conviction by a Stuttgart court. He received a double life sentence, a rare punishment by a West German court in the 1960s. But it turned out to be largely symbolic: he was pardoned in 1973. He died a decade later. See Dieter Pohl, *Nationalsozialistische Judenverfolgung in Ostgalizien, 1941–1944: Organisation und Durchführung eines staatlichen Massenverbrechens* (Oldenbourg, 1996), pp. 392, 417.

looking for evidence of guilt: Gertrude Segel Landau statements of 29 May, 2 June and 17 June 1947, and 17 Feb. and 27 Feb. 1948. VCA, Wien Stadtarchiv, Vg 8514/46.

183 witnesses who accused her: Regina Katz, who had worked as Block's personal tailor in Drohobych, was one of the witnesses against Block. Ms Katz had two reasons for going to the authorities. When the Jewish ghetto was liquidated in 1943, Katz's life and that of her daughter were at risk. Block retained Katz as a labourer, but not the one-year-old daughter. Katz wanted to find her child, and she wanted to make sure Josefine Block would be punished. Statement of Regina Katz, 3 Oct. 1946, VCA, Amtsvemerk, Haft, 19 Oct. 1946, Polizeidirektion. Niederschrift vom 19 Okt. 1946, Hausdurchsuchung, Wien Stadtarchiv, Vg 8514/46.

'friend of the Jews': Statement of Josefine Block, 14 Nov. 1946, VCA, Vg 8514/46. Josefine Block statement, 12 Feb. 1948, Investigation of Gertrude Landau, VCA, Vg 3b Vr 7658/47. The former Birkenau guard Irma Grese claimed she was a victim of the privileged Jews who really controlled the camp; see testimony in Donald McK-ale, *Nazis after Hitler: How Perpetrators of the Holocaust Cheated Justice and Truth* (Rowman & Littlefield, 2012), p. 41.

in that Vienna courtroom in 1949: The investigative process had dragged on for quite a while, with Frau Block remaining in jail until early 1949. Austrian authorities made little effort to locate key eyewitnesses, 'foreign' Jews who 'spoke poor German' or had left Austria to live in a less hostile environment. The Austrian prisons were full of suspects, and there were too few layman lawyers and judges to handle the cases. After some time everyone wanted to move on, with perhaps the exception of a prosecutor, Altmann, who on 3 March 1949, issued a one-page indictment against Block, charging her with the torture and abuse of one girl. The other charges were dropped, and the only witness to the crime against the girl was gone. Another prosecutor stepped in and rushed through the half-day proceedings. Block was unanimously acquitted on 15 September 1949, on the grounds of insufficient evidence. Beratungsprotokoll bei dem Landesgericht Wien, 259/3 stop.

Exhibiting little understanding: A similar bias appeared in the Hermine Braunsteiner case, also held in the Viennese People's Court in Austria. Braunsteiner, a camp guard, got only three years in 1951 because 'a Viennese woman could never be so brutal'. In 1981 she got a life sentence in a Düsseldorf court. See Claudia Kuretsidis-Haider, 'Täterinnen vor Gericht: Die Kategorie Geschlecht bei der Ahndung von nationalsozialistischen Tötungsdelikten in Deutschland und Österreich', in Krauss, *Sie waren dabei.*

184 'Do you remember . . .': Vera Wohlauf interrogation, 19 Nov. 1964, BAL, B162/5916, 1655–1658.

187 eight thousand Jews: Christopher R. Browning, *Ordinary Men: Reserve Police Battalion 101 and the Final Solution in Poland* (HarperCollins, 1993).

Gustav was killed in action: For more on Gustav Willhaus (1910–1945), see Pohl, *Nationalsozialistische Judenverfolgung in Ostgalizien,* pp. 333, 423.

188 'went against all preconceived notions . . .': Lemberg Trial, Indictment, BAL, 162/4688, p. 274.

'whose conscience cannot . . .': Quoted from the German newspaper coverage of the trial, 'Das Urteil im Lemberg Prozess', 30 Apr. 1961, which was included in the Stuttgart prosecutor's press clippings file, BAL, 162/4688, 208 AR-Z 294/59.

perpetrators tried in East Germany: Published work on female perpetrators who stood trial in the GDR focuses on the camp guards, especially the SS-Aufseherinnen Ravensbrück. Thirty-five were tried and received relatively light sentences in East German and Soviet courts between 1947 and 1954. See the interesting analysis by Insa Eschenbach, 'Gespaltene Frauenbilder: Geschechterdramaturgien im juristischen Diskurs ostdeutscher Gerichte', in Weckel and Wolfrum, '*Bestien' und 'Befehlsempfänger*', pp. 95–116.

By the time Erna Petri was arrested: My analysis of the Petri trial is adapted from material I published in an earlier article, 'Male and Female Holocaust Perpetrators and the East German Approach to Justice, 1949–1963', *Holocaust and Genocide Studies* 24, no. 1 (Spring 2010): 56–84. I thank Oxford University Press and the US Holocaust Memorial Museum for permission to use passages (in altered form) from that article.

189 the local agricultural commune: Landwirtschaftliche Produktionsgenossenschaft (LPG), an East German term for a Soviet-style collective farm. About this time West German prosecutors investigated and launched trials against perpetrators in the same region of Ukraine. Erfurt officials did not benefit from this coincidence; they focused on collabourating with Polish and Russian authorities. On the West German trials in Galicia, see Omer Bartov, 'Guilt and Accountability in the Postwar Courtroom: The Holocaust in Czortkow and Buczacz, East Galicia, as Seen in West German Legal Discourse', paper presented at 'Repairing the Past: Confronting the Legacies of Slavery, Genocide, and Caste' (Yale University, 27–29 October, 2005).

confessions extracted under duress: The files do not reveal the duress, though the times of day noted on the interrogation reports suggest that the sessions were long, exhausting and conducted at odd hours without interruption. The signatures of the defendants on the transcripts are shaky and irregular.

190 'most severe war crimes . . .': Erfurt, General Stasi Records, Allg. S 100, BSt U 000111–113, Allg S 73, BStU 000019–21, BAB, Archiv-Nr. 403/63, BSTu aussentselle Erfurt, twenty-two volumes/folders, plus ten audiotapes and two photo albums.

'Thank you . . .': Audio file of the trial of Horst and Erna Petri, Eft. AU 403/63, Archives of BStU, BAB.

'18 to 20 years ago . . .': Petri case, no. 10733, *DDR-Justiz und NS-Verbrechen*, Lfd Nr. 10733, 271–272.

191 'Which crimes . . .': Erna Petri interrogation, 15 Sept. 1961. Case Against Horst and Erna Petri, BAB, Archives of BStU Berlin, file number Eft. AU 403/63 GA 1, USHMMA, RG 14.068, fiche 565.

'Why have you denied . . .': Erna Petri interrogation, 18 Sept. 1961.

192 even an embarrassment: In Kathrin Meyer's analysis of the denazification proceedings against German women, she found that gender expectations raised the moral standards for women, who were not supposed to behave brutally. Such expectations

coloured the judgement of American, West German and East German jurists and officials alike. See Meyer's *Entnazifizierung von Frauen: Die Intierungslager der US Zone, 1945–1952* (Metropol, 2004).

'those people . .'. and 'I admit that my wife shot': Petri letters. BAB, Handakten Staatsanwalt Erfurt, BStU 000379.

194 Jewish women as troublemakers: BAB, Abschrift, 7 Aug. 1961, Untersuchungsvorgang, Erna Petri, Stasi, Erfurt, 3493/61, Band V, Archiv-Nr. 403/63.

In the next few months: According to a law of September 1990, a person could be rehabilitated if a West German court, or German successor court, found that the Nazi crimes one was convicted of were not substantiated with evidence, if one incurred serious violations of human rights in the investigative process and trial, and if the trial was carried out in an unlawful manner. One in six prisoners (or his or her descendants) applied for rehabilitation, amounting to 106 applications; of these, 43 were declined or rejected outright, but the rest were altered or revised in some manner. Of the thirteen convictions overturned, many originated in the Waldheim trials. Two prisoners were released. See Günther Wieland, 'Die Ahndung von NS-Verbrechen in Ostdeutschland, 1945–1990', in *DDR-Justiz und NS-Verbrechen: Sammlung ostdeutscher Strafurteile wegen nationalsozialistischer Tötungsverbrechen* (K. G. Saur Verlag, 2002).

She came home in 1992: It is possible that Petri was released on 12 December 1991, in accordance with the ruling of the Stollberg court. The decision and a quote from Petri, who gushed about her visit with Gudrun Himmler Burwitz, 'the most wonderful woman', is in Oliver Schröm and Andrea Röpke, *Stille Hilfe für braune Kameraden: Das geheime Netzwerk der Alt- und Neonazis* (Aufbau Verlag, 2006), pp. 104–5. Author interview with Petri family, 24 July 2006.

195 If Petri had resided in West Germany: Historians disagree as to the higher conviction rate of women who were tried. In the highly publicised trials, such as the Majdanek trial, the female guard Hildegard Lächert received a twelve-year sentence, whereas her male counterpart received a sentence of eight years. A general analysis of all West German cases, however, led another historian to conclude that most women tried were acquitted or received sentences of less than three years. See Michael Greve, 'Täter oder Gehilfen?' in Weckel and Wolfrum, *'Bestien' und 'Befehlsempfänger'*, p. 202. Also see Claudia Koonz, 'A Tributary and a Mainstream: Gender, Public Memory, and the Historiography of Nazi Germany', in Karen Hagemann and Jean H. Quataert, eds, *Gendering Modern German History: Rewriting Historiography* (Berghahn, 2007), p. 161.

The images of Nazi propagandists: This was first argued by the former Nazi Hermann Rauschnigg, then echoed by the historian Joachim Fest.

'men organise life . . .': Quoted in Ute Frevert, *Women in German History: From Bourgeois Emancipation to Sexual Liberation* (Berg, 1989), p. 215.

created false narratives: Roy Baumeister, *Evil: Inside Human Violence and Cruelty* (W. H. Freeman, 1997), p. 46.

196 historian Katrin Himmler: Katrin Himmler, the grand-niece of Heinrich Himmler, has pursued her own personal and scholarly reconciliation with the Nazi past, pub-

lishing a study of the Himmler family as well as marrying an Israeli. See her essay, '"Herrenmenschenpaare": Zwischen nationalsozialistischem Elitebewusstsein und rassenideologischer (Selbst-) Verpflichtung', in Krauss, *Sie waren dabei*, p. 73.

amount of material booty: Götz Aly, *Hitlers Volkstaat: Raub, Rassenkrieg und Nationalsozialismus* (Fischer Verlag, 2005). Some of the people interviewed for this book proudly showed me items that had been brought back from their wartime years in the East and which are now displayed in their homes.

197 sensationalistic press coverage: Among the more prominent defendants were Ilse Koch (the sadistic seductress accused of making lampshades from the tattooed skin of prisoners), Hermine Braunsteiner (the mare of Majdanek) and Irma Grese (the beautiful beast from Birkenau and Bergen-Belsen). See Sybil Milton, 'Women and the Holocaust: The Case of German and German-Jewish Women', in Renate Bridenthal, Atina Grossmann and Marion Kaplan, eds, *When Biology Became Destiny: Women in Weimar and Nazi Germany* (Monthly Review Press, 1984), pp. 297–333; and Sarah Cushman, 'Women of Birkenau' (PhD diss., Clark University, 2010). For East German cases against women in particular, see Insa Eschebach, '"Negative Elemente": Ermittlungsberichte des MfS über ehemalige SS-Aufseherinnen', in Annette Leo and Peter Reif-Spireck, eds, *Helden, Täter und Verräter: Studien zum DDR-Antifaschismus* (Metropol, 1999), pp. 197–210.

'sensationalised Nazism . . .': Koonz, 'A Tributary and a Mainstream', p. 161.

EPILOGUE

199 post-war population exchanges: On the interaction of Hitler and Stalin in eastern Europe, especially in Ukraine and Poland, see Timothy Snyder, *Bloodlands: Europe between Hitler and Stalin* (Basic Books, 2010).

201 An informant in the 1960s: The eyewitness was a former Jewish POW who was in the ghetto in Miedzyrzec-Podlaski. Franz Bauer was known as the henchman with the dog, who often declared, 'I cannot eat breakfast until I have shot a Jew, and cannot sleep until I have shot a Jew. With this pistol I have shot 2000 Jews'. Sworn testimony of Daniel Dworzynski, Linz, 28 Feb. 1962. Correspondence between Wiesenthal and Staatsanwalt Zeug, Zentrale Stelle der Landesjustizverwaltungen, 8 AR-Z 236/60, 5 Feb 1962. An investigation was opened in Dortmund, file no. 45 Js 28/61. Correspondence from Wiesenthal to the Investigative Office for Nazi War Crimes, Tel Aviv, 28 Mar. 1963, SWA.

I interviewed a survivor: Author interview with Gisela Gross, 3 Nov. 2005, Baltimore.

202 If one chose to *help* victims: An SS report on the misconduct of Reich German men and women in Galicia cites a few cases in which German couples illegally employed Jewish labourers, allowed the Jews to eat in their kitchens, and allegedly provided one family with papers to escape to Romania. Frau and Herr Gilke, an architect who also managed the German railway station in Kolomea, interfered with an SS action to deport Jews from the station, and may have hidden and saved five Jews. This case, among others, was investigated by the SS and police. An official named Roth who

helped Jews escape across the border to Hungary from occupied Poland was punished and sent to a concentration camp. SSPF Katzmann to HSSPF Krueger, Verhalten Reichsdeutschen in General Gouvernement, 14 May 1943, ITS.

sentenced to death: Ulrich Frisse, 'The Role of the Local Judiciary: The *Sondergericht beim Deutschen Gericht Lemberg* (Special Court at the German Court Lemberg) and Its Contribution to the Holocaust in Eastern Galicia' (Yad Vashem Summer Workshop Presentation, July 2010), pp. 8–10; archival source, Sondergericht bei dem Deutschen Gericht Lemberg, Strafsache gegen Liselotte Hassenstein wegen Judenbeherbergung, 1 Oct. 1943, 3 KLs. 103/43. See also Jill Stephenson, *Women in Nazi Germany* (Longman, 2001), p. 111.

final months of the war: Richard Evans, *The Third Reich at War* (Penguin, 2010), p. 686.

'The streets of Danzig . . .': K. H. Schaefer, 'Die letzten Tage von Danzig im Jahre 1945', Pfingsten, 16 May 1946. I am grateful to Wolfgang Schaefer for sharing his father's manuscript.

I learned that one of my interview subjects: Author interview with Maria Seidenberger and Dr Boris Neusius, 6 June and 20 Oct. 2010, Hebertshausen, Germany, deposited in USHMMA.

# INDEX

Page numbers in italics refer to illustrations.

www.vintage-books.co.uk